Yellow Meat Watermelon

DW Hennington

Edited by Belisa Serna Hennington

TABLE OF CONTENTS

FOREWORD

"Counselor?" "Counselor," I heard as I answered the phone during the summer of 2018.

It had been more than fifteen years since that voice addressed me—yet I knew it could only be one person--- Mr. Damian Hennington. We remain forever linked given my representation of him, as his attorney, in *State of Texas versus Damian Hennington* during 2002. "Yellow Meat Watermelon" presents his story and journey from free man to the bewilderment and anguish of finding himself locked up for a crime he didn't commit.

The conviction and incarceration of a factually innocent man haunted me for many years. Unquestionably, Damian was shocked and what follows herein is his story. I invite you to read this book. Become enlightened, saddened and angered at a system that would impose a burden of proving innocence on an accused.

Damian was naïve about the criminal justice system, believing that a jury would clearly see his innocence. Accused of possession of marijuana after giving a pregnant co-worker a ride home (the weed was in her bags), Damian became aware the notorious "G" (Gary) Brown, the primary police officer involved, was dirty. He learned that "G" Brown often extorted drug dealing for his personal gain from those he would "investigate." Damian refused all such demands, being a man of integrity. Damian believed, however, the other officers would testify truthfully at trial. Rejecting all possible plea offers, his case was set for jury trial in Bowie County (Northeast), Texas.

As his attorney, I faced a daunting task—the representation of an atypical criminal client---a factually innocent one. How would we prove to the jury his innocence? While our criminal justice system, in theory, does not place such a burden on an accused, reality is quite different. Alas, the odds were overwhelming against Damian. From a corrupt cop, "G" Brown; a prosecutorial-friendly, conviction-driven and racist white judge; a cocaine-snorting assistant white prosecutor; and a prosecutorial-oriented all-white jury,

Damian faced incredible odds. The presiding trial judge, Bill Peek, apparently fond of me, stated: *"Dan'l, why are you working so hard for that nigger?"* Unsurprisingly, Peek did not see himself as racist. His comments were hardly novel and often stated within earshot of the jury--one composed of entirely white people who unconsciously perpetuated a continued pattern of racism. I endeavored to educate the jury and send a shocking wake-call and confront their indifference to a black man's exclamations of innocence.

The facts surrounding Damian's arrest weren't unusual. Yet, the State's primary players were eager to pretend that no police officer would lie, nor prosecutors suborn perjury. Damian's co-worker was very well known by "G" Brown of the Texarkana, Texas police department for her drug use and dealing. She was highly motivated to fabricate any story for the prosecutor and jury to avoid a lengthy prison sentence. Indeed, she was given the proverbial "slap-on the wrist" in exchange for her perjurious trial testimony and so she did. Of course, and contrary to Texas law, there would be no corroboration that Damian had knowledge of the Mary-Jane inside Jackson's luggage. To an all-white East Texas jury, Damian was yet another black man peddling dope. Damian, however, was a hard-working man of honor and good character. Facing a felony conviction and possible prison sentence, he eagerly wanted to maintain his good name and reputation.

In capital cases where the accused faces the death penalty, our system of jurisprudence attempts to afford an accused the protection of every one of his constitutional rights and heavily scrutinizes the trial and appellate process. Still, however, it is beyond dispute, our system has convicted factually innocent people in such cases. Such wrongful convictions occur even when the stakes are at the highest. It would not be surprising that we also routinely convict the innocent in cases where a mere felony conviction and a stint in prison are on the line. But to quote the maxim of Voltaire, *"that 'tis much more prudence to acquit two persons, tho' actually guilty, than to pass sentence of condemnation on one that is virtuous and innocent."* Zadig, chapter 6, p. 53 (1749, reprinted 1974). Once, our criminal justice system honored that maxim. Sadly, no more. Our "prison industrial complex machinery" cares little about throwing out the good with the bad.

So, despite a sincere and vigorous defense, the jury convicted Damian and returned a sentence of 4-years of incarceration. Being found guilty and becoming a felon devastated Damian. Shackled and headed for a prison sentence in the Texas Department of Criminal Justice, Institutional Division. Sounds benign? Far from it, TDCJ, ID is an old-school prison system where the guards regularly engage in cruel debasement of its charges. Often, the guards do so for their perverse enjoyment.

I am honored to have fought for Damian Hennington and for being asked to provide this introduction. This book is a moving and poignant portrayal of all that is wrong with our criminal justice system—from the initial encounter with a corrupt cop, a one-sided grand jury process, a hypocritical prosecutor and the conviction-driven trial judge and the indifferent appellate process and insidious incarceration of an innocent man.

Yellow Meat Watermelon is a brutally honest and unflinching exploration of race and personal struggles, told with a heart of an honorable man. Laugh and cry, but don't remain on the "sidelines." Judge if you must but condemn those truly worthy. Damian's book should touch you deeply. Come feel his hope, his fear, his pain and his journey back home.

As you read this book and account of Damian's personal struggles, I trust that you will be moved to a place of righteous indignation and closer to becoming genuinely active in your community for meaningful justice reform. It is incumbent upon all of us to seize control—eliminate the power imbalance between an overreaching, ambitious and blindly corrupted system and its citizenry. For without such vigilance, who watches the watchmen?

Daniel Siler, JD

1

I begin this expose of corruption where any good manifesto of the street should begin. Here at life's proverbial crossroads in the confines of a 5 x 9 state sponsored public storage unit known as the pen, the clank and La Casa Grande and a cold concrete slab amid the putrid stench of 150 years of decomposing blood, piss and shit.

I find myself locked down in the worst place this side of creation. A place where I was told I might end up, but never thought I'd be. A crossroad where legit business meets the streets, where corruption rots in the soil and where I learned, in my short tenure, I ain't got to be wrong for the man to be right.

I'm working a straight gig check to check. My cars' radiator goes out and I have just enough cash to get it fixed. Just then Homegirl calls. She sells me a sob story about her failing relationship with her husband. She's is pregnant, he's sleeping with one of her sisters and she can't take it anymore. She's at a motel with her other sister and wants me to take her to her mom's house in Texarkana, 200 miles east of Dallas. All I need is gas and couple of bucks for my pocket. She obliges and I do her this solid.

Before I drive 400 miles, I head to south Dallas to get a dime bag of smoke. I arrive at a motel across town where Homegirl and her sister are staying. She's not close to being ready, so I grab her duffel bag and a few plastic bags filled with clothes and put them in my car. Homegirl is finally ready. We light a blunt and roll out.

Homegirl and I come from Texarkana, an east Texas border town. As we travel east on Highway 30, I reminisce about my childhood. I tell her about my summer vacations spent in this small town eating yellow meat watermelon and visiting Grandpa'nem. When I turned 13, we travelled back to Texarkana from California. The five of us - pop, mom, two older brothers and I- are staying at The Howard Johnson. My Uncle Rasheed, aunt and cousin came with us for a short stay. It's 1:30 am and my uncle needs to get to work. He turns to me and asks if I would drive him and my auntie back to Dallas. "You damn skippy!" I said with excitement in my voice. I look over at my mother and see that worried look trying to tell me I'm too young. My pop cosigns and says, "Let the boy go." My 11 year old cousin wants to come with us; my two older brothers are already sleeping which is a win for me. If they go, I won't be driving. I'm in the front seat with my cousin; auntie and uncle are in the back. One more concerned look and a word of caution from mom and we hit the road in my uncle's 1982 Olds Delta 88. It's midnight blue with power everything and Earth, Wind & Fire singing *That's the Way of the World* on the radio. I set the cruise control to 80 and we're flyin' low. Uncle Rasheed says in a semiconscious state every 50 miles, "Slow down nephew." We pulled in to Oak Cliff just in time for my uncle's shift at the Post Office. My uncle says, "Right on Nephew."

Homegirl brings me back into focus by telling me her exit is coming up. As I get off the highway I notice two police cars parked on the grassy median just ahead. Both cop cars pull up behind me and my street instincts kick in. I make a right into a gas station located just off the highway. I'm not too concerned. If it comes down to it all I have is a dime bag and can swallow it. I go piss and get a soda just in case I need a chaser. I get back into the car and the cops continue to follow me. We twist and turn through Texarkana back streets and the police match me right for right, left for left. Homegirl says take the next right. I hit the signal, turn right and the cop hits his lights. Unbelievably, her mother lives only two houses away. As I look in the review mirror, I notice the cop is black. It's been my experience black cops tend to overcompensate in front of their white counterparts so as not to appear weak or soft on the brothas. Given the history between black people and the police in America, any brotha who chooses to wear the blue is suspect. I'm expecting him to be an asshole. He does not disappoint.

Cop says, "Do you know why I stopped you?"

I reply, "No."

Cop says, "Failing to signal 50 feet before the turn."

I ask, "Are you serious?"

Cop replies, "That's right. License and insurance. Step out of the car sir."

Meanwhile, his German Shepard is barking and slinging slobber all over the back seat of the cop car. "Hands on the hood", he says. During my preliminary pat down, the cop missed the dime bag in my t-shirt pocket as I knew he would.

Cop says, "Can I search your vehicle?"

I ask, "What will happen if I say no?"

Cop says, "Then we gonna be here all night."

I reply, "Damn, go ahead man."

The cop already missed what he was looking for, so he can search all he likes. His partner finishes his interview with Homegirl. She's standing there looking anaphylactic. The white cop is easy going; a typical "just doing my job" type of cop. He's trying to keep my mind off his partner giving my car a rectal exam. The black cop comes over and starts to cuff me. I say, "Hold up, is this normal procedure?" He replies, "Yes!"

In my peripheral, the white cop is trying not to let me see his confused expression which tells me this isn't standard procedure. He goes back to my car and pulls out her duffel bag full of weed. I look at her and ask who it belongs to. The black cop shouts "shut up!" I notice the white cop attempting to hide the fact that he's uncomfortable and taken aback by what's happening. I'm taken in handcuffs and placed in the back of the white cop's car. In the meantime, a third cop shows up who quickly put Homegirl in his car. An undercover cop rolls up, climbs into the cop car with Homegirl and begins questioning her. Once he's done he gets in the white cop's car to talk to me. He says, "We know where this stuff is coming from and we know where it's going. Tell me what you know and it'll be easier on you." This hillbilly is fishing in a dry pond, but what he said may be true because the cops were waiting on that exit for someone. "I don't know anything man," I say. I don't know if I'm more pissed off at this bitch for getting us caught up or because she didn't tell me. If she had, Buford T. Justice here couldn't catch me with Tony Hill's hands. The undercover cop gets out and the white cop gets in; I remember his reaction to the black cops' attitude, so I see an angle.

I say, "Say man, if you don't mind please give me some room in these cuffs. I have an old football injury in my shoulder."

A Texas white boy ought to have some sympathy for an old football injury. He obliges me by putting two handcuffs together; he helps me out of the back seat and uncuffs me with a warning, "This is a felony. If you give me any trouble I will treat you like a felon."

With the cuffs hanging on one wrist he turns his back to me and walks over to the third cop to get his cuffs. I'm looking around for an escape route, but this is a strange hood. I don't know which fences to hit. Plus, something tells me black cop is just waiting on an excuse to turn that dog loose. I'm standing still like a good nigga and white cop links two cuffs together and sits me back in his car. On the way to the county jail I want to see if this guy is the Lone Ranger or Barney Fife.

I say, "I've never been through this before. Can you tell me what I'm lookin' at?" The ranger let me know everything I could expect.

He says, "Hey man, I'm just doin' my job."

We arrive at the county jail and I still have a dime bag on me. They'll have to outsmart me for this little sack. I finally make it into the holding cell, angling and trying to figure out my next move. The irony is not lost on me. How can I smuggle this shit into jail? Some may say get rid of it, but they haven't spent their life trying to get away with shit just to see if they could. My mindset has always remained the same – the system is rigged, no one is following the rules so why should I. Fuck the consequences! There aren't any if you don't get caught. Such is the rationale of the Black Sheep.

My life started this way. I'm the youngest of three Air Force kids who travelled the world and witnessed first-hand what it's like to be different in an unknown land. It starts with the one child in the house who requires more discipline than his siblings and parents who were preoccupied with their marital problems. I was a hard-headed young man with time to burn and fun to have. I rarely ever paid attention in school; books and term papers were never my forte. I was a regular visitor of detention and Saturday school. I even found my way into a police station one 4th of July weekend. By the time I was 11 I managed to get myself in trouble for arson and burglary. The street afforded me a first-class education. It's how I knew that pig would miss my stash.

The black cop is interviewing me. He says, "Now's your chance to state your case. You can write down your side of the story." He's looking for me to self-incriminate. I write one line, "My only involvement in this is driving a friend to her mother's house." I saw the look in his eyes, smug satisfaction to uncertainty and concern, "So that's all you gonna write?" The rule on the street says never say or write anything down especially when it comes to the law. No one should ever assume the law will do the right thing with your words. The more one talks the more likely it is you will talk yourself right into a rendezvous with old sparky. When you talk, you limit and severely curtail the number and variations of lies your lawyer will be able to tell on your behalf. I have no need for a lawyer's lies. I ask the attending correctional officer (CO) to use the bathroom which is a single bathroom the size of a closet. He escorts me into the stall and locks me in. Now's my time to get rid of the dime bag these idiots didn't find when they took me in. I lodge the sack behind the toilet; I have every intention of coming back to retrieve it after they issue the orange jumpsuit. I return to the booking area for a full body search, "Lift up your nut sack! Bend over and spread your ass cheeks!" All I can think of are slaves greased up and standing on the block awaiting inspection and sale. I'm finding out what I'm worth the hard way. Dressed in prison orange, I ask a different CO to take me to the bathroom. I returned to the stall to get my stash. I take the sole out my high top, compress the bag of weed and ever so carefully arrange it on the arch. I cover up the sole and I'm on my way. The CO fails to search me again.

After my bathroom run I'm moved to an intake room with 60 other inmates. Another CO is yelling orders.

"If you have anything you should put it in the trash now! Don't let us find it later. If you get rid of it now, we won't add another felony charge, but if we find it later, we will!"

Several of us are dirty with contraband, but not one of us moves. The consensus is fuck them and just as I thought, COs don't check shit.

I'm moved upstairs to a cell and it's a sight to behold. I'm in concrete hell, caged like an animal. This jail has two stories of ten mass cells, fifty to a cell, twenty five bunks, two showers, three toilets and four pissers. I'm not from around here. This is a small-town jail and everyone knows each other. These inmates went to preschool with the guards. I don't know what gangs are popping, who's clicking with whom or who's beefing. This is an unknown battlefield. I don't know friend from foe, so I watch and listen. I managed to get a bunk in the back against the wall so I can see them coming. I relocate my stash for easy access just in case they come busting in. I get close enough to the men running this tank so I can listen without getting caught ear hustling.

My recon says this place is wide open. Inmates are stashing pounds of weed and here I thought I was doing something with my little ol' dime piece. I see a big head, high-yellow nigga nicknamed Tweety standing at the bars flirting with a female CO. His eyes are blood burgundy and flying half-mast when he looks her in her eyes and says, "That's right, I'm fucked up!" I'm struck by his uncanny resemblance of my father as young man. I have to stop myself from staring at him. I keep Tweety in my peripheral because if it's going down, it's going down around him. I've got nothing to do but wait so I roll one and light it up, and ponder the thought of just how close I came to being from around here. I was born in San Antonio, but my home is California; I've smoked some of the best green this planet has to offer. I'm smoking dirt-packed weed - all sticks and stones - yet this is one of the best highs I've known. Fuck them guards, fuck them bars!

Sitting in a sea of nothingness, I can't help but think about Texarkana and the irony of being locked up in this country jail. There are two kinds of people in any small town - those who love it, live and die without ever leaving the county. The others are haunted at birth by an overwhelming compulsion to catch the first thang smokin'. My father was of the latter because his father cast a long shadow. First thang smokin' for him was the Hercules C-130, an Air Force cargo plane he flew in Vietnam fresh out of high school. He was a high yella rich nigga which was hard on him. Most people he knew were barefoot poor and blacker than the law allowed. Next to none were educated, black or white, so they gave him mad shit. As a child I could see he still hadn't gotten over it. My grandfather was superintendent of the Jim Crow schools in Texarkana; the kind of man who wore a three-piece suit and a fedora to the Piggly Wiggly. He drove a showroom floor mint green 1976 Coupe DeVille long as the block. Grandpa Hennington made sure his only boy had four years of Prairie View paid for before graduating high school, but my pop had other ideas. After my father's efforts to escape the Mason Dixon, his youngest son has been ensnared by slave catchers.

Samuel Houston Hennington, Sr.

Grandpa's Cadillac

My father Samuel Houston Hennington, Jr. & his sister Charlotte

My brothers and I

2

Its lights out and I'm anything but still. The realization is setting in. I have nothing but time to ponder the irony of my presence in such a place. No slumber this night; contemplation is working the graveyard shift. I make a concerted effort not to allow myself to wonder and worry about my legal problems at this point; there are more pressing issues at hand. I'm attempting to ascertain whether I can close my eyes without regret. I sit in my bunk quietly hunting blind, concealing my eyes in the shadows so I can watch without being watched. I see it all – alcohol, tobacco, firearms, drugs, gambling 24/7. I'm aware of the inherent dangers of attempting to steal anything in the den of thieves even if it's only a glance. Anything they're doing doesn't need a witness. If they get caught for anything guess who's the snitch – you – and once you get a snitch jacket, you keep it forever like luggage. Inmates run the joint and do all the paperwork; sooner or later, no matter how many transfers you request, someone you've done time with will have you back in baggage claim. If you're caught snitching expect to find fists, shanks, broken glass, boiling water or a lock in a sock. You won't see it coming, but when they come, they aren't coming one at a time or playing fair. You can request protective custody (PC) where you'll do your time with child molesters and the rest of the snitches, but if they want you bad enough, they'll pay the guards to set you up.

It's the middle of the night. With nothing to do I watch how the inmates get down in the dark; I see many things, but what I see the most is honor amongst thieves. My voyeuristic activities allow me to see the soul of a crook – dirty, but not evil. The difference? Dirty may pick your pocket, steal your car, assault you, break into your house and take you for everything you own. It may even kill you. Evil will wait until you and your entire family is home, then he commits a heinously unspeakable crime and makes you watch. There's no evil here, but what's here is dirty. It's count time. All inmate and personnel movement is stopped so COs can account for everyone. Strange how both sides of the bars work to minimize the time this takes though for different reasons. For us it's like on the outside, when the cops are around you slow down. For the COs it forces them to come amongst us; a not so subtle reminder they are locked up as well.

It's breakfast time at 2:30 am. This is where I start my infiltration. I've got one angle - I don't eat pork. This is a country jail; the damn corn flakes have pork in them. And so begins the trade,

"Say man, I'll give you a bag of chips for the ham." says an inmate

"A'ight, cool," I replied

"Where you from nigga?" asks an inmate named Tennessee

"Cali", I replied

"Whuuut? Westside!" he said

"Right, right," I replied

"What the fuck is you doin' off up in this muthafucka?" he asks.

"I got drafted," I replied.

"I know that's right!" he says.

Tennessee said they got him for 250 pounds of weed so we're instant simpatico. He was busted a couple days before me which means he'll see the judge before me. He'll serve as a barometer on what the courts will try to do to me. Plus, it seems he's been on a recon mission of his own. There was no sleep for us. We stayed up all night. He tells me about the goings on in this place, but what's more obvious is the information he's not saying which makes clear to me he's a pretty cool dude. He clued me in on what I needed to know without me having to ask because he knew it was helpful to another outsider. He knew to watch my back and I his with just a glance. He's intelligent enough to recognize the value in this kindred crook and cunning enough to check me out in similar manner. Still, this being jail, caution is warranted. "Pretty cool dude" is standard issue camouflage for evil.

We go about putting out our feelers in an attempt to find out what's on the wire. This is all about making our stay as Cadillac as possible. For me, it's about getting as even with these crackers as much as my current situation will allow. I'm settling in, unloading what little property belongs to me when an inmate yells, "Yo Tweety! They got the dogs downstairs!" An inmate trustee who just finished mopping saw the dogs and clued us in.

"Fuck! How long they been down there?" Tweety says.

"Bout' five to six minutes", says the trustee.

"Aight't den we got about five mo'e minutes", Tweety replies.

Inmates are running in all directions. They do their best to hide contraband in their possession. You name it, we had it - weed, rocks, powder, crystal, cell phones and even a couple of 22 caliber semi-automatic Smith & Wesson's. Dudes with the big stashes and reputations to go with them get the best spots which are usually up high. It's very difficult to get a dog's nose up there. Prisoners do this with speed and military precision. I'm at a distinct disadvantage, uncertain of how the sheriff conducts his shakedowns, so I palm my dime bag and a slight of hand trick in plain sight allows contraband to be concealed, adjusted, relocated and discarded with a flick of the wrist. This allows me the most options in my attempt to evade and elude.

Sure enough and right on time, COs call rec (recreation); our one shot for air and the outdoors. We line up and head out to the yard. I hang out in the back of the line so whatever they throw at us will happen to me last. I've got three to five seconds which is more than enough time. They didn't search us on the way out which was strange. On the yard, the ominously palpable tension makes its presence known. I look around and see brothas hoopin' just like we did as kids at play during 4th grade recess. The game keeps the guards distracted. The yard's propensity for violence is infamous and not just because we're so close together which gives us ample time and opportunity, but because it affords us the greatest opportunity to get away with it.

All of a sudden, tension ignites. The diversion is a free throw line tomahawk dunk over two in the paint that shakes the goal post to its foundation. Just as the whole yard turns to show proper respect with a rumbling OOOOHHHHH, an inmate is hit from behind and goes down. While the guards are distracted with the stretcher, the prime stash real-estate can be accessed without being spotted. Tennessee and I walk the perimeter so we can smoke what we can. We eat the rest. From the extent to which these niggas are going to conceal the spoils, I can tell it wouldn't be prudent to take mine back in, so I swallow the last of my sack- sticks, stones and all. It's over. I see the K-9 unit exit and discreetly disappear around the corner. As we line up to go back to the cells, I'm taking mental note of the security procedures. I'm looking for cracks in their modus operandi. The cracks are in plain sight much like their policing.

All told there was a loss of 15% of the hidden contraband which is acceptable. If you wish to stash your stash, you're required to contribute to the cause. As such the collection plate is passed and all offerings are hidden in places known to have been recently discovered by the COs. Their subterfuge allows the guards to think they're doing a good job and justifies the K-9 budget. It also gives the COs enough to smoke, shoot or snort for free which saves them money. The time and trouble of having to go across the tracks to deal with less than savory individuals who are the same motherfuckers they'll see on this side of the bars sooner or later. We're smoking big blunts and talking shit to the COs.

"Fuck you!"

"Bring yo scary ass off up in here. Punk bitch!"

"Have you in here screamin' for backup! What you gonna do, lock me up? You still gonna have to explain to your wife how you got that black eye and busted lip and why you need Preparation H."

There's one thing about being locked up - when one has nothing to lose, one can find freedom even in a hell hole like this. It's liberating.

An inmate who works in the kitchen tells us the hooch will be up here after dinner. Hooch is jailhouse wine made of sugar, fruit juice, bread for the yeast and time. In California they call it pruno. Our cocktail of choice is stored in the refrigerator and kept in 50 gallon drums all in plain sight. One of my cellies tasted it last night and said it was fire. It takes 3 trustees, 3 mop buckets and a few supplies. Inmates fill a small trash bag with hooch. Then tie off one bag inside the other to ensure air tightness and to spot leaks. Next, they place the bag of hooch at the bottom of the bucket and fill it with dirty, soapy water and use the mop to hold the bag down. The inmates' ingenuity is impressive. They've figured out how to send written notes and contraband orders known as "kites" through the toilet system. By now its common knowledge I don't eat pork so the bidding for my lunch begins.

An inmate says, "Say bruh, I'll give you 2 bags of chips fo' yo' bologna."

Another inmate says, "I'll give you a box-o-cookies and a bag of chips."

Pork is a commodity on this exchange. I hooked up a deal for $25 of store (jailhouse 7-11) for the rest of this week's swine. Just in time, too. I didn't have a dime when they booked me.

Sitting on frigid stainless steel picnic tables are 50 men striving to avoid his brand of imminent blues. Some are playing chess, spades, dominoes; some are reading books. Some are getting into things they shouldn't. I'm watching TV and shooting the shit with Tennessee. A mutual grin and knowing looks are exchanged as we bask in our triumphant efforts to escape even if only for a few hours. I best dust off my chess game.

It's chowtime and the whole tank migrates to the bars. Our wrangling reminds me of the subjugated Sioux awaiting rancid rations. Rancid for the same reason - some public official is pocketing the profits. This doesn't bother some. Inmates are laughing joking, eating and sleeping without giving a fuck. Still, there's something to be said for the ability to, day in and day out, maintain your nonchalance. This is one of the ways manhood is quantified on lockdown. After lunch the conniving begins where it left off. Tennessee came up on some weed and who doesn't like to smoke after a meal. In order to mask the smell, Tweety unrolls four feet of toilet paper, rubs deodorant on it and twists the paper. He lights one end, blows it out and let's it smolder like incense.

"What the fuck is that burnin?" says a CO.

"It's just deodorant man. We just tryin' get rid of some of the funk in this nasty muthafucka," we explain.

The CO's hate the stench too. If by chance we run across a guard that gives a fuck and tells us to put it out, we switch to a smoke screen which consists of socks filled with medicated talcum powder. We beat them on the white brick so as not to leave any traces. The ensuing cloud of fragrant powder masks and defuses the weed smoke. As I'm smoking, I watch self-imposed segregation play out. The Buffalo Soldiers over here, Poncho Villas' gorillas in the back, and front and center are some of old Stonewall's brigade. Each group is full of criminals who are collaborating and commiserating. The subject matters range from meth cooking and crack sales to breaking and entering.

As we're smoking, an inmate tells us how he committed his crime, "Yeah man, she just left her car window down. I reached right in and took her garage door opener off the visor. She was at work; I was in and out of her house before she even thought to look for it. I rigged it to open any garage door of the same brand."

Another inmate offers his help, "I can teach you how to disable a home security system. I used to work for ADT."

Littlewood has been in and out of this jail since he got out of juvie. I like him. He's a laid back white boy who doesn't give a fuck. He tells me how to make silencers out of a corn cob and two 2-liter bottles. If guns were my thing, I'd have two more reasons to use them, two less reasons to worry about getting caught and four more reasons for you to fear me on the street. It isn't me with which you must concern yourself considering the element within ear shot of these conversations.

A few of us are bullshitin' when an inmate gets to talking about dirt he got away with. I see it come over him - the realization that Tennessee and I aren't local boys, and may be snitches:

"What you two niggas in here fo'?"says the inmate.

"Weed, man" I reply.

"Boaf y'all?" he asks.

"Yeah" Tennessee replies.

"Where'd they get yuh?" an inmate asks

"We didn't get busted together," Tennesse replies.

"Naw man, I just got here last night," I reply.

"Ooh! You dat nigga dat got caught wit' o'girl," the inmate says.

"Yeah man," I reply.

The inmate yells across the cell, "Say Tweet, dis du nigga right here."

I knew exactly what happened to me – it was a straight set up. She had me run interference. That's why the K-9 cops were waiting for us on that exit. Either she was running off at the mouth or the cops got a tip from the dude she's running for. I don't know the particulars, but I recognize this subterfuge. In the six seconds it took me to see this angle I realize these niggas were expecting me which is good news. They weren't waiting on me which would indicate someone gave the order. If that were so, they would've been discreet. Today's paper will show a picture of the heroic police and K-9 unit victoriously fighting the scourge of drugs in the community with a headline that reads "Keeping poison out of the hands of our children" as the cop stands awash in righteous fortitude while taking a cut of the drug deals to finance his retirement. In any penitentiary in America, COs and inmates alike can indulge in organized crime, drug trafficking, alcohol, prostitution, extortion and gambling. All of this occurs 24 hours a day seven days a week on maximum security lock down.

Many of these cats will see the judge in the morning. Most men are in here for drug offenses, domestic violence, B&E (breaking and entering), robbery, aggravated assault and DUIs. Tennessee and I find our way to the marijuana caucuses. When it comes to the legal statutes, precedents and mandatory sentencing, the men in here are Rhode Scholars, every single one. I notice Tennessee is paying full attention in class; he's seeing the Man in the morning, but just for an arraignment. He may get a bond set which is the one way to find out what it's going to cost him to see daylight again. The boys say his bond will be about $250,000. Upon hearing this prediction, Tennessee turned to me and said the same thing I was thinking - "time to lawyer up."

Tennessee is settled back in his bunk; he tells me he'll have his girl call a lawyer he heard about in here.

"Ain't heard nothin' but good shit from muthafuckas about this white boy", Tennessee replies.

"Word! What have you heard?" I reply

"Last time Littlewood had him for a PD he got him off so smoove, Littlewood went home and broke off $5,000 out of his re-up stash and gave it to him. He said if he would've had to hire anybody else, it would've cost him twice as much for half as good." Littlewood has no doubt this investment will yield high returns. Another dude said after the counselor got him off scot-free he still owed him $1,500. Daniel Siler told him to keep it", Tennessee replied.

"Damn! A lawyer told him to keep his money!" I exclaimed.

A few more people start telling Siler stories. "Man, you should hear these convicts in here campaignin' for this lawyer like he was the second comin'." They finally fray off into good and bad stories about other PDs and lawyers. No one in here has heard anything bad about this lawyer.

We're going down to the chow hall for dinner. This ought to be educational. I'll get a chance to see how things work when we're all on the move. Movement is key to any contraband trafficking and trading; it opens the entire inventory of black market merchandise. Tennessee said he got the hookup on brand new underwear from a dude that works in laundry. This isn't a big deal to some, but that same some have never had to place their private parts in public underwear. I'm working on getting a thicker mattress because two inch foam on a steel plank isn't cutting it. I found two extra mattresses and I'm doing my damnedest to turn this bootleg mattress pad into a Serta Perfect Sleeper, doubled over and propped up against the wall.

It's 3:30 pm and we're going to dinner which will make for a long night. What the fuck am I talkin' about? I'm locked up. They're all long, but that's how quickly and easily it happens. We're lined up and marching out in a prompt and orderly military fashion. There are too many hands moving in too many directions. To the COs, it looks like chaos. It's anything but. A hand shake is a transaction. A simple "what's up?" is a prelude to violence. A head nod is conformation of a successful venture, exchange and/or 3rd party sale.

In front of the cells, along the tier and down the stairs, 150 convicts are going east and west. I find the collations between this and a grade school cafeteria disturbing. There are plenty of rules around territory. If you're over there, you better be handling business. If you're sitting over here you better have an invite. If you're hanging out in the back it's because you belong in back. Tennessee and I don't participate; we aren't invested enough to trade stock on this exchange. One must be grandfathered in.

Plastic tray, plastic spork, plastic chili mac. I'm eating without chewing, inhaling so as not to taste. At the same time I'm taking in my surroundings. I look down the table and see something that affirms one of my opinions about poor white and black folks especially in or from the south. Four white boys in unison crumbling cornbread into their black-eyed peas callin' each other "Wood", short for pecker wood. In the south, black and white folks have more in common than not. They eat black-eyed peas the same way even in the clank.

I notice some are enjoying this dining experience, consuming provisions like they just came out of Big Mama's cast iron skillet. They're soppin' the corner of the plate which is evidence the most dire consequence of prolonged incarceration is mental institutionalization. I sit here quietly pondering how such a thing like incarceration came to pass through my life. I'm not hungry enough to joyfully ingest Lord knows what. Even more of a quandary, I wonder if my stay will be extended enough for such a thing to happen to me. Chow is over. We're on our way back to the cells.

I see and hear something that for some reason I failed to notice at rec - a railroad switch yard where diesels sit idling, rumbling and spewing exhaust day and night. The air ducts are down wind and facing the tracks which explains the radioactive aromas in the cells. I wonder what kind of medical repercussions exposure to prolonged train exhaust will hold. This shit is strong enough to circumvent the severest of sinus infections.

We finally make our way back to the tank; it's relatively tranquil and I'm happy my belly is full after such a long, arduous day. I want to chill and watch TV. There aren't any women here and I'm lucky enough to be in a tank with very few youngsters, so there's no excess talking. Like most men with a full gut, we covet the silence. I forgot all about the pruno and it arrives right on schedule. Made with apple juice, this drink is surprisingly smooth. I don't know why I should doubt these country boy whiskey making abilities. These field niggas been brewing this shit right under Massa's' nose for centuries. I'm not a drinking' man, but the circumstances are special. You would think introducing alcohol into dynamics such as these would be about as intelligent as drinking kerosene and pissing on a camp fire. Quite the contrary. Give a man a full plate and a full glass, and he is as content as an Alabama tick on back of a Georgia hound dog. All understanding it won't last, but the relative reprieve is well received. In this tank, most of us are of a mature age which means there might be a lot of shit, but there won't be much bullshit. Most bullshit comes from young men attempting to assert and/or prove their budding manhood. This is tolerated maybe a little more than is prudent because it wasn't that long ago when we did the same damn thing.

The magnitude of the situation is starting to show on Tennessee. He's on his way to see the Judge in the morning. He came over to my bunk hoping for some distraction. We ceremoniously pour out a little liquor for our homies who've gone before us either to prison or to the grave; we're from the streets so this is how we show our respect. As we drink, he starts in, "Man this ain't shit. My homeboys' granddaddy showed me how to make this shit from corn. He used to run his 49' Mercury on it," Tennessee explains. Moonshine stories abound. They all start the same way, "Remember that time we drank that shine?" Tennessee continues with his story about the one time he drank too much and how he threw up, and what happened after he passed out from the hooch. The lies about whiskey are almost as good as the lies about pussy and just as telling. Just the same, we can't wait to hear the next one. Guess we could all use a little distraction. For Tennessee, the storytelling isn't working; he's contemplating and calculating on how he's going to handle the judge in the morning. He's trying to play the point spread; the unknown variables are killing' him and I know he knows better. All of what he's doing requires too much effort, yet yields no fruit. Even a hard man hates to gamble with his future.

In order for us to hear the TV we use headphones which requires inmates to sit on cold stainless steel day room tables, but not Littlewood. He hooked himself up with a job in maintenance which gives him access to, amongst other things, 15 feet of speaker wire on his headset allowing him the luxury of watching from his bunk. His cavalier, devil-may-care disposition may seem innate; it requires years of devotion and dedication to fucking up. Unless you've had the honor of fuckin' up a time or two, you will never be able to fathom both the length and breadth of the constitutional fortitude, instinctual cunning and the unmitigated gall to tell the judge in open court to "suck my dick!" All are prerequisites to achieve this Zen like state.

It's time for spread, inmate's version of a jailhouse meal prepared in the cells. Those who've been to store begin cooking. Everything looks nasty. The things I see getting mixed together don't look or smell appetizing in the slightest.

I ask, "Say Tweet, what the fuck is you making?"

"Spread nigga," Tweety replies.

"You gonna eat that shit?" I ask.

Four or five of them start to laugh. Tweety smiles and says "you will too." "Oh hell no, not Cali," I explain. He grins like he's heard that shit before. Spread consists of ramen noodles, summer sausage, corn chips, nacho squeeze cheese and jalapenos. This is the nastiest shit I've ever seen or smelled. I'm uninterested completely. Still, Tweety has done more than his share of time in the county, so he feels no compulsion to convince. Everyone is heaping this shit on bread and while Tennessee is trying to convince me, "it's good Cali." I'm not that hungry – yet.

The hooch is chilled in the commode. A stainless steel pot is designated, bleached and scrubbed with Ajax, then rinsed with boiling water from the spigot for coffee and ramen noodles. Then the pot is lined with plastic trash bags, flayed and spread. They line the bags with paper so if it's snatched out and discarded it looks like a bag of trash. Bags of hooch are then laid on top. All ingenuity born in the clank is consequently twice as ingenious.

The hour is late and it's lights out. There's not much going on and the judge is the foremost thought tonight. Even if you aren't seeing the Man in the morning, you'll eventually see the Man. No sense in worrying myself. I'm going to sleep. I'm attempting to bring my first 24 hours of incarceration to conclusion and trying in vain not to concern myself with what is most certainly to come.

3

I awaken to the return of the damned back from court. The expressions on their faces range from quiet concern to fearful disbelief. Some got the news about high bail, no bail, extra and dropped charges. I notice a young white boy with eyes full of sympathetic sorrow. He says, "Man, they sendin' y'all to the pin!" He's referring to the disproportionate number of blacks who receive disproportionately stiffer sentences for the same crimes white folks commit. He sees with his own eyes the lies he was told about black folks. Now he's thinking them niggers might not be bullshitting about racism and discrimination. He slowly walks to his bunk and sits in dismay, visibly shaken and gratefully thanking the Lord for making him a good ol' white boy. I would be remiss if I neglected to mention the other side of that still burning cross of "them niggers deserve it." They don't voice these opinions too loud. This is the clank. They're acutely aware that in here they're the minority. This poor kid is ill-equipped to handle this situation, a fact not lost on the brothas. Some of them enjoy and abuse this reversal of fortune a little too much for my taste. Then again, I don't live down here with these ignorant, incestuous and inbred crackers either.

Tennessee says $200,000 is his magic number. His PD advised him to plea five years or receive deferred adjudication - ten years on probation at the end of which your record is wiped clean. The catch is for ten years you can't get so much as a parking ticket. If nine and a half years later your girl decides to call the cops, forget about it. You have to do the whole 10 years on the inside. If you don't pay now, you'll pay more later. Just like the credit card company, despite all their efforts to ensure repayment, the last thing they want is a zero balance - its business and prison is big business in the United States. A zero balance yields no revenue. If the same logic is applied to the business of corrections, lawyers and politicians will campaign and complain about the recidivism rate. You must consider who built the revolving door into the very foundation and framework of this our penal system. Only then does the motivating and mitigating factor in this contradiction reveal itself. Prison and the caged animals inside are simply revenue – not human. All of this is playing out before me like a midnight matinee and it seems so surreal, yet all too real. All the things in this life that I've done and I now face the penitentiary for something I didn't do. Every risk I ran was calculated with a high percentage and probability of escape.

I always keep a fat resume. When it became necessary for me to procure gainful employment, I'm more than qualified. I've never been cut out for manual labor. I learned early on, contrary to what I was told, the harder you work the less they pay. Digging ditches is hard work. One must reckon with the street's finite existence. Any imbecile knows the street holds no longevity, but the risk is commensurate with the reward. If I'm burdened with an X on my back and thereby forced to check the little box on any employment application, I will consequently be forced to reconsider my need and desire to coexist peaceably within respectable society.

As a child I endured many a punishment, restrictions and butt whippings most of which I had coming, but the ones I remember are the ones I didn't have coming. Civil decorum suggests I should acquiesce my anger, digress and demure. I did nothing wrong therefore I have nothing to fear. I should just wait for my portion of due process that's every American's birth right. Truculence is unwarranted and less than prudent. I do my best to have faith in truth, justice and the American way. The truth is there's no justice in America. Not for us, anyway. This is a subject with which every red-blooded American nigga must contend with. When our mothers sent us out to play it wasn't with the admonishment to watch out for strangers. Our mothers tell their children "watch out for them goddamn police!" They grew up in a more sinister America with full and intimate knowledge of the police and their ignominious evil. "Boy!" she would say, "You ain't got to be wrong for them to be right."

Tennessee is on the phone with his girl. His body language is textbook. He's eagerly listening to the ring and his relief when she picks up. He's impatient with the automated collect operator and feels ashamed for putting his loved ones in this predicament. His girl provides a little sweet consolation that only good news can bring. She tells Tennessee she spoke to his lawyer, Mr. Siler. She says he's on the case which put a pimp back in Tennessee's limp. There's nothing like a good woman when you're locked up. Something she said must've reassured him of her resiliency and wherewithal. In here, a man has only his doubts. The lady that she is, she left him with no doubts about her. As long as he lives I don't think he'll ever be able to make her understand what this means to a man. The lady that she is, he'll never have to. I'm not the type to keep a girlfriend; I just keep a couple places to stick it. These are not women one calls collect looking for bail money. These are women one calls for an amicable exchange of pleasure.

When it comes to spending any length of time with a woman, I'm particular more than some might say I have a right to. I'm not saying she has to be a cover girl, but she must attract me in some way. For my purposes, goodness is paramount. I've found this to be a most alluring and rarefied trait. We've heard the arguments "women are bitches, men ain't shit." They're speaking in half truths. The whole truth is people aren't shit. Before I spend my time with shit, I'll spend it alone.

I had a good woman once. For me, pussy itself is not all that difficult to come by. I assign it no undo value. The treasure I covet is in her goodness. I've had women from around the world. From time to time I still lust for some of those women, but I covet only one. When the tender rhapsodies of the unrequited come over the airways, invariably it is the scent of her memory I taste. Time and space hold no relevance, not for Babydoll.

My synapses are firing on all eight. I'm attempting to disseminate all I observe and apply what I've learned to my own dismal circumstance. As a child, my pop would always say, "Boy, I don't know why you insist on doing shit the hard way, but you gonna learn. Oh yeah, you gonna learn." To which I replied, "Pop, when you were my age and Grandpa was telling you the same thing, did you listen?" "Hell no boy, but you gonna learn!" My indignation gave him the impression I wasn't listening. Time will tell if I have indeed learned my lesson. My thoughts tend to travel to different times and places. It's one of my ways of coping. It's the way I keep my cool and defense against the onset of emotional instability. Letting emotions get the better of me is a feminine characteristic and this is not the place for that. A man is to control his emotions, but all too often he simply represses them which cause a surplus of other issues. I can't afford either. If I'm to get myself out of this fix, it will require at least a sound mind. In a cage, that's usually the first personal possession lost.

I've been called to the infirmary. These fools opened the gate and let me walk downstairs by myself. As I get to the ground floor, three inmates are standing around the bottom of the staircase. They're being entertained by a pretty little red bone. She's been shitting in her hand and throwing it at the guards, so they put her in psychological segregation. Through a 6 x 6 Plexiglas window she's giving a peep show. She's inventive and enthusiastic when it comes to her auto-erotic activities. It seems her fingers have proved inadequate to the task at hand and simply won't do. I don't know how long these niggas have been without pussy, but she has their undivided. A CO notices us and tells us to move on. True to form, he doesn't bother to wait for us to go around the corner before he starts enjoying the show. The only difference between COs and inmates is they haven't been caught yet.

The nurses are a pleasant surprise. It's been my experience in situations such as this that women tend to over compensate for their fully justified fears. They've been told not to let it show so the best they can come up with is bitch. They think if they act tough enough it will save them. The problem is they haven't had much practice dealing with their mortal fears. These two little old white ladies have no such issues with their Aunt Bee accent and a well-placed "sweetie" or "honey." They beguile instead of bully. They sooth with southern comfort. In return we go out of our way to be helpful and gracious. I'm grateful to these ladies for treating us like men when they don't have to.

I've been asked to piss in a cup. Before I can say anything, she attempts to convince me it's not for drug testing so naturally I assume it's for drug testing. I don't care. With all the shit being smoked, shot, and snorted around here, the weed and hooch in my system won't even raise an eyebrow. So I piss. I will prolong this outing as long as possible; I'm in no rush to get back to that cell. Since they've seen fit to allow me to roam the halls unescorted, that's exactly what I intend to do. These halls hold the promise of untold mischief so I do some recon work. The ground floor holds not only women, but men back from the big house. There's no way to get to the women in here; they're electronically locked and guarded by what can only be described as the quintessential female corrections officer. She gives the impression of a person who enjoys guarding caged and helpless women like the way a necrophiliac enjoys his job at the morgue.

I go back around the corner to see about that crazy little red bone. The CO had his boy keep a look out while he tried to get some. Now his look out is on the floor laughing hysterically while the CO has her bent her over the toilet/sink. He didn't even get it in good before she shit all over him. He scurries off to the bathroom to clean up before he has to explain. I regain my composure and go back upstairs. I'm not one for gossip, but I can't wait to tell it. Back in the tank and the word beat me back, but they didn't hear about the shitting. I leave out no detail. We laugh a long time. The judge is expecting me in the morning. Some unknowns will no longer be, but I know it won't be good. It's my turn to impose upon Tennessee and I'm glad he still has a little smoke; I'm mixing this shit with hooch tonight. I'm trying to get as high as the Himalayas. Tennessee doesn't say much. He already knows and I don't have shit to say.

After holding it since I arrived three days ago, it's finally time for me to shit. Some things are private and I would prefer to relieve myself by myself. Wiping my ass in front of 50 men is unsettling, but I'm past the point of deliberation. Inmates are holding entire conversations on the toilet, speaking in mid grunt. I find myself wondering, again, if I'll get that comfortable. In jail, even a bowel movement can't be taken lightly. I've seen some men drop their pants and remove one leg from the bundle at their feet. I was curious, but that's not a topic of casual conversation. I realized the right leg is freed up as a safety measure. If they come for me while I'm shitting, I don't want to fight for my life with my ants around my ankles.

It's 7 am and I'm in a containment cell with 20 inmates. All of us are waiting on the judge. I saw Homegirl on the other side of the hall. She attempted to give me the "it's all good" look like she put the fix in, but it fails to bring me inner peace. She's working for herself. Everyone is discussing their case with each other like someone in this cell could actually help. We're dealing with our nerves and guilt. If you don't suffer from one, you suffer from both. These are the very emotions the police are hoping will get you to self-incriminate.

They put me in a closet with a closed circuit TV. This is a security measure intended to protect his honor. The judge is not safe on his own bench in his own courtroom. This usually happens when they try to railroad the wrong people. The judge has been attacked one too many times which is indicative of oppression. It's the same kind of oppression that makes a man throw a rock at a tank. This is the seed that sows revolution. I have a female public defender which is always good news. A woman in her profession has to be good; if she where a man, she could get by with mediocrity, but not a woman. Looking at her on the monitor, the district attorney tries to strong arm her to no avail. It would appear she has the situation well in hand. My bail is still $150,000.

Upon returning to the cells, two young white boys are making a severe mistake and have no idea. They're whining and complaining about receiving relatively minuscule sentences of 3 to 6 months. They don't see the anger building up all around them. Men looking at real time have no tolerance for such childish whimpering. I look at Tweety and he just shakes his head and goes about his business. He just found out tonight is his night; he's going to the big house for the first time on a 5-year bid. He's on the chain and understandably apprehensive.

An inmate asks, "Say Tweet, what you think about bein' on that chain tonight?" He says, "A little nervous, little scared like any man."

The bravery in his honesty at such a moment and in such a place is surprisingly refreshing. One of his dark and imposing looking homeboys walks over to the crying couple of white boys and chastises them with a skill usually reserved for an episode of "Scared Straight" paralyzing his young victims with fear. For a moment, I thought he would beat them both like rented Georgia mules. He leaves them wet and smelling like piss. As they quiver he turns my way, smiles and winks. Little bastards won't be making that mistake again anytime soon.

It's Friday morning and over the intercom they announce "Muslim services, get ready." Being in the Bible belt, they have church services four times a week, even in jail. Still, it's a surprise to hear there are enough Muslims to hold services. Most people are under the mistaken impression it's easy to get religion in jail as if there is nothing else to do. This isn't true. What a man has is a lot of time to think; a luxury not afforded to a man on the outside. Life on the outside leaves little time for introspection. On the inside guilt ridden remorse tends to fester with an acidic burning in some men's gut like fire water, so they look for some absolution. Most deal in contraband. I'm curious to see if my Muslim brothers are any different. As I get ready, I hear a muffled southern drawl, "he's a Mooslem too? Figures." Tennessee says, "That's why you don't eat no pork. Should'a known." To be honest, I didn't think this establishment would even recognize the Islamic faith, a huge testament to the Muslims around here. I'm pleasantly surprised. There are 6 of us and everyone is well-organized and learned. Out of respect the contraband is kept to a minimum. Just food and coffee, things Muslims should be sharing.

As we go through the ritual of prayer and worship, I

wonder if they're orthodox or Nation of Islam. The Nation is led by Farrakhan. They've been taught things that aren't Islam. Most notably, black man is God and the white man is Devil. In these back woods, I could see how they would hold on to that hate, but I've never read anything in the Qur'an about no black or white. Such prejudices have no place in the word of The Creator. Racism is strictly a human institution. I hold no ill will though. There was a time when I was real militant so I know what they know. I just don't believe it. I was fortunate enough to have been enlightened, but there's no light down here.

The Imam lets me know in the most unforgivable way possible that most of the Muslims here are affiliated with the Nation of Islam. At the end of his speech he tries to make a point and at the same time tries to justify the Nation killing Malcolm X. He tried to do it respectfully because he knew it wouldn't go over well. For me it didn't. I'm polite and stay until the end, but I won't be back. Malcolm was my hero. I have few. It's not Islamic of me to judge what others do, but I'm not that good a Muslim yet. My faith is a work in progress. When I return to the cell Tennessee asks me how it went and looking for me to elaborate. I just say it went and leave it at that. He says cool, hands me a joint and tells me he has good news. He's getting out; his woman will be here to pick him up Monday. Siler got his bail reduced. This dude is good. Up until this point, my cynicism would not let me fully believe, but if Tennessee walks out of this jail Monday morning I will be his very next convert. I congratulate him and give him a pound. Cool as he is, he doesn't rub it in by enjoying it too overtly in front of me. It's time for me to call my people. I've been gone for four days without a word. I know the job is trippin'; they must think I up and quit. I wonder if I still have a job. I have no love for this jailhouse phone, so I make one call. The one person I know will handle everything for me. She also happens to be the one person I don't want to know I'm in this predicament – my mom.

I don't know if a mother can ever become accustomed to this type of phone call, but there are precedents. The first time my mother received this call I was 11 years old. My brother, six of our friends and I were at a Security Police station for arson on an air force base. It was not our intent to start that fire, but we burned up a lot of land. One of the neighborhood kids in dire need of acceptance told us he knew where to get illegal fireworks. He said a family friend just got back from Nevada and he watched them unlock and put them in the shed. He even remembered the combination to the lock. That night we all asked if we could sleep over each other's houses. We slept in our tree fort up on Pine Cone Hill. At 2 am in the morning we went on a commando raid. We hid in trees, bushes and behind cars. We kept lookout while the kid with the combination did the dirty work. All night and well into the next day we popped and cracked all over that base until we got word from our homeboy, the Police Chiefs' son. He told us we better take that shit off base. We found the perfect spot - a place we called Farmer's Land behind Volcano Hill. Right on the other side of the fence we rode our bikes on a dirt trail when the cows let us. We headed a little farther out where we knew there was a stand of eucalyptus trees encircling a sand pit. Funny how we walked two miles through four foot high dead grass and not one of us considered the obvious fire hazards. We find out why these particular fire crackers are illegal. These are all the best ones. We had a good time until a bottle rocket caught a cow patty on fire. We managed to put it out, but it ended the fun. As we headed back, one of my friends glanced over his shoulder at what looked like the last day of Sodom and Gomorrah - black billowing fire and brimstone. We tried to do the right thing, but it was too far gone. If we put one part out it started right back up again, so we had no choice but to call the Man. They in turn called our parents. There were one or two other times, but after that I stopped getting caught.

I call mom. She's understanding and helpful all the while trying not to let me know how much it hurt her. I'm her baby boy and she's having a hard time hiding such things from me. She knows this isn't my MO, but that doesn't do anything for her pain and disappointment. I can hear it in what she doesn't say; pain can't begin to describe what this does to me. When I was young she had to get me out of sticky shit. She beat my ass for most of it. Through it all, never once did I doubt she was coming to get me. Mama loves you when nobody else does.

That's why a bad boy will kill and die for his dear mama.

Just as I hang up the phone, a fight breaks out. Two young brothas are exchanging blows and rolling around the floor, each giving as good as he's getting. I'm glad they waited until I got off the phone; I wouldn't what my Mom to hear and have something else to worry about. It doesn't last long because someone yells "CO, CO!" Both stop on a dime and retire to neutral corners huffing, lumped up and a little bloody, promising each other a round two. There's no real anger, both are just trying to show how scared they aren't. For the onlookers, it's something to pass a little time. The fight will be commentated, discussed, debated and laughed at for hours to come.

The Warden decides it's time for a shakedown. They come busting in like storm troopers. This is supposed to be the elite squad of the COs – the Special Response Team (SRT). They're wearing grey and white camouflage fatigues and combat boots. There are 30 of them each doing their best Billy Badass impersonation. In actuality, they're simple-minded Bubbas with control issues who shout orders at us in an attempt to intimidate and give an air of no nonsense. The loudest, most obnoxious of all of them is a short stocky bastard who looks like a little Caligula nigga. He's malicious due to his cowardice and insecurities. They invoke no fear, only a chafing annoyance. These aren't the demographics to attempt the sale of woof tickets. Ordered to stand against the walls, we're all a bit surprised we didn't get advanced warning of this raid. They ransack what little personal property we have and enjoy it far too much like crack head burglars. They just missed the party and found nothing. It's the end of the week; most of the good contraband comes from visitation. Visitation days are Saturday and Sunday, and like the day before payday, rations are low. All they get is a couple of jack mags and extra blankets. Frustrated with their meager quarry, not to mention the smug looks on our faces, they holler, huff and puff for a minute or two before slinking out in dismal failure. These dumb sons of bitches didn't even get my extra mattress pad. Granted, it's not what they came in for, but it's not like them to permit a man an extra measure of comfort. Forest for the trees I guess. Good thing because I've grown accustom to the cushion. I'll do my damnedest to stay that way if for no other reason than to keep a smirk on my face when they come busting in.

This untimely raid has Tennessee's blood pressure elevated. He had his shit packed and ready to go. Now all of it looks ran over by a plow. They had to knee him in the nuts once more for good measure. We go about the business of straightening up; it looked like a tornado hit a Texas trailer park. A single unanimous murmur is audible throughout the cell; all of us hoping we get the opportunity to catch one of these SRT motherfuckers on the street. For most, it doesn't matter which one. Littlewood says he knows where the little tyrant lives and says he won't see it coming or know who's responsible for the disastrous calamity that will befall him. Knowing what I do about Littlewood, he'll get his get back. I'm standing at the bars looking at the guards, up the tiers and down the halls watching oversized dim-witted hillbillies with shotguns doing their best John Wayne. There's nothing more dangerous than armed ignorance. I wonder how cocky they'd be if they knew they weren't the only ones armed and dangerous.

I just returned from laundry with a change of sheets and socks. I was also issued a coat - green with a reflective yellow encircled X across the whole of the back just in case we make a run for it. Billy Bob will have an iridescent target at which to aim. The absurdity of this tactic is confounding. We're cunning enough to escape, but not enough to take the jacket off or simply turn it inside out? Does the warden believe us stupid? Is he right or is he ruthless and diabolical enough to employ Machiavellian psychology?

It's Saturday and some are coming back from visitation. A few inmates are dealing with more bad news about women and kid problems. The loot looks promising. They don't say anything. It's on their faces. They're happy they got what they were expecting and happy they didn't get caught. We're happy we'll be high tonight. Inebriation dulls the blade just a little.

After the initial celebratory gluttony, we go about the business of stashing the surplus. We found out the hard way we can't rely on our early detection system. We know the powers that don't be are eager to assert the figment thought to be their authority. The trick is to allow them to believe they're in control. As long as they believe, we have little reason for concern. Most anyone employed by corrections suffers from severe control issues. The only other reason to work in a place like this is a dire need for a job. If that's the case, you don't get any real promotions. Those positions are reserved for the dedicated. It's difficult to foster dedication in a cesspool of corruption. So what's left in this shallow employment gene pool? Control issues. These backwoods suffer from no shortage of such simple men. We learn to make the best of our circumstances.

It's Monday morning and I've lost my co-pilot. He woke me to say goodbye. I gave him a pound and wished him good luck. We were up late dreaming about getting out. I asked him about it so he wouldn't feel bad about bringing it up. I don't know if he could tell because I tried not to let it show, but I will miss our collaboration. A good friend is a rare and precious commodity especially in hell. Don't get it twisted, I'm elated for my nigga, but my misery was rather fond of his company.

I've fallen prey to another asinine and ineffective security measure. They've decided to split us up; they're moving a few of us to different tanks. They think they can disrupt the black market. Shit like this only serves to facilitate trade. Redistribution and relocation eases the availability of products and services. They moved Littlewood and me down one tank. Now I've got to start all over. The demographics in this tank are a little different - an odd mix. A few older white men and a few younger black men. I find a top bunk against the back wall and close to the TV. A middle aged white man offers me his bottom bunk because he prefers the top. I can't tell if he's afraid of me or thinks I'll offer some protection. Either way, I got a bottom bunk.

The bottom bunk next to me is inhabited by an old white man. If I have one prejudice, it's old southern white men. I can't help it. On sight, the first things I think about are the pictures and stories of lynchings I've seen. Every white person in town standing around laughing and pointing at castrated, beaten, burned and hanged black bodies. Most of the older ones are already dead or so decrepit they wish they were. Lynchings were a family affair; 7 year old boys and girls watching and enjoying. I can't help but think that's who I see next to me now. I feel a compulsion, almost a duty to look him in the eye and cut his throat while my young brothas and I stand around laughing and pointing as he bleeds out. I know it isn't fair or right, but I ask you, what's fair or right got to do with lynchings?

Here I sit, trying to be a better man. Though I must admit, it's hard to see the benefits at this particular juncture. The fact that he's old and docile makes me sick. It means if I hall off and fuck him up then subjugate and oppress him, that makes me an asshole. Then there's always the possibility he could've been one of the two white men in the entire south that didn't actively participate in the viciously vial oppression of my people. I'm not talking about 100 years ago. I mean my mother and father. I'm not too happy about these pups either. They don't know how to sit still. They're gang related, so they're too afraid to live and die on their own. They will tell you in a minute "I don't give a fuck", trying in vain to act hard. I watch the old white man intently. I'll let him decide whether or not I should regard him as an enemy. In the interest of not being an arbitrary asshole myself, I'll have to factor in when and where he was born, reared and raised, none of which he chose. I can't blame him for being a red neck any more than he can blame me for being a thug. While I watch them, they watch me.

James, the one who gave me his bunk seems to be a man of some education. As such, he's less apprehensive about revealing his curiosity. Believing me to be a man of reason, he asks questions. He's not from the street; he doesn't know he's in violation so I tolerate his naiveté. Asking a man from the street personal questions is a good way to catch a snitch jacket. For his own good I interject a quick admonishment, "you ask more questions than the police." I say it with a smirk so he knows he's in no danger. He gets the point, smiles and backs off. This old white man is altogether different. He's a crook from way back. You can't tell him shit. At first I thought he was being kind and generous to minimize people fucking with him. He's the same with people who can't offer any threat. He's the original good ol' boy. He and Littlewood have conducted business in the past. To my surprise, even the young brothas bestow upon him a measure of respect; they call him "School"

- short for old school.

It's Wednesday and I'm back in court to talk with my public defender. My former PD has gone on maternity leave, so his honor has seen fit to appoint me another. The word about my first PD was pretty good; a rare thing for someone working for free. The word on my new one is all bad; lazy, corrupt and an immense lack of skills. I don't find this out until after our brief meeting, but I gathered as much from the way he handled me. He asked me questions as if I were guilty, "what was all that liquid fabric softener for?" "What are you talkin' about?" "The bag with the 27 pounds of marijuana had a lot of fabric softener in it. Why?" "Man, I don't know!" He never asked me what happened and just like that, the meeting was over. This is the law's idea of equal representation.

As I get back to the tank my first and only thought is Counselor Daniel Siler. I might have stayed with the first PD, but he's at best a double agent. James lends me a note pad and pen; I had to buy a stamp and envelope. I got the counselor's address from Tennessee and decided to write a letter the likes of which he has never read. I let him know I'm not the conventional convict with which he's become accustomed. To that end, I compose a Shakespearean masterpiece, calling forth my eclectic phraseology from every unnamed source I've forgotten. The couple of paragraphs I've written took me all damn night. They're time consuming not just because I'm going 15 rounds with Webster's Dictionary, but because I've never been panic stricken before, not even while being shot at. I don't like this afraid shit. I'm not a man without fear, but the fear I deal in is tempered with excitement and laced with adventure. This shit here is uncut.

I'm back in my jail bunk with all of my fears and hopes folded up in an envelope. How corrupt is this institution? Will this letter even get past the nearest trash can? How many corrupt officials will read and laugh at my desperation? Will super lawyer even give a fuck? Will my cry for freedom end up discarded upon a pile of neglected cries for freedom? Then again, he could just say no or worse, say nothing. I have no business doing this to myself and I won't anymore.

It's Friday morning and we get five more lost souls. One immediately stands out; a very young brotha who doesn't look old enough to be in here. It's his first time. He's frightened and despite his best efforts is unable to conceal any of the emotions betraying him. He's quiet and to himself. His bail is only $25. No one, not even his mother will come get him. I wonder what he did to get his mother to turn her back on her baby. How long and how many ways has he earned her apathy? 17 at most and you've alienated everyone in your life? How has this come to pass? The whispers are of pity for this boy, but not me. Something tells me he has well earned his isolation. I'll have to keep this hard head under surveillance; glad he's on the other side of the tank. He doesn't have any business hanging around over here. James is wondering why I lack compassion for him. He can see the boy is scared, so he feels for him. Time will tell. Our conversation mutates into a discussion about my people. James and Old Man Carter have questions, and they're chomping at the bit for answers.

Old man Carter says, "Maybe you can answer a question that's been doggin' me for years? Why do y'all call each other nigger?"James chimes in, "Yeah!" Mr. Carter says, "I mean that just don't make no sense." I reply, "Look man, we don't live in the same America. Our experience is altogether different. Our skin makes us outsiders. It's something we all have in common. Miami to Seattle, Los Angeles to the Hamptons. Rich, poor, educated and ignorant, we're all niggers which means white folks are allowed to rape, beat, torture, torment, castrate and kill us with impunity. The law is our chief persecutor which by the way is the reason you can't say that word now. Amongst us, it started as a self-inflicted admonishment like`Nigga you know them white folks ain't gonna let you do that` or `That nigga done lost his mind.` We never used it in mixed company; we knew you would not understand. Now that word doesn't have the same power. The youth didn't grow up with that yoke on their neck. Therefore, they lack the proper respect. Consequently, I don't give a fuck what white people don't understand. It's a black thang." "A black thang huh?" asked Old Man Carter I reply "Yes. In the interest of a proper subjugation it was necessary to eradicate all traces of Africa. Public Enemy said it best, `It takes a nation of millions to hold us back. `We had to start from scratch. I mean from the flour, sugar and eggs. We had to do all of this under the watchful eye of Massa. Having nothing else to go on we emulated white folks, but a lot of the things y'all do and the way you do them are too stale. If you've noticed, we don't walk, talk, cook, dance, fuck or even shake hands like white folks. We're of the opinion you do these things with a T-Square lodged in your rectum. White folks are entirely too ridged, devoid of any natural rhythm, seemingly stemming from the arrogant belief in the superiority of civilized man - white man." James asks, "Why do y'all walk like that?" I explain, "The walk comes from slavery. Captured runaway slaves were issued a ball and chain. Young boys admired the courage an escape attempt required, so they honored the bad niggers by imitating their walk. It evolved into body language. Man, the length white folks will go to preserve their belief in their superiority!" James says, "What makes you think white people believe in their superiority?" I respond, "Here below the Mason-Dixon, here in the last bastion of the Confederacy, y'all don't believe in white supremacy?" James responds, "Well, we all don't believe that." I reply, "Really? Nigger, kike, spic, chink, jap, wop and all the other colorful colloquialisms are used to communicate one fact – we ain't white. In America not being white is a grave insult."

We're interrupted by SRT again. This time they have us face the walls while they do their dirty work; trying but failing to prevent us from seeing where and how they search. Poor bastards. They had bad timing again. Our contraband is well-stashed. A rookie SRT has old man Carter hemmed up in the corner stripped and assuming the position. Of all the bad bastards in this place, he picks on an old man. Its things like this that fosters contempt for law enforcement.

The elite squad comes up with nothing, but they'll be back. I pull an OG player to the side and suggest giving SRT sacrificial bones and scraps to keep them off our backs. Charles says, "These little niggas ain't smart enough for that. They'll let SRT run up in here every day befo'e given'm shit." The young men are risking everyone's stashes for the sake of greed. As we're cleaning up SRT's mess, James asks, "Of all the tanks in here, why do they keep running in on us?" I say, "Cuz they haven't found anything." Mr. Carter adds, "And they'll be back 'till they do." The conversation doesn't stay light for long;

it's my turn to ask questions. "How does a whole town sleep after a night of lynchings? Does no one feel remorse? Does no one think what they've done is reprehensible? I'm not talking about just the sheriff or his ignorant minions. I mean the Mayor and the DA, the mill owner, the town doctor and barber. "James replies, "Some do feel real bad. Sometimes it was your friend in that tree, but what can you do? Mob rule, ya know."Mr. Carter chimes in, "When I was a kid it wasn't nuthin' to see somebody hangin' in a tree. Seen it all the time. Most people don't know this, but you was almost as likely to see a white man hangin' from a tree as a black."
I ask, "What you mean almost? What like 70/30?"
He replies, "Pert'near." I say, "Not one was hung simply for being white." Mr. Carter says,"Naaw, but they had plenty uh other reasons to hang yuh." I reply, "Guess you right. If they almost lynched Sam Houston, ain't noboby safe."James chimes in, "Who tried to lynch Sam Houston?" I respond, "A bunch of crackers in Dallas." "No they didn't, did they?", James responds. Mr. Carter answers, "M'fraid so." James asks, "Well why? I mean what for?" I respond, "For bein' a nigger lover." James says, "That's not true."Mr. Carter responds, "M'fraid so."

I'm called to the bars by an inmate trustee who tells me Homegirl got out. She made a deal with the DA to turn states evidence. I'm angry, but not surprised. The game down here is real dirty. They turn on each other at the drop of a dime, so an outsider like me can forget about it. She gave four contradicting written statements. I guess they finally got one they like. The truth is a hindrance which means I'm fucked. This is why it's said in a court of law, if you're guilty you got a 50/50 shot. If you're innocent you're going to jail.

The 17 year old hard head is in some shit already. He made an error in protocol and judgment. OG Charles is reproaching him profusely to the point another brotha says, "Man Charles, don't hurt the boy." Charles responds, "He ain't even worth the trouble of takin' the time to slap upside the head, but he ain't gonna do no shit like that no mo'e!" We all laugh. The boy is momentarily embarrassed, but he figured out no one is going to fuck with his little ass. Despite how scared he was, he's too stupid to be grateful. He'll try and take advantage mistaking kindness for weakness. If he isn't careful, he'll make someone regret being nice to him.

I'm not from these parts, so the white boys don't show me the same aversion they harbor for my brothas. One white boy has a Muslim sir-name Rockmon; he's here for cooking meth. When it comes to interacting with the brothas he's more compatible than most white boys. This has given him some credibility with us. Still, he said something that had me blowing hooch out my nose. In the middle of a meth cooking symposium he said, "I thank God for meth." I reply, "Now why in the fuck would you go and say some shit like that?" He replies, "Because meth puts more white boys in the pen." Even with his considerable crossover skills the reality of being a minority is unsettling.

For lack of anything better to do a few us find ourselves sitting around talking about how we ended up here. The variations are boundless. It's amazing how many have been snitched on by their best friend, girlfriend, cousin and nephew. It makes me think of all the people who've been snitched on throughout history like Dillinger, Bonny and Clyde, Jesse James and Jesus. The DA's office is an active participant; snitches' names are listed in the paper as witnesses for the prosecution. I can remember a time when that would've made them an accessory to murder. It's no wonder I got caught up in this tangled web. This place is like a parasite with nothing to eat, so it feeds upon itself. Strange as it sounds, I find myself feeling grateful my circumstances aren't more dire.

Rockmon's little brother is locked up in the tank down the hall. He's in here for meth, too. They have the market cornered inside and out. I can tell he's square dealing, straight forward and honest. He's the one that told me about that bullshit public defender they're trying to give me. When he asked me what I intended to do, I told I wrote to Siler. He said, "He's yuh best bet." Rockmon is waiting to go to the big house. He's already got his sentence – eight years. We talk awhile. I tell him I'm innocent and that I'll beat this case. I don't believe my own words. Rockmon looks me in the eye wondering why I don't know better. He says, "Well, good luck. But just in case, if I see yuh down there, I got yo' back." My self-righteous arrogance has suffered severe damage. Rockmon's expression makes it impossible for me to remain in denial about the dire nature of my situation. When I return to my bunk Mr. Carter tells me someone stole his last pack of cigarettes. My anger gets the better of me.

I yell out to the entire tank, "Not one of you muthafuckas can say he ever said no if you asked him for a smoke, but you simple fucks gotta steal from the one person that would give it to you. Fuck anyone who got some'm to say and fight go wit it!"

I don't know what came over me. This goes against my grain. I don't want to be anyone's benefactor, least of all an old white man. Mr. Carter says, "Thanks, but you didn't have to." I reply, "I know, but I did. Keep'm from thinkin' they can do whatever they want." James is in shock. He never thought he would ever see a black man stand up for a white man especially in jail. I had to explain to him for me it isn't about that. It's about right and wrong. While I haven't always been right, I can only be so wrong. My world has never been that small. My short time in Texas has served to narrow my outlook. And I know better. I've had good and bad experiences with enough people from around the world to know color ain't got shit to do with it.

It's mid-November and it's getting cold which has severely curtailed most inessential activity. They've turned on the heat and it's stewing the train exhaust. The combination of train smoke and thirty unfiltered, hand rolled cigarettes a day is wreaking havoc on Mr. Carter's respiratory system. He's coughing, wheezing and smoking simultaneously while rebuking all attempts at advising him to quit. He'll get no such reproach from me. I believe he's earned the right to do as he pleases.

James gave me a book to pass the time. It's a science fiction/action adventure. He assumes I'm well read. I don't have the heart to tell him I don't read at all. In fact, I've only read two books. Black like Me by John Howard Griffin was the first. A 10th grade teacher who thought I was becoming too militant made it required reading for a book report. The second was Alex Haley's Malcolm X because he's my hero and I have few. I'm dyslexic. The written word has always given me fits. I came up before our modern age of enlightenment. There was no diagnosis or help at school and at home. The school system stuck me in the dummy classes, so I learned early on how to live without much reading. I put the book James gave me in my foot locker.

4

It's Thanksgiving. The jail provides us with a traditional meal with all the fixings including dressing and sweet potato pie. I don't know who put the pecan smoke on this turkey leg, but he got skills. They even got the pie right. I never thought I'd enjoy a holiday meal behind bars. We've smuggled everything from turkey and cranberry sauce to dinner rolls and gravy back to our cell. Each one of us walks away with at least three pieces of pie trying our damnedest to make it like home. We have plans to eat, drink and smoke while we tell stories about turkeys past until it's time for the Cowboys to be play.

I've been locked up for a month. I haven't received any word about my court case. As soon as I resign myself to living in a testosterone cauldron, they bring in a new female guard. She isn't a dime piece, but in here she's a super star by default. To make it worse she neither likes nor wants the attention. She wants to do her job and go home. As I was standing at the bars waiting on a weed delivery, she walked by. Her scent alone gave me a sweet and sour aching pain way down deep in places you don't mention amongst polite company.

A new shipment of inmates has arrived. One of them is Mr. Carter's cousin. His name is Steve. He's in his 40s and like his kin a crook from way back. He too has no overt issues with the brothas. Steve is quite popular with the entire jail. Weed is his thing. I saw Rockmon talking to Steve at chow. He must've told him how I looked out for the old man because there was a fat joint waiting for me back in my bunk. Steve comes over and says, "Preciate what you did fer ole cuz. Need more, let me know." I reply, "You and I are gonna be good friends." I dig the way he conducts business. The 17 year old was moved to the bunk above me. I hope I don't have to hurt him. James gives me a foreboding look and shakes his head. Mr. Carter says, "This ain't gone be good at all." He's come down here because it's close to the TV, another bad decision. Everyone in this tank knows it but him.

It's early Saturday morning and we're playing spades. Steve and me versus Charles and Littlewood. We're winning 4-0 and talking big shit. We laughed so hard we lost the last game. It didn't matter. The point was to pass the time. We're smiling and laughing during count time. The COs like it quiet so they don't lose count. We're simply unable to comply. After failing to coax us into shutting up, a young white CO turns to me and says, "You're in a good mood." I reply, "Well, I didn't get it in here. Plus, if I ain't, that means you win, don't it?" He replies, "You got a point." I omit the part about being high and drunk; it sure makes it easier to smile in his face.

Its way past lights out. On the table directly in front of the heat vent is an empty plastic grape juice bottle and cap. The cap pops up about three inches. Four inmates in the line of sight jump straight up out of their bunks. Eyes about to pop perplexed and petrified. One of them says, "You see dat? Dat ain't right. Ain't nothin' but the devil!" I have no tolerance for unbridled ignorance. Life is hard enough without your own stupidity making it harder. I said, "Goddamn you some ign'nt muthafuckas! That's just the heat expanding the air in the bottle!" They reply in a simultaneous mumble, "oh." The one that convinced himself the bottle was possessed by the great Lucifer himself, after coming face to face with his own ignorance, decides to take exception with me calling him on it. He says, "Yeah, but I ain't no ign'nt muhafuckuh." Seeing no purpose in arguing the point I tell him he's right. It's the new millennium and these poor bastards still think like them book burning, witch hunting, inquisition fucks.

James is shaking me from sleep. A prize fight is at hand. Littlewood is lacing his boots. He's bright red and quietly resolute. They've put an adversary of his in this tank so Littlewood is salivating. As soon as the coast is clear, Littlewood looks him in the eye and says, "Bring yo bitch ass over in the corner." This tank has a built in blind spot. The front wall is cinder block. The rest of the tanks are barred. Those who wish to maintain prolonged combat choose to do so behind the cinder block wall. As soon as he gets within arm's reach, Littlewood unleashes a blistering barrage of textbook rights and lefts nearly all reaching their intended target. The contender is clearly out matched. He tries in vain to mount an adequate defense. He even manages to get off a shot or two. They lack the desired effect. There goes his eye. Blood has blinded him. His nose looks like a faucet. Having no taste for his own blood, he tries to switch tactics. He reaches out to grab and hold. No good. Littlewood catches him with a punishing uppercut. His knees buckle, but he's saved by the bell. The ref yells, "CO, CO!" like roaches when the lights come on. Everyone gives their best "we ain't doin' nothin" look.

The vanquished has managed to drag ass back to his bunk. The guards come in, look around and know exactly what's happened. Pointing at the pummeled, a CO says, "You come here! What happ'm. Never mind. Take'm to the infirmary." If he talks, they'll stack another charge on Littlewood - aggravated assault. If they come looking for Littlewood, we'll know his opponent snitched. This is the third time this week. Every time it's the same thing. They come running in here huffing and puffing. If it didn't work the first time what makes them think it's going to work now. It's like being impotent in a whore house - no good to nobody, yet still they come. Getting all dressed up just to come in here and fail again and again must be frustrating.

On the way out of the cell Caligula tells me to get a haircut. On the outside my grooming habits are meticulous, but in here I don't give a fuck. I'm locked up. Fuck what my hair looks like. It's impossible for one to look good in jail, so I make no attempt. I see brothas primping and trimming like they're going on a date. They're obsessed with their waves and hair lines, dismantling disposable razors and putting the blades on the teeth of a comb so they can keep their fades tight. The barber shop downstairs stays busy. I don't think I've even combed my hair since I got here. Now that I know my hair is of some annoyance to the COs, I damn sure won't do it for them. After SRT leaves, I ask Littlewood how long he's been waiting to put his hands on that dude. He said about two years, "Used to be in bid'ness with my little brother. Stole from him. Made his count come up short. Almost got'em killed behind it. He's been runnin' ever since." I reply, "Felt good to catch up with his ass, didn't it?" He says, "Oh it ain't over. Every time I see his bitch ass, it's on. Gonna beat him 'til I get tired. Shit, better hope my brother don't catch up with'em. After that, ain't gonna be no next time."

The next morning I wake up early to the sight of my own breath. The heat isn't working. It's ball-shriveling cold in here. I look around to see no movement. I didn't get up for the 3 am breakfast so I'm the only one who doesn't know the power and heat are out due to a fucking ice blizzard. I have to piss, but it's too damn cold. I go about putting on every piece of clothing they've given me and shiver my way back to the pissers. The pipes are frozen. We can't flush and the water already looks like antifreeze and reeks of ammonia. 50 men, four urinals, two toilets, no water and no heat in the worst ice storm in 30 years. I can't wait to get back to my bunk. I managed to commandeer three extra blankets from those coming and going. Up until now I used them for padding. Here I lay. Five gray woolen blankets, two towels over my head, two t-shirts, two shirts, two pants, three boxers, three socks, boots, and a coat, and still I shiver. I heard somewhere it's not good to put all these clothes on; they only make it worse. I must admit, right now I can't for the life of me remember how less clothing is supposed to keep me warm. I can't talk myself into removing a single stitch. The warden is coming around making speeches in an attempt to reassure. We all know it's to keep us from starting fires, rioting and shit. All of east Texas is shut down. The last thing he needs is a jail in upheaval. I don't think he has anything to worry about. It's too damn cold for any such foolishness. The frigid temperature has turned us all into affable gentlemen. The warden says there will be no movements. Nurses will bring meds around to all the tanks.

Food will be brought to us as well. That's fine with us. It means we don't have to get out from under these blankets.

It's 1:30 pm. The cold is no longer crippling. We're up and about with blankets around our shoulders. We're moving and stomping trying to get blood flowing. They brought us lunch called "Johnny sacks" - a glob of congealed peanut butter and jelly in the center of two pieces of soggy bread, a stale baggie of chips, an orange and a juice box in an oil-soaked brown paper bag. There's an eerie silence as we scarf it down, hopeful the digestive process will generate some internal combustion.

My box is full. I have people who care enough to keep money on my books and I make a few dollars off the sale of swine, so I'm as comfortable as a man in a frozen jail can be. When I look around at the state of the average inmate I can't help but be grateful. The county will never feed an inmate enough. In fact, the minimum daily calorie count minus the skim is what we get fed. Those with little commissary suffer as well. Ramen noodles require hot water. There's no hot and no water, so some are eating it raw. There's no telling how long we'll be without heat and water.

Without a damn thing to do I'm reading the sci-fi book James gave me. It's good. Anything is better than staring at these four walls. Reading gives me a headache, so I avoid it. Without any distractions I finished half of the book in one day. I have no headache, so I read on. Reading keeps my mind off the cold until I have to turn the page. My fingers are freezing and I can't get them back under cover soon enough, but I keep turning pages. Just as the book is getting good, the warden comes calling for help. He wants clean up volunteers to go out in the cold to cut trees off power lines and houses for old affluent white folks. He says it's our chance to do some good for the same people who refer to us as incorrigible heathens and think jails are too soft. There the same people who still brag about their families having owned slaves. Fuck them! I hope they freeze to death one toe at a time. They fought hardest and longest to keep my people under their boot. When it was time for a lynching it was these white people who sent the Klan to drag you out of your house in the middle of the night in front of your wife and kids.

Some inmates decide to help. They're country. They like the

outdoors. Some like the idea of helping out, some are thinking about getting their hands on some tools. Whatever the reasons, a man does what he thinks is right or what he thinks he can get away with. Unlike amongst the commonwealth, in jail a man has no need to construct a facade of decency and righteousness.

An unexpected bonus today - just me and the older crowd are left. There are roughly 10 of the original 50. Quiet, cold and still; shivering', smoking' and reading'. Mr. Carter and I are languishing in the frigid and stillness. We don't say anything. He roles a cigarette, I role a joint. He lights it with his contraband lighter and passes me his cigarette to light my joint. He's counting every spark. COs are the chief donators of lighters, but not during an ice storm. They worry inmates may burn this motherfucker down. I can't tell if it's arrogance or ignorance that allows them to believe they could stop us if we decided to release the hounds of hell; another example of the systemic brilliant stupidity.

The sun is going down and the incorrigible heathens are returning from outside. They're tired, cold, sweating and dirty; 40 of them and no functioning showers. The sweat is making them damn near hypothermic and now they have one change of clothes which means they can't double up. They strip down and try to dry off, funking up their one remaining change of clothes. I'm beginning to hear the low moans of regret. Any satisfaction reaped from a good deed done is long gone. Charles says, "Out dere tryin' to help dem rich white folks. Should'uh stayed right here like you Cali." I reply, "Man, y'all look fucked off! Hope you had fun." Charles says, "Fuck you Cali." I try not to laugh too much because the cold ain't no joke, but it sure is funny. The commodes are full of mounded lumpy shit, piss and toilet paper. One good thing about the cold weather is the lack of stench and steam that permeate during the summer months. That's another reason why I bunk far from the toilets. I'm not looking forward to dangling my precious tender loins so close to such repugnance. I'll have to hold it.

One of Rockmon's long time clients is continuously working his way into conversations. He's the after in the before and after. He's strung out on crystal and he's been in and out of jail for mostly stupid shit. He wants acceptance. Each time he comes to talk he asks to sit on the foot of the bunk. I tell him, "Say man, why you keep askin'? I told you I don't care." He looks at me with an intense hollow fear. He replies, "You ain't never been down before have you?" I reply, "No, why?" He says, "Cause if you had you'd ask every time too." I don't believe much of anything he says, but I believe that.

Mr. Carter saved his Johnny Sack for a late-night snack – a salami sandwich. He tells me he likes the salami seeds. I say, "What is you talkin' bout old man?" He replies, "These little black seeds in the salami." I say, "That's pepper, Mr. Carter." Stunned, he asks, "What?" I explain, "Yeah, whole black pepper corns. That's what pepper looks like before its ground up." He looks at me in disbelief like he thinks I'm fucking with him so I shoot back a reassuring glance, "Yeah man, no bullshit." He bites into one and for the first time recognizes the flavor, "Well hail, I guess you never stop learnin' do yuh?" I reply, "I hope not old man, I hope not." I want to ask him how it's possible a man of his years could think processed meat would contain seeds like a piece of fruit. As if you could grow salami from the ground, but I say nothing. I have no wish to ridicule this old man.

My stomach is in knots. I need to figure a way to shit without getting close to the commode. It's not late enough for me, but the choice is no longer mine. I ask a CO for a trash bag. I spread it open over the toilet and shit. After finishing, I unravel half a roll of tissue for cover, wrap it in another bag and set it outside the bars. The guard picks it up and adds it to his trash. Charles makes a point of letting me know my shyness isn't a secret. He says, "That nigga must'uh really had to shit. He couldn't even wait til 3 in the mo'nin' this time." It would appear I'm not the only one with a problem bearing his balls over a septic tank. Another inmate does the same with the bag, but fails to cover his shit with gobs of toilet paper and trash. When he finishes he sets his bag of pissy shit outside the cell in front of the guard. The CO takes one look and loses his mind, "What the fuck is this shit?" The whole tank erupts in a roaring laughter. An inmate says, "Yep, that's exactly what that is, shit!" The CO yells out, "Oh y'all thank this is funny? Well I got some'm fer y'all!" He's telling his coworkers what's in the bag and they hit the roof, "You mean I'm stuck in here while my family is sittin' in the cold and dark while their fuckin' friends are probably lootin' right now, and these som'bitches are shittin' in the halls? Oh hail no! We'll fix them!" One of the young brothas says, "They cain't do shit." I know better so I ask Charles what they have in mind. He says, "Probably gonna take us outside in duh cold and let us freeze." So a couple of us go about bundling up. Just as I put on all I can, the Warden comes in and says, "Awl the thangs I gotta deal with and you sorry som'bitches are throwin' shit bombs! I see some of y'all are bundlin' up. That's good cause we're goin' outside." The Warden has all 50 of us shuffling out to the rec yard. I hang out in the back again, this time for different reasons. It means I'm the last one out in the cold and first one in.

We walk outside and I see darkness I had no idea existed. The blackness is boundless-no street lights, no houses lit, no stars, no moon. We're all hardened men, some more than others, but not one of us has seen this type of dark before. As we walk out into the yard, the wind demands our attention. Despite my layering efforts, I can feel every gust of wind; I might as well be butt ass naked. We all know we can't allow any visible apprehension to betray us. If the COs think they're getting to us we'll be out here all night. Without saying a word we suck it up and don't so much as shiver. Our contempt for authority is hotter than the ice is cold. Well, almost. The warden is colder than we are. Realizing after less than five minutes he's failed in his attempt to teach a lesson, he starts his concession speech, "Now I know you guys got it bad with the toilets an all, but if I hear any more about y'all throwin' shit bombs, I'll keep yuh out here all night. I'm serious now. Don't make me bring y'all back out here. Now if yuh thank y'all can act right we can go back inside. That is unless y'all just wanna stay out here a little while longer." We muster a begrudging, "No sir." As I turn around I can't see where we've just come from. Warden yells "Well, get goin'!" I make an approximate 180 and head out.

The COs have been poking around in our personal belongings so I immediately check my stuff. It's been riffled through but intact. Mr. Carter and James both notice their lighters are gone. Mr. Carter goes right into a cursing fit, "God damn mutherfuckin' cock suckin' sorry assed no good sum'bitches!" I must say he looks 20 years younger - cheeks full of color and no arthritic pain hindering his movements. He wasn't this mad when they stole his last pack of tobacco. Steve says, "Don't worry Cuz, I'll make you a light." He says he can light a cigarette with 2 AA batteries and 2 staples; he isn't' the only one having nicotine fits so we gather around to watch. I see the regret in Steve's' eyes; he realized he should've just did it and not announced he had the ability. Now he's feeling the pressure. Littlewood retrieves 2 staples from court papers he got in the mail. Charles gives him the batteries from his FM Walkman and we tell everyone to spread out. Steve stands the batteries on the flat iron rail at the foot of the bunk and thumbs the staples on top of them. He touches them together but no spark. He realizes the 17 layers of paint on the bunk are interfering. Finally, he hits metal. As soon as he's done he turns to me and says, "Don't know why I just don't use a screw." The screw failed him. Just when the crowd gets restless, he put the batteries back on the iron, touched the staples and it sparked! Low and behold he's smoking! He sucks on that cigarette like a malnourished infant on his mama's nipple. He passes the cigarette to Mr. Carter and in one drag his lustful desire for tobacco is fulfilled. Overcome by the realization he would have to go through the same thing in about 10 minutes, he realizes he doesn't want to rely on Charles and his batteries, and neither do we. We can't make a wick without the COs having a breakdown, but we're in jail and we aren't about to start following rules now. I twist up a wick, catch a spark and light a joint for my trouble. Another catastrophe averted so I return to my book.

Unaccustomed as I am to reading for pleasure, the anticipation of turning a page holds an unfamiliar thrill. I never believed teachers who claimed the book was better, but they were right. I thought that was some bullshit they said to get me to do my homework. I've seen the movie Lady Sings the Blues many times, but the Lady Day biography I'm reading is better. I can't explain it, but it pisses me off profusely. Even in this ice box, the book is better. In retrospect, Alex Haley's Malcolm X was better than Spike Lees'. It makes me wonder what I've been missing. As I'm reading I learn that James and

Mr. Carter are big Lady Day fans. With all the Conway Twitty, Merle Haggard and Hank Williams around here, it never occurred to me they would've even been allowed to listen to "jungle music." Mr. Carter said his mama wouldn't let him listen to it in her house, but that didn't stop him from listening. I say, "James, man, I know you must've taken a lot of flak for liking nigger music." He says, "Yeah but it didn't stop me either." We reminisce and recall old records – *Love for Sale, Good Morning Heartache, Ain't Nobody's Business, Don't Explain*. Given our prior conversations, we consciously omit Strange Fruit.

As soon as I put this book down it seems to get even colder. All I have to do is look at old Mr. Carter to know it could be a lot worse. The old man is three shades of blue, but he's too tough to complain. I don't know what he's going to do if he catches the flu or pneumonia. He's damn near coughed up a lung already. No movements mean we can't get to the warming hooch. Steve, James and I each gave him one of our extra blankets, but his circulation is shot. He can't get warm enough to stay warm. This old man is in jail for a probation violation - an old possession charge from 8 years back. He took some prescription medication that wasn't prescribed to him and failed a random piss test. On any scale of justice this man's debt has been paid.

It's 4 am and the power is back on. A great and joyful roar echoes through the halls. It's strange to hear from every single soul on the block after 5 quiet days. Mr. Carter is the first one to stand in front of the heat vent. Inmates are standing around the electric cigarette lighter on the wall and pushing the button over and over. No one even thought to turn on the TV until a CO wanted to see the news. The toilets and urinals were flushed and luckily for us and COs the pipes are holding. Littlewood constructed a coffee pot from a glass jar and soldered aluminum and tin; Steve combines coffee with hot coco to create which I coined "Mocha De La Pinta." I don't know about the other shit they make in this motherfucker, but this shit right here is good. Mr. Carter has his hands around his cup like the plump and tender breast of his first love. His fingers are no longer blue and the veins in his face are not as prominent. Charles says, "Good to see you ain't lookin like the

Grim Reaper no mo'e." Mr. Carter replies, "Thought I'd meet that sum'bitch before the week was out myself." We all laugh, but there was a time when it looked like even money. I woke up many times glad to see him still breathing; I caught James looking down from his bunk, eyes full of fear and hope. It got to where his coughing was a good thing. Dead men don't cough.

It's Saturday morning and we got trouble. During visitation, a young white boy bumped his knee on a weed delivery taped under a table. The crook that he is, he couldn't pass up this opportunity so he stuffed it in his crotch and scurried back to the tank. He doesn't get back to his bunk before coming out with it, "Look what I got!" Had he been quiet, he could've gotten away with it, but his excitement got the better of him. Now that he's announced his plunder he's strongly encouraged to share. I get my cut. It isn't two hours before the intended receivers in the next tank over figured out what happened to their stash. Inmates coming and going from visitation pass the bars and let us know they know. They don't know who exactly, but it won't be long. The boy is trying not to worry and he's holding up well under considerable pressure. The young brothas in our tank are fucking with him profusely, "What you gonna do man? They gonna fuck you up! Man them niggas gonna kill you! You gonna wish you left they shit alone." He's lying in his bunk, smoking and seems unaffected so the young brothas lose interest and leave him be.

On the way back from dinner a few brothas corner Steve in the stairwell. As I pass through, they got him jacked up in the corner. They're threatening to bounce him off every bit of steel and concrete in the stairwell. Its common knowledge he runs the weed in our tank so if he didn't do it, he damn sure knows who did. If I stop to intervene it they would assume we're guilty and exact their revenge so I keep walking. Steve isn't talking, but his eyes are as big as pool balls. One minute after I get back to the tank Steve comes in. He doesn't waste any time and goes directly to the young white boy and jacks him up. He says, "You better tell them you got their shit cuz I ain't takin' no beatin' for you!" The boy says "Ok, ok, I'll tell them." He has the nerve to tell Steve he could've told them he had their stash, "Yeah you little shit, I could-uh, but I ain't no snitch!" The young brothas couldn't wait to send word over; they all know who the weed belonged to and are eagerly anticipating the retribution. Either this white boy is suicidal or he should get an Oscar for this performance. Rockmon asks him, "What you gonna do man when they get somebody in here on your ass?" The crack in his armor is starting to show, "I don't give a fuck man. Let'm come." He's nervous like a rabbit in a hole and comes to the conclusion that he can't do shit now and resigns himself to the situation. There's a strange kind of peace that comes with coming to grips like when you know death is at hand. The only question left is how you die. He has decided to go out holding his nuts even if his hands are shaking. It's Monday morning and I can't believe my eyes. The young white boy is rolling up his bunk - his bail has been posted. It must be the luck of the Irish. The whole tank is in disbelief, "Can you dig this shit? This white boy must be blessed!" He's doing his damnedest to conceal his relief, but it's not working. He's grinning and moving fast; he'll be going out just as his assassins are coming in. The young brothas hate to see the white boy get away with it.

I've been sent for and told to go downstairs. I'm directed by random COs to the front office. They ask me to identify my personal property left in their charge, "This is my watch, but this ain't my band. I don't see my wallet. What the fuck is this? What happen to my shit?" A CO explains, "Well, we had a break in and some of the property has been stolen." I reply, "What? Who would break into a jail property room? Never mind. I know goddamn well who did it." There's only one explanation - guards conspiring with inmates. The jail has been on lockdown and frozen in for the last week. No movement was permitted, but someone was moving. Whoever it was had time to choose what they wanted to steal and had time to switch my watch band. The CO says, "Is this your stuff or not?" I reply, "It's some of it! Guess I'm just ass out of the rest?" He replies, "We'll get back to you on that." On my way back to the tank I over hear inmates talking about rings and watches they bought and sold on the wire stolen from the jail safe. You can buy your own belongings from the person(s) who stole them while you, he and your belongings are all locked up in jail. While I'm contemplating the irony I can't help but wonder what the guard's cut was. Were they homeboys from way back or was it blackmail? Both Littlewood and Rockmon tell me this isn't the first time this happened, "You can forget about gettin' your shit back." I said, "Figured that." Rockmon says, "But don't worry, ain't gonna be long before we know who did it. It'll be a big fight in one of the tanks soon as they try to sell a nigga his own stuff." No sooner than the sentence is spoken it starts - loud, chaotic rumbling at the other end of the block; all the guards start running in that direction. I can tell this isn't an ordinary fight; everyone on the cell block wants to know what the fuck is going on. We're at the bars to catch a glimpse of the motherfucker responsible for this treachery. When the guards come back this way they're escorting 10 inmates and recording the whole thing. This is when I lose interest. I know the local boys will handle this situation.

James says he's getting out tomorrow; I think he'll be missed most by Mr. Carter. No one else has as much in common with the old man. It was no surprise when James gave his jailhouse possessions to him - radio, tobacco, store, extra clothes and blankets. This is usually a time when the scavengers start to circle, but no one even asks for so much as a candy bar. We all watched Mr. Carter suffer in the cold so we wish him all the comfort possible. Besides, the old man would give anything one of us might need. Nevertheless, I can see he'll miss James. So will I. James and Charles are both gone this morning. Charles didn't even know he was leaving. He came over gave me a pound and his radio. The goddamn SRT again! Don't these simple bastards ever get enough?

This tank provides an ingenious stash spot. The air duct hangs in the center of the room so if an inmate is standing on a bunk he can hide almost anything back behind the adjustable vents. As many times as they've run up in here, not one of them has so much as looked up in that direction. Having failed to find contraband, SRT quietly leave our cell. As they're leaving, Little Caligula stops and says, "Didn't I tell you to get a haircut?" I reply, "Yes." He asks, "Why ain't you do it?" I reply, "The last thing I'm concerned with is my appearance." He says, "Well, you gonna get a haircut." The conservative mindset in this region is stifling. Even the liberals are conservative. Before

I can finish my thought a CO calls me to the bars and instructs me to the barber shop.

I'm back downstairs heading into the shop. I can already hear the shit talking just like any black barber shop. Football, basketball, pussy and the streets are the topics at hand. All of a sudden I feel like getting a haircut, but I'm in no rush. I intend to prolong this respite as long as possible.

An inmate barber asks me, "Damn nigga, what's up wit yo' head?"

I reply, "I know man, just cut it."

He asks, "What the fuck you want me to do with this shit?"

I reply, "I don't give a fuck man just shape it up."

He says, "You asking a lot fo' a free hair cut! When was the last time you put a pick in this shit?"

I say, "The night I got busted."

He says, "Yeah, it look like it."

Another barber says, "Man Ray you might have to take that down to the slab."

He replies, "Nah, he got good hair, just ain't takin' care of it."

I say, "I got good hair cuz I take care of it. Just not in here. Wasn't gonna cut it till this little black bastard in SRT said I had to."

He says, "I know just who you talkin' bout."

The other barber interjects, "Shit nigga, we all do. That little muthafucka got problems. Hell ain't hot enough fo' that nigga." My barber says, "I'm gonna cut it just this side of regulations."

5

It's the weekend before Christmas which is of no consequence to me except this being the Bible belt I know the municipal business will come to a grinding halt. I haven't heard anything about my case. Not so much as a letter from that bullshit PD I was assigned. Not surprising, but I had hoped to hear from Siler. With the ice storm and now Christmas there's the distinct possibility I won't. It's as if the calendar and weather are conspiring against me. Come to find out, the DA has 90 days to charge or release me; 30 days to go and no news is good news.

I'm reading Fredrick Douglass' autobiography and one thing's for sure; it makes me not want to complain about anything ever again. Fair, just or right has nothing to do with nothing in this world. The information in this book is not new to me. As I'm reading I have to stop myself from hating crackas anymore than I already do. I had to learn early on in my life to manage the anger already within. I work continuously to keep from compounding the issue. Funny how our doctors tell us our fried, salty, pork rich diet is the reason for the disproportionately high percentages of hypertension and heart disease. They fail to factor in the pent up, frustrated and unmitigated hate.

It's Christmas and we're eating another traditional meal, but this time the pie is apple. Once again there's a spike in the smuggling. Dinner is served around 3 pm, but we'll eat late into the night. I'm making some hellacious turkey sandwiches with dinner rolls I took from the chow hall. I have gravy everywhere when Mr. Carter says, "It ain't good til' it gets on you," - a belief that can only be derived from a land of BBQ. It's times like this when we all sit around and talk about the food we're going to eat when we get out. From salivating over the thought of what's the first thing coming off the grill to lusting after a drive-thru. We clean up the contraband in a hurry. The warden is visiting soon. I never could understand this phenomenon known as the "Christmas Spirit." The rest of the year they won't give a man the dog shit off their shoe, but one day out of the year they want to show compassion like people aren't starving in July.

Here he comes. The warden walks in here all smiles like the Santa Claus. No one in here wants his fucking gift. How about getting my wallet back muthafucka! Bet you didn't come to talk about that shit, did you? I say nothing because it might put a damper on the spirit. The warden seems to think he can fool all of us. We're in jail. We aren't fools. He gave us each a wool cap, a brilliant gift. Since everyone's got one, and only one head, it isn't good for trading or stealing. It must've been a bitch trying to figure out a gift to give people who might use it for causing someone else pain. The groans of discontent grow audible, "This ain't good fo' shit! Should've gave us this shit when we were freezin'." It's damn near New Year's Eve and still no word from Siler. I guess I didn't make the impression I'd hoped which troubles me. With this woefully inadequate fuck up ass of a PD, I will more than likely be forced into a plea of guilt. This is America.

I'm racking my brain to make sure I do as little penance as possible. It's the only way I know to get even. That's why I have not and will not spend one single solitary sober day in this man's jail. You're goddamn right I'm keeping score. This villainous system is getting over on me, so I kick it in the nuts every chance I get. I sit in this jail cell gathering rust and dry rot; snatched out of living my life for damn near three months now. No word from no one about nothing. I lie in this bunk and go 15 rounds with anger every night. Sometimes I win, sometimes I lose. There's an inexhaustible torrent of emotions that torment an incarcerated man's soul, but like most men, they all tend to coalesce into anger - one of the few emotions our relatively simple constitutions can comprehend.

We get word the warden is retiring; the 31st of December is his last day. His going would have gone unnoticed except he's passing out new jail house handbooks. That's right, handbooks. Like when you get a new job. They're intended to help prisoners get acclimated. So why would a retiring warden need to issue new handbooks on his last day? The new is an exact replica except for one page. It says the warden is not financially responsible for the stolen personal property in his jail because the warden can't be responsible for what he's responsible for. We're to sign it and hand this one page back. Fuck him, I'm not signing shit! I have no delusions of ever getting my stuff back or getting justice for that matter, but I won't give him a legal back door either. We've been allowed to watch the ball drop on late night television. I remember celebrating the New Year on Okinawa as a young boy. Now at the tender age of 30, on this New Year's, I find myself jailed in Texarkana. I must admit I have until now taken this journey for granted. I didn't have time to revel in it because I was entirely too busy living. This season, time is all I have.

It's the 10th of January and Rockmon is going from jail to prison tonight. In my time here I've seen men go home and go to the penitentiary despite what the courts have decreed, without rhyme or reason. In a place such as this, one gains the ability to discern a danger to society quickly. Ones' well-being depends on such information. Incarcerated, a man is at his worst; free to indulge in every fanciful debauchery. I can tell you first hand the police, district attorney and all the judges on the bench are all woefully and shamefully inadequate. Not simply incompetent, but complicit. Perpetuating and fertilizing the very element they are charged with eliminating. Doubt my words? Check the steadily increasing crime rate. The construction crew, the engineers, the architects, and the fucking foreman of justice are all lawyers and politicians. Most are both. We the people have the nerve to wonder why shits all fucked up. The system is working as designed.

I'm back in the courthouse again; I'm in a little room with this bullshit PD. He asks how much money I have; I didn't know so I guessed $50 or $60. I was finally getting out. The man hasn't charged me yet so they must let me go. I sign all the proper paper work and wait. I couldn't stop smiling, I mean ear to ear. I don't know how, but I'm going home. For what felt like an eternity, my time behind bars seemed ominously indeterminate. It doesn't anymore. Friday morning' motherfuckers!

Back in the tank I'm spreading the news like butter on all four corners of the bread. My cellmates give congratulatory shakes. I know most are waiting for me to start handing out my jail house belongings. This is a ritual as old as hand cuffs, but it's only Wednesday so they'll have to wait. Littlewood and the old man seem genuinely happy for me. I start calling my people to tell them the good news. I call Mom and she already knows; she's been on the courts ass to get her baby out. They tried to tell her all kinds of stuff. They told her they have no one by that name, told her they found a syringe in my car, but my mom is from Texarkana and has worked in corrections. You can't tell her shit she doesn't already know first-hand so she raised a little hell and got the job done.

Thursday evening and Steve is back from his job in the kitchen. He said he's got a bucket of hooch coming up tonight to celebrate. We're going to smoke all my weed and drink all his hooch. I didn't come in sober and I'm not leaving sober. Plus, I'm not trying to smuggle weed out of jail. So, we consume. This being my last night, I try and take it all in. It has been a hell of a ride. I've learned things about myself a man can't learn in the world. Don't get it twisted, I won't miss this place, but I will remember. Littlewood kicks it off, "What's the first thing you gonna do tomorrow Cali?" I reply, "Don't know man, but I know what I want to do - fuck! Everything else can wait. All I wanna do is lay up in the pussy for a full 24 hours straight. Mr. Carter is teasing me saying I won't last but 24 seconds. I say, "Well then, I'm just gonna have lock jaw." Steve tells me the last time he got out after 6 months he and his girl fucked until it hurt. Til' it hurt sounds good to me. The next thing I'll do is hit up the first drive-thru I see.

I'm in this bunk for the last time and it's like the first, no sleep. I'm good and dizzy. The cell is spinning. It's 4:30 am and I couldn't eat a bite of that shit they pass off as breakfast so I gave it to Littlewood; he didn't have a problem with it. Matter of fact, I can hear him snoring. Mr. Carter is up smoking a cigarette; he offers me one, but I don't want anything. Drinking isn't my thing, but I drank more last night than I had since high school. Now I remember why I stopped. At least this hangover is keeping my mind off the time. When I look at the clock I swear it's going backwards. I get the call, "Hennington, roll it up." I'm in the middle of giving my stuff away; I don't want to keep shit. I gave most of my food to those who didn't have any. I made a deal with Littlewood for my radio. One of his homeboys on the outside will leave weed for me on the side of I-30 West. He said it'll be in a paper bag at a gas station phone booth. Well worth a radio.

After 3 months my weed hook up is probably long gone, relocated or busted. Dwayne, one of the young brothas said, "Man Cali, you know you supposed to give that radio to one of us." I reply, "Yeah man I know, but Littlewood paid for it." I know how he feels; music sooths the savage beast. For a young brotha it can take him far beyond these walls, but a deal is a deal. I'm finally changing out of these county blues and back into my own clothes. I can feel the freedom come over me as I pull up my own underwear. And I managed to get my watch, but when I ask for my wallet I was told, "Don't know what you're talkin' bout." I knew that was coming. The COs let me know I go to court on Monday which means I have to stay in this truck stop town all weekend.

As they open the gates I see a man I haven't seen him since Big Mama's funeral in 1980. My big brother put in a call to Cedric; we smile and embrace.

"Long time man," I say.

Ced replies, "Yeah. Too bad it had to be like this."

I say, "Man who you tellin'? How you been Ced?"

He says, "You know, livin'."

I reply, "Well let's get the fuck out of here."

Ced replies, "Sho'e you right! You wanna get some food?"

I exclaimed, "Yes!"

He asks, "What do you want?"

I reply, "Right now I want a Big Mac and a Whopper."

He asks, "Both?"

I reply, "Yep, fries from McDonald's and onion rings from Burger King."

The chocolate shake is too thick to get through the straw. I take one bite of the Big Mac, one from the Whopper, couple of fries and a couple of rings. The shake is too thick to get through the straw. Cedric looks at me and says, "You ain't got to chase it man. The food ain't goin' nowhere." Crumbs on my cheeks and lips shining, I smile and he just shakes his head. Before we get back to his house I've finished every last morsel. We get to Ced's house where he sparks up a joint, takes a couple of hits and passes it to me. He asks how such a turn of events has come to pass. "So D, tell me what happened?"

By now, I've had enough of reliving this remarkably low crux in my life all the while knowing I'll to recount this allegory for every single person in my life. I understand its news to them. I run down the short and skinny in the hopes of quashing his curiosity. To no avail, he's got a trunk full of questions so I go about answering them. He wants to know how it was.

"It was jail man!" I explained.

He replies, "I know that, but what happened in there? I know it must've been hell in that ice storm."

I say, "Yeah, that was real fucked up, but what really had me buggin' was the absolute corruption."

He responds, "Yeah man, I know it's bad. The DA is an acquaintance of mine."

I say, "Oh, so you do know!"

Ced explains, "It ain't no secret. This town is too small to be this fucked up. Don't you know that's how they get away with it? Everyone's dirty so nobody says nothin'."

I say, "Ya, self-insulating. Say man, you're a Navy man. You've seen the world. How can a man such as yourself stomach living in these back woods? The shallow gene pool, the narrow and small minds, lest we not forget the racism. How can a man who knows better and has seen better deal with this ignorant shit day to day?"

He says, "Well, this is home."

I reply, "Fuck that man, the earth is home."

Ced says, "Sometimes it's harder than others, but my hat is hangin' over there on that wall."

I reply, "How do you live with these white folks down here? I mean they still think and act as if they were right, as if they did us a favor."

Ced says, "Not all of them D."

I say, "I know it ain't all of them. Just the ones in positions of power."

Ced says, "Now that ain't fair."

I reply, "You goddamn right it ain't fair, but it's true. Regardless, I'm more interested in the day to day relations. How do you keep yourself from becoming a mass murderer?"

Ced explains, "I ain't as militant as you D, but I get your point. I got white friends, associates and coworkers. Some have real bad race issues, some don't. Like this one white boy I work with said he's around when they get to talkin' bout nigger this and nigger that, so I asked him what he says when they start talking like that and he said he says nothing. I told him that makes him just as bad as them."

I say, "I see you didn't let him get away with that Sweden shit."

Ced says, "Now, you know better than that. He looked me dead in the eye and told me he goes huntin' with these guys."

I say, "Their great-Granddads use to go huntin' together and you're tellin' me he's afraid if they so much as suspect he's a nigger lover, he'll become a hunting accident?"

Ced replies, "Yep."

I say, "I knew it was deep, but damn!"

Ced replies, "Yeah, this here's the New South."

We smoke and talk late into the night. Ced tells me one of his lady friends is coming over tomorrow night and asks me if I want her to bring a friend. I reply, "You damn skippy! You know where I've been for the last 3 months." I wake up in the morning harder than Damascus, never mind the fact I promised my dick we'd be back in Dallas by now. I'm not a morning person, but I'm grateful to be outdoors breathing free morning air on the porch. "Tell me Ced, you got feelings for this woman of yours?" I ask. He replies, "You mean is she more than just a fuck? Yeah, she's good people." I reply, "Good because I feel like cooking." This isn't something I usually do for a woman I don't know especially for a booty call, but I got plans. I intend to be shamefully carnal with this woman. I have orgasm on the brain so I need a distraction. Cooking will do the trick.

"What you gonna cook man?" says Ced.

I reply, "You feel like Italian?"

Ced says, "Sounds good."

I tell him about tonight's menu, "How about some chicken cacciatore, linguine in red clam sauce and sautéed mushrooms? I need some wine - red and white. "

Ced says, "Damn, where did you learn to cook like that?"

I reply, "I'm an international nigga." Ced says, "You're full of shit!"

I reply, "Maybe, but tonight we dine well. This is gonna take me all day so let's get busy."

I feel like a teenager - nervous and excited over a woman I've never met. She doesn't disappoint – a pretty little cinnamon skinned sista. Her beautiful mahogany eyes tell me she's just as pleased. I give her a smile, a glass of wine and offer her a seat on the couch next to me. The conversation is smooth and easy; she's got more questions than I like to answer, but her eyes and sweet smile are disarming.

"How did you learn to cook like this?" she asks.

I reply, "An old man named Pietro taught me. I was 15 and it was my first job. Now I cook for pleasure."

She replies, "What else do you do for pleasure?"

After dinner and the second bottle of wine, she pulls out a fat blunt full of the kill. When we emerge early the next afternoon, Ced can't resist, "Damn D, Whopper and Big Mac?" I'm going to court in the morning, but I don't know what for. I haven't been so much as charged with a crime. Ced, seeing me in a state of angry contemplation, asks me what's on my mind. "I'm going to see the judge in the morning: I explain. Ced asks, "For what?" I say, "Don't know. I was told when they let me out; guess they want to make sure I don't run for the boarder." Ced says, "Well ain't shit you can do about it tonight so hit this and chill." We smoke and reminisce about the days of old; family memories of when I was a child and Ced a teenager.

It's 8:30 in the morning and I'm sneaking to the courthouse. I'm afraid I'll be arrested for driving without my license which was stolen with my wallet. I park adjacent to two police cars; I still have yet to find a better hiding place than plain sight. As I walk up to the courthouse, I take in the architecture. The long, wide white steps and towering monumental alabaster pillars are all designed to give the impression of official pomp. Inside the courtroom is no different - square, nude oak frames the official state seal with the state flag on the left and American on the right, carefully measured to flank the old white man in his long black robe. All I see is the con.

As I walk through the doors, I can't believe who I see - Tennessee. There he is sitting on a bench, talking to someone who instantly brings to mind Matthew McConaughey in "A Time to Kill." It can't be anyone but Daniel Siler. When Tennessee sees me, he breaks into laughter.

"Glad to see you got out. When?" He says.

I reply, "Friday."

He says, "Hey Cali, this is..."

I say, "You ain't got to tell me. This must be Counselor Siler."

With a strange look on his face Siler asks, "How would you know?"

I reply, "Let's just say you fit the description."

He says, "You must be the one who wrote me that letter."

I reply, "Oh, so you did receive it?"

Siler says, "Oh yes, I got it. Forgive me for not responding. I've been busy more than usual."

I ask, "What's up, some big crime wave?"

He says, "No, my office was burned down."

I reply, "What? Damn!"

He explains, "Yeah, the fire was so hot it burned the bricks."

I say, "Damn man, brick don't burn!"

He says, "That's what I thought too."

I say, "Who the fuck did you piss off?"

He says, "More than a few I'm afraid, but recently I filed a multi-million dollar lawsuit and won a large settlement for one of my clients against the city. The police burned and tortured him during interrogation."

I reply, "Damn, was he black?"

Siler says, "What does that have to do with anything?"

I say, "A lot down here. That makes you a nigger lover."

He says, "Yeah, I've heard the term."

I explain, "Something else you're going hear – can't blame a nigger for being a nigger. That's like blaming a dog for being a dog. But a nigger lover, well he's worse than a nigger. He's a traitor to his own kind."

Siler says, "I've heard that as well."

I say, "And you're going to hear it again. You got time for one more client?"

He says, "Sure, but one at a time."

He leads Tennessee into the courtroom. I follow. Both Tennessee and I draw a judge that's a stickler. He gives no leeway, but at least we know where we stand. Tennessee is hoping for some of that deferred adjudication, but there will be no ruling today. Siler gets up, says a few words, sets another court date and that's it. For me, it's a similar story.

Awaiting my turn with the judge, I watch a young brotha receive probation and a stiff fine for 300 pounds of weed. He buys his freedom by reaching into his pocket and pulling out a mass of wadded up cash; balled up bills of indiscriminate denominations are falling at his feet. His lawyer puts his hand on his client's wad of money and whispers, "No, not here." There's a low chuckle throughout the courtroom. I thought about the money in my wallet; the bills are straight and in sequential order. I know exactly how much. My money comes hard so I respect it. This brotha has no respect for his money because it comes easy. Every person in this courtroom knows he's going straight back to the block, yet there he goes. They all know he'll be back. The courts will double dip to maximize their profit potential. He'll commit a plethora of other crimes with an indeterminate number and variations of victims before he's recaptured.

As I stand before the court, I'm hard pressed to contain my contempt. The pretense and formalities make me sick. Court employees work diligently for the mere appearance of justice pretending they don't see the judge's school girl crush on the cocaine addicted Assistant District Attorney (ADA) whose skitzing and sniffling in open court. The judge says I can go until the DA decides to charge me with a crime which could take up to a year. In the meantime, I live in limbo.

The judge says I have to drive from Dallas once a month to piss in a cup - a vain attempt to keep me from smoking weed. These people can't keep drugs out of their jails or out of the DA's office. What makes them think they can stop me 200 miles removed? This municipality is deaf, dumb, blind and crooked. I'll have to take off work - if I still have a job - and come back down here for the express purposes of pissing. Fuck that! If that DA bitch can sniffle, scratch, twitch and shake in open court, I'll be damned if they get half an ounce of obedience from me. This angry line of rationale will just get me locked up again. I'm angry and quite possibly rationalizing, but I'm not stupid. The law and this municipality are both conceived and constructed with nothing but rigid right angles. I'm alive. Life is fluid, unpredictable and random like a paint splatter. 5 will get you 10 it won't take long to find the perforations. To have faith in the law and the justice system is to have faith in lawyers and politicians.

I say my farewells to Tennessee; he's on his way back home. Siler breaks me off a little more of his time. We get some things straight; I tell him how it all went down. He tells me not to worry for at least 8 or 9 months and says he'll call me when it's time. I tell him to be careful, "You're a nigger now. Make sure these crazy crackas don't burn down your house next. There's nothing so dangerous as an honest man." We shake hands and part company. Despite the odds, in all of five minutes Siler has calmed my nerves. Even with the fact I just allied myself with a man so vilified by the powers that be, they've seen fit to set his office ablaze.

I go upstairs and take care of some paperwork. I'm out on bond. Being from out of town, I must get some things transferred. I go to one office and they tell me this isn't the right office. I say, "Not two minutes ago I was told to come to this office." A clerk says, "No, you want the office down the hall and around the corner." I go to the other office and I'm told to go back to the first office. I explain, "I just came from there. She told me to come see you." Another clerk says, "Hold on one minute." She keeps me waiting for 20 minutes only to tell me she has no idea. She starts pecking at her computer then gets up and goes in the back again. 10 minutes later she comes back to her computer. A couple more minutes of pecking and she says, "Here you are. I got you." Low and behold, therein lays the perforation. I'm in-between offices - neither here nor there. None of them are looking for or expecting me. I will come and piss next month. If I get the same run around, that's confirmation enough I won't be missed.

I tiptoe back across town to say thanks to Ced for all he's done and hit the freeway. I stop at the first gas station outside the city limits to pick up a package and just like Littlewood said it was right under the pay phone. Light green and fluffy. Good looking out Littlewood. I fill up the tank, cop some zags and rollout, headed back to what, I don't know. After three months I have no idea what's left of my life, but for the next 200 miles the smoke will help me forget.

Traversing this outstretched and unbending thoroughfare between Texarkana and Dallas, the unflinching burn of the late day sun compels me to see the light. Memories betray me like a promiscuous lover and all I can recall in this moment is my pedigree. Grandpa was a legend. The City of Linden saw fit to memorialize him in bronze. My father was motherfucking Geordi La Forge. He was a war hero and retired Chief Flight Engineer of the USAF's Galaxy Class Flagship. My eldest brother left with a master's degree in 5. He's one of them cum laude niggas. I'm the last of my name and I leave as a reputed felon. This sad song I sing is the ballad of the black sheep.

6

It's been a month now and I'm on my way back to the courthouse to piss. I've got my life back together; got a new job doing PC Tech Support fixing computers, so I secured a substitute urine sample just in case. I get the run around again. No one knows what to do with me. When they finally show me to the bathroom I leave them the substitute, but this is the last time they'll see me. I had to make up a reason to leave work; I like this job and I won't lose it behind this foolishness. I will not allow them to take anything else from me. Each time I leave this place I count my blessings like the fly who has somehow escaped the spider's web. As I hit the front doors, I see a friendly face - my old celly Falcons. He's leaving just as I am. He says he's walking, so I offer him a ride. As soon as the offer leaves my mouth, it dawns on me this how I got caught up in the first place. We shoot the shit about being locked up. Strangely enough we manage to get a few laughs out of the memories. We get to his grandmother's house and he invites me in. It's clear from where he gets his home training. Grandma don't play. She reminds me of all the older black folks I've visited over the years in this little town - good and strong people. She asks me if I would mind running her to the store; there's no way I could or would ever say no, so off we go. She's a matriarch endowed with the ability to instantly return you to a state of childhood.

10 months have passed. I finally heard from Siler and just as I thought not a word about the nonexistent urine samples. He tells me we have a court date and not to worry because he's getting an extension. Life is just starting to get good again. I don't need any interruptions. I ask Siler how he's doing, "They haven't set fire to anything else have they?" He replies, "No, not yet." I say, "Well, watch your back." Siler replies, "You, too." We agree to let the bureaucracy take it's time.

I'm seeing a pretty little Puerto Rican girl from Queens. She's far too selfish for this to last, but she's a petite Latina, so naturally I'm enchanted. Late one Saturday night while we're lying in my bed with the Oasis jazz radio station playing in the background, I suggested we go to a jazz brunch they host in the morning. She says she can't because someone she knows might be there. I ask, "Who?" She says, "I have a boyfriend. Well, I had a boyfriend. He's in prison. It's complicated. I told him I would wait." I replied, "Well I know he ain't gonna be there." "No, but his parents go all the time." She has no idea I'm out on bond. As we lie here together I'm forced to recall all the long lonely nights in that cell. I think her man was foolish to believe she would wait. Locked in his cell, I think he knows she won't and it's killing him softly. Even though it's self-inflicted, it's strange to be lying here with her and feeling for his pain.

I'm back in the courthouse. Siler tells me this is just a preliminary hearing, but says there's a way out of all this.

He says, "You can take a lie detector test. If you pass they will drop the charges."

I reply, "Is that right? What's the fine print?"

Siler says, "Well, you won't pass. It's run by their man, so it will say what they want it to say." He tells me Homegirl has already failed.

I ask, "What do you think I should do?"

Siler says, "You can take it if you want, but it isn't admissible in court."

I reply, "So it's futile?"

Siler says, "Basically."

I reply, "Tell me something man, is this place as corrupt as it seems?"

Siler replies, "Yeah, it's pretty bad."

I reply, "What about the DA's office? Was I trippin' or was that woman ADA going through withdrawals?"

Siler says, "Oh, you noticed that? Yeah, she's in and out of rehab."

I ask, "Ain't that grounds for something?"

Siler says, "Depends on who you know."

I say, /"I heard some things about the DA taking payoffs."

Siler responds, "That ain't the half of it. My daughters go to high school with his son. They told me something I didn't want to believe."

I reply, "Yeah, I heard he's the biggest ecstasy dealer in the high school."

Siler says, "Man, you guys hear about everything in that jail, don't you?"

I say, "Shit, you don't know the half of it. The shit we hear is so bad it's hard to believe, but sooner or later we always get confirmation."

This judge is reputed to be an old school cracker. He's known for referring to black defendants as niggers in open court. My chances for a fair trial look bleak.

7

More than two years have passed and it's finally time for my trial. I don't know why, but there's an air of optimism in my lungs. Today we pick a jury. On the steps of the courthouse I overheard a young black couple talking about having to serve jury duty. Brotha said "Better be glad I ain't on that jury. Whatever it is - not guilty! Fuck these dirty muthafuckas! Not guilty!" So I asked him, "gonna be on a jury?" "Not me man, her. I just got out of this jail for some bullshit. These dirty ass muthafuckas cain't tell me shit! Babe, when you get in there, fuck what they talkin' 'bout, - not guilty."

"Counselor, good to see they didn't get you." Siler and I converse a little before they bring in the prospective jurors. He says he would like my input on the selection so my eyes are wide open. Out of about 50 prospective jurors there are three black. I can tell you now, not one will make the cut; I can also see about 10 I know have had dealings with the man. It isn't hard to tell. The rest are George Bush's constituency; never even had a free dream much less a conscious thought in their entire lives. Even worse than that, they aren't even aware of the fact they aren't free.

Siler begins questioning jurors by asking each one if they can be fair and impartial. From the first three or four he receives the obligatory "Yes I can." Siler asks one of the prospective black jurors the same question. He replies, "Well, duh police and duh DA's office is all professionals, right?" Siler replies, "Yes." The prospect replies, "Well I'm sure they wouldn't be here just wastin' all our time fuh nuthin', now would they?" The remaining black prospective jurors simultaneously drop and shake their heads while the rest of the jurors reply in a slow murmur,"Uh, yeah" as if this simple bumpkin had uttered something profound. There aren't but three black prospects and this one is a bonified house nigga. This conglomerate of honest, decent and hardworking American men and women have the audacity to look at Siler like "what do you have to say to that?" My heart stalled on the spot as it dawns on me that I'm going to prison. If the police say you did it then you did it. Siler goes about talking the tightrope and explains to the prospective jurors their stupidity and does this without insulting all these "good Christian folk." Despite our best efforts, we ended up with a prosecutor's jury. Several older southern white gentlemen, a few older white ladies and a few of their offspring including a young white southern minister. Not one person of any color. Not one poor white person. Siler objected to the lack of integration to no avail. Arguing for a black man's rights down here is futile. A trial date is set in 30 days. Any sense of optimism I had has been eviscerated.

The night of my trial has arrived. Both Siler and I are full of doubt and apprehension. It's no secret the deck is stacked, so I've got a couple of witnesses with me. Cedric and my former boss, Theo will testify on my behalf. As we walk the courthouse halls I run into Homegirl's brother. He was cool with me, so I feel no animosity toward him. I can only imagine what she told him. He happens to be fresh out of the pen himself; he got caught with a gang of weed a few years back. I think he's aware of the lies his sister is telling. I turn to go into counsel with my lawyer and there she is. I can't even look at her without a dangerous spike in blood pressure. Nothing left between her and me except murder. Sitting at this big oak defense table, I'm afraid. This is a kind of fear I've never known. I'm not going to let it show; I refuse to play the part of the prey. To everyone else this is just another day at the office.

The court goes about preparing and shuffling the files that may send me to the land of the Philistines.

"All rise!" The judge is a thin, white-haired Klansmen who's considerate enough to remove his white robe before entering the courtroom. The Office of Persecution's opening remarks paint me in a most unfavorable light. If you let him tell it, I'm the black Pablo Escobar; he's chosen his weapons - fear and racism. This way he doesn't have to present an actual case. All he has to do is titillate and insinuate; stereotypical ignorance will do the rest. I lean towards Siler and whisper, "You got your work cut out." He shoots me a reassuring glance and gets up to address the jury. He has a subtler approach, short and sweet. The first witness for the persecution is Homegirl. She proceeds to tell a tale about her just going along for the ride and how I was on my way to Tennessee on a drug run. She said I offered to drop her off on the way - a story so ridiculous it's scary. While running 30 pounds of marijuana across three states, I take the risk of coming into this jerkwater town as a favor to this woman? Is this the best they could come up with? This can't be it. The cops were too cocky for this to be it. Siler must be thinking the same. In cross examination, he simply makes her repeat that story real slow, exposing the stupidity. It falls to me not to appear that stupid.

Next up is Black Cop. "I pulled him over for failing to signal 50 feet before the turn. He looked nervous, so I asked if I could search his car." The DA asks, "What did he say?" Black cop replies, "He said yes." The DA gets the opened duffel bag of evidence and sets it on a table directly in front of the jury box making sure they can see and smell it. Siler on cross examination says, "If my client knew the drugs were in the car why would he submit to the search?" "I don't know," he replied. "Some suspects think we won't find it." The undercover cop is cocky and arrogant, and all too sure of himself. Being in narcotics no doubt he's done this countless times before. Siler asks him if he had prior knowledge or if he got a tip. He says no. "You didn't tell my client "we know where this stuff is coming from and we know where it's going?" "No." He's lying in open court because he doesn't want to expose his drug dealing snitches.

The truth has no place in a court of law. This is about who

has the better lie. That's why the guilty have a 50/50 shot and the innocent ain't got a shot in hell, statistically speaking. The Lone Ranger, the only cop here who's just doing his job, comes from behind the courtroom in time to take the stand. He gives concise yes/no answers to both the prosecutor and defense. When the truth contradicts what his brothers in blue have already testified to he says "I don't recall." From his body language, he's clearly uncomfortable with all that's going on, but he will not rat on his fellow cops. It's either loyalty to the blue or a fear for his life, most likely a combination. For this cop, I hold no animosity. He did not go out of his way to lie. I don't blame him for not putting his life on the line for me. When he leaves the stand, he asks to be excused from the court. The excuse of a prior engagement did nothing to hide his contempt. He just wants to do his job. Some might say his job was to tell the truth without the omissions. It's obvious to everyone in this courtroom that he's an unwilling participant which is more than I expected. "No name" cop is called to the stand and I wonder what for. He didn't get to the scene until it was damn near over, but he doesn't waste any time. The prosecutor asks him one question, "What did you hear the defendant say when you got to the scene?" "I over heard him say he was on his way to Tennessee." I blurt out, "Complete fiction, a total falsehood and a bald- faced lie!"

I quickly apologize to his honor because it's too early in the game to piss off the ref, so I add the numbers up and this is what I continue to ask myself - why would a police officer risk his career by committing perjury? The answer is in the brilliance of the lie itself. How does one prove in a court of law this officer of the law didn't hear what he said he heard? This is the reason they chose this particular bullshit story of Homegirls', it allows them the easiest corroboration. They've done this before. As reputed, Siler is very good. He makes No Name recount the accounts of the arrest, but he can't afford to treat him with any hostility. It would only serve to further alienate the jury. Siler must force No Name to incriminate himself. With the subtle skill of a neurosurgeon, Siler makes him admit he didn't even arrive at the scene until after I had already been placed in back of Lone Rangers' squad car, alluding to the fact it would have been impossible for him to hear anything I might have said. At which point Siler turns to the jury and shrugs his shoulders and says "no further questions." I wonder if the jury even got his point. With that, the persecution rests.

It's our turn now. Siler calls Cedric to the stand, "How long have you known Mr. Hennington?" Ced states, "I've known Damian since he was in diapers." With a loud boom, the DA says, "Objection your Honor!" The judge replies, "Sustained." After two more questions and two more sustained objections the persecutor succeeded in getting Ced off the stand on the grounds of relevance. I get a sinking feeling this won't take long. The DA is getting' all the home cooking'. Siler can't get the table scraps. He calls Theo to the stand, "How long did you work with Mr. Hennington?" "More than a year." "In all that time was he reliable." "Yes." "Objection." The DA is using an old trick - object to everything. If the defense does this it looks like they're trying to hide something. When the DA does it, it looks like the defense is trying to get away with something so he can't lose. "Did you have any doubt Mr. Hennington would show up for work the next morning?" "No sir." A couple more objections, couple more sustains and no further questions. Siler says, "I have no questions for this witness your honor. I call Mr. Hennington to the stand." I jump out of my seat and stride towards the stand. I can't wait to put my two cents in. This is where most defendants hang themselves. Despite the prosecutor's considerable years of experience, I'm unimpressed. Without the lies he has no case. That's why he felt it necessary to fabricate. "Mr. Hennington, how did the marijuana get in your car?" "I put it in there. I didn't know it, but I did. She told me she was moving to her mother's house, so I put a lot of her bags in my car. She was pregnant. I got a mother, ain't no way I would let her carry all those bags." "You couldn't smell it?" "No, because we had been smoking weed. I went all the way to South Dallas to get a dime bag." "The officer testified you were nervous when he pulled you over. Were you?" Yes." "Why?" "Because they followed me all the way from the freeway." I figure brutal honesty is my hold card. There's no way they would expect me to tell this much truth. Never mind the fact I ain't got shit else. The persecutor starts right in, "Tell the court about all your drug acquaintances." I replied, "Whoa, whoa, all what drug acquaintances?" "You said you know" "No man, you said that, I didn't." "What about the drugs you said you bought?" "Man, that's a half second transaction. I bought $10 worth of weed. It would've lasted me all week. How long would $10 of alcohol last you?" In my peripheral, I notice his honor sit up and grin. "I'll ask the questions. When you go to law school, then you can ask the questions." I can't and make no attempt to hide my satisfaction. I'm entertaining the judge and annoying the prosecutor. So far, so good. "You said you were nervous when the officer stopped you? "Yes." "Why?" "They were waiting on the exit ramp, so they knew we were coming." "How would you know that?" "Because the narcotics officer said so. He said we know where the stuff was coming from and we know where it was going." "He said that?" "Verbatim." The judge snatches his head in my direction surprised I used that word, and correctly no less. He's no doubt unaccustomed to a black man with shoulder length cornrows and a vocabulary. "That's not what the officers testified to." "Yes, I know." "Oh, so they're all liars?" "Well I don't know if they're liars, but I know they lied!" The judge smiles and sits back.

I purposely avoid eye contact with the jury. I'm told I have an intimidating gaze and I don't want them to personalize my animosity. Siler is grinning profusely. A defendant on the stand is for the defense at best a crap shoot. More often than not it comes up snake eyes. Seeing Siler's quiet amusement, I know it's going as well as I suspect. Now I can't wait for the prosecutors' next question, but true to form he punks out. "No further questions." The office of persecution starts his closing arguments. While he's calling me everything but an agent of Al-Qaida, my mind wanders to all the people who've had the horrifying misfortune of occupying this particular hot seat, both the deserving and undeserving. How the office of persecution vilifies every occupant indiscriminately just as he's doing to me at this very moment. He makes a point of saying I-30 is a known drug thoroughfare conveniently omitting the fact it's the only thoroughfare. From Perry Mason to Law and Order, as many of them as I've watched, I've never given the dynamics of this procedure much thought. Needless to say, I am now. "That is a lie! I'm sorry your Honor, but is he allowed to just lie like that?" As I sit back down the DA glares at me. I wonder if he really expects me to just sit here and let him lie or does he realize my outburst has a dual purpose. He was working up a good head of steam so I decided to interrupt his rhythm. He's laying it on extra thick because I beat him on the stand. Now that he has the floor, he's trying to stick it to me. True to his cowardice form, he figures at this point I can't fight back. This is not now nor has it ever been a pursuit of truth or justice. The office of persecution is taking his job personally as if it's his life on the line and not mine. Do I risk contempt of court and alienating the jury for one more outburst? "No, that's a lie! I apologize your Honor, but it's difficult to sit here and listen to this."

Good thing the DA is wrapping up because I have pushed his honor to his limits. Siler addresses the jury in a low and steady tone perhaps compensating for my truculence. He's calmly laying out the facts of the case; his is an exact opposite tactical strategy compared to the persecutions'; he's appealing to reason, logic and rationale. Siler is a cool customer, "Ladies and gentlemen, this man has been honest to a fault. He is the one with the job. He is the one with the life to get back too. She is the one without a job, life or hope. Ladies and gentlemen of the jury, this is a smart man." Fear and uncertainty are now to me both tangible and palpable. As the jury is excused and turns to leave, I try and fail to get a reading. Walking slowly, silently and heads bowed, almost somber, I lean over to Siler and ask, "What do you think?" He says, "Well, you can never tell with a jury, but I'd say we've done very well. Better than the DA expected" I say, "Yeah, I thought so too. That's why he spread the mustard on so thick." Siler says, "Yeah, didn't think you noticed that." I reply, "Couldn't help but. Ain't he a little too old to be so childish and petty?" Siler says, "Apparently not."

I'm out on the 3rd floor balcony in the country night air and I'm laboring to take in enough oxygen. Ced and Theo are full of reassuring words and back slaps; wanting to, but unable to believe, I stare into the night sky replaying the trial forwards and backwards. Of course, now that the point is moot I come up with a few more pertinent bones of contention like the fact I was absolutely broke the night they arrested me. Matter of fact, my bank account was $25 in the negative. God damn overdraft fee, so how could I be planning to drive across three states with absolutely no money? They could say I was planning to sell some of the weed. If that was case, they could have charged me with intent to distribute as well, but that would have forced the persecution to prove that charge as well. They felt they had enough to get the job done and we shall soon see.

Siler comes out of the court room and on to the balcony expressionless. The kind one might get from a doctor trying not to give you undo cause for concern. It doesn't work then and it's not working now. Siler says, "The jury has requested to review some testimony." "Who's?" "The officer who testified he heard you say you were on your way to Tennessee." "All they want to know is what that cop said? That don't sound good." "Maybe, but it could go either way." "That's all they want to review so far." "Say counselor, I know it's irrelevant now, but why didn't we bring up the fact I had no money to cross 3 states with?" 'The prosecutor would have argued intent to distribute. With almost 30 pounds intent is almost a given and that comes with a stiffer minimum sentence. That one bit of evidence wasn't worth the risk." "Damn, fucked for telling the truth!" "Yeah that's just about the size of it." I don't know how long it's been because I refuse to look at my watch, but the night air is getting cold. Ced and Theo suggest we go back inside, "It can't be much longer now man. Yeah let's go back in D." "D, man sit down and stop trippin'. You got this. Yeah man, you goin' home."

The courtroom door pops open and Siler says, "It's time." I have no breath. I compose myself before I hit the oak double doors. Though I don't know why, at this point the verdict has been rendered. There's nothing left but the anticipation and formalities, "Will the defendant please rise. Has the jury reached a verdict?" Wouldn't you know it? The young preacher is the jury foreman, "Yes, we have your honor." What say you?" "Guilty."

I can't see or hear anything. The only thing I feel is the wood grain of an oak desk pressed into my forehead and Siler's arm around my shoulder; I have no idea how much time has passed when my senses start to return, but I begin to recognize

Ced's' voice calling my name. Regaining enough motor skills to turn my head, he tells me to keep my head up. As the court goes about its procedures, the weight of what has just transpired is more than I can bear. Physically I'm having difficulty standing; heart palpitations and erratic breathing, falling forward on my palms. My chin is on my chest and Siler is doing his best to console me. It's clear the verdict has severely shaken him as well. A normally relaxed man, he is plum red and his face muscles are all contracted. I admit this verdict doesn't come as all that much of a surprise. After all, this is Texas and worse than that, rural Texas.

I look over at the jury and try to take in the faces of my condemners. I'm taking them in one at a time and I see something that shocks me to my core. One of the younger female jurors is in tears, face in her hands and streaming shameful crocodile tears. Two or three others are visibly afflicted with the same doubts. The look on my face is one of confusion and disbelief. How can this be? If you disagree with the decision, then how did you unanimously come to this verdict? Just as quick as the question manifested itself, so did the answer.

Everyone in this courtroom is now aware of the jury's uncertainty which is turning the prosecutors' sweet victory a bit sour. He found it necessary to re-close the case. I've never heard of a prosecutor feeling compelled to re-close a case after procuring a guilty verdict, however ill gotten. But here he is, "How dare you look at them like that as if you are angry with them." "Mine is not a look of anger sir, but one of disbelief." "Ladies and gentlemen, don't feel sorry for this man. He did it to himself. Look at him. Does he look sorry for what he's done? No, he's cocky and arrogant. He's not the least bit remorseful." "That's because I'm not guilty!" "Ladies and gentlemen there is no need to feel sorry for him. You've done the right thing here. He brought it on himself." I lean over to Siler and in a not-so-low whisper say "Can you believe this shit?" With that the DA glares at me, turns and stomps back to his table. He makes a motion to have the jury deliver a sentence tonight. Siler and I agree. I have no desire to prolong my agony by waiting for them to render my fate. The DA mindful of some sympathetic jurors, he takes this opportunity to twist the dagger one last time, "I think he needs to go sit down somewhere and think about what he's done. I don't think a fine should be imposed. He's a drug dealer. As such, he will just get the money from dealing in drugs. Therefore, I recommend no fine."

As the jury exits Siler is beside himself, "I'm sorry man. There's just no way it should've come out like this." "I know. I still can't believe it. So what do we do now?" I asked. Siler says, "Well, we can appeal. Do you want to try that?" I reply, "You damn skippy! As appeals go do we have a shot?" Siler says, "Yes, but it's a long one." I reply, "Damn, you're full of good news." Siler says, "I know. Feels like I let you down." I say, "No man, you did a damn good job." Siler replies, "Yeah, but it wasn't good enough. I'm going to get the ball rolling on the appeal."

I've just been sentenced to a Texas penitentiary for some bullshit; I can't get my mind around it. The ramifications are unfathomable. How could this be? A convicted felon? Not me! I don't deserve to be locked up. This just can't be happening. Just as I'm about to drown myself in this pity puddle, I hear chuckling laughter. Over my shoulder there they stand - three cops pointing and laughing at me like playground bullies just got me detention for some shit they did. Instantly the self-pity evaporates and is replaced with cold, raw, malevolent and unmitigated hate. Look at them! They couldn't be more pleased with themselves, so they find more pleasure in taunting and tormenting me. It makes me wonder how many others they've done this to being that this is standard operating procedure. I'm small potatoes, a drop in the bucket. These dirty cops have railroaded more people than Amtrak. They've extracted their last ounce of pleasure from me and they know it.

The jury returns 30 minutes later with a sentence of four years like they're handing out Halloween candy. As I watch the jury leave for the last time, I wonder if they think they've done a good thing. If I survive four years in purgatory, will I be better for it? Will I be a more affable and civilized citizen? Is that the aim? Is that the intent? Despite this, I hold no ill will towards them. Sure, I was angry at them at first, but I realized they're just simple, credulous people naive enough to believe if a man puts on a police uniform he's a good guy.

Siler and the DA are arguing a point at the bench. His honor rules before I can focus in. The DA is not pleased, so naturally I am. The judge has ruled in our favor; I have no idea what the ruling is, but I'll take it. The bailiff, another stoic and aging white haired southern gentleman comes to me and says, "I don't know what you did, but in 25 years I've never seen him do what he just did for you." "Is that right?" "Yes, so be grateful." Siler comes back to the defense table. He's regained some of his color, "I've just gotten bail granted pending appeal." "What? I didn't expect to get it. Well shit! Guess I made an impression on the old judge after all," I reply. I'm grateful to be going home tonight. I have to be at work in the morning. Ain't that a bitch!

As two deputies take me downstairs for transport I'm a bit paranoid. I don't know how deep the dirt runs, so I'm looking for tell-tell signs. It's late at night and very few people around. I'm being escorted by two redneck cops through this backwater east Texas town; I'm in handcuffs and in the back of a police car- anything is possible. I say, "Can I ask you guys a question?" "Yeah, what do yuh want?" "How do you feel about your fellow cops lying on the stand?" "What do yuh mean?" "I mean telling bald-faced lies while testifying in open court." "What did they lie about?" "To start with, the nark cop told me he knew where the stuff was coming from and where it was going." They look at each other with patronizing smiles, "Did you ever thank that might be just an investigative technique?" "Oh I have no doubt that's what he was doing. My question was why did he find it necessary to lie?" "Well, I don't know." "Oh so I guess you don't mind working with dirty cops?" A dangerous question, but if they are dirty as well it will invoke a telling response. "What do you mean dirty?" "I mean they just got me sent to the pen for something I didn't do." "Oh come on! Do you know how many times we've heard that?" "Probably a lot, but you tell me this - how many 30 year old drug dealers do you know with a clean record?" They look at each other, shrug and nod. "Yeah, you got a point there. But that ain't got nothin' to do with us. Our job is just to take you to jail." With that, I'm a little more at ease. They gave me true and natural responses with no emotional attachment - just doing their job. Subtle reassurance makes these dark, lonely back-country roads a little less ominous.

The smell. That fucking jail house smell. By itself, it incarcerates a man's consciousness. How I'd hoped to never have to infect my respiratory system with this rancid stench ever again. Yet here I am standing in front of a CO getting booked in. Along with the smell, nothing has changed - same guards, same furnishings, and same sounds. Before I can even get through the booking process, I feel a hand on my shoulder. "Counselor!" "Yeah, I'm gonna get you outta here right now. Have a seat over there and I'll be back in a minute." He's right on top of it. I can't tell you how a little piece of mind changes this whole process. With a public defender I spent 3 months in jail without even being so much as charged with a crime. Here I've been tried, convicted and sentenced in one night as a felon and with private counsel. I'm getting out before they even get through booking me in. Siler is so good; I'm walking out of jail before they can even give me that orange suit. He bailed me out for no money. Anyone who's had to make that collect call from behind bars to a bail bondsman knows they don't want to hear about shit except the mother fucking money.

Ced and Theo are waiting in my car outside. Siler says I need to sign papers at the bail bondsman's' office and then I can go home. "Don't worry, I'll stretch out the appeals for a couple years, but I must tell you the odds aren't in our favor." "No doubt. Go through the motions anyway." "Don't worry." He has repeatedly apologized for the verdict and I've repeatedly said it's not his fault, but I can tell it's going to keep him up nights. After seeing the bondsman and taking Ced back home, Theo and I head back to Dallas. On the outskirts of New Boston, we stop to fill up, roll a fat one and ride out. Theo knows the weight of things on my mind. As a youth, he spent a few months in Huntsville. We don't have to talk to communicate. After an hour or so, the radio station has long since faded out. Neither of us bothering to change it, Theo breaks the silence. "Damn man, I didn't think shit like that still happened. That was like one of those civil rights movies."

Three years have passed and the time has come. All of my appeals have been exhausted and Siler says I'm to turn myself in Monday morning. Barring a miracle of mercy, tonight I breathe free air for the last time. Theo is having a Super bowl party; I'm surrounded by friends and acquaintances trying in vain to enjoy the end of life as I know it. Everyone is full of encouraging words and all of them are sure I'll be out in no time. I smile and agree if only to keep from fuckin' up their good time. Theo is the only one who knows and right now all he can do is keep my glass full and my blunt lit. Simultaneously suffering from dread and the munchies, I'm stuffing my face with chips and dip, peanuts, brownies, cake, candy and soda. It's difficult to enjoy knowing it will be the last time for a while.

I'm going to see a lady friend after the game also knowing she will be the last for a while. I can't wait for the game to be over. Now more than ever, time is precious. I wish to spend the remainder wallowing in femininity. The game is over and I'm leaving. I give daps to the homies and I hug all the girls. I'm enjoying each sensation these women bring - the softness, the curves, the way their breasts press against me, the difference in perfumes and scents, the way my hands sink into their supple flesh, the way their hair brushes against my cheek, the subtle condoling moans, the soft sweet look in their eyes. There's just no way to adequately convey the agony life without these pleasures inflicts on a man.

I have to be in Texarkana by 9 am and it's a three-hour drive. I say goodbye to my lady friend with one last hug and kiss, and set out to begin an incarcerated life.

8

My mother and father have flown in from California. While it's good to see them, I wish they hadn't come. I don't want them to see their son in such a state, but Mom insisted. She said she wants them to know I have people that care for me. Personally, their opinion of me is of no consequence. I'm late getting to the court house. Fuck them! What can they do to me - lock me up? My outlook is bad, so I don't care. The way I feel now I'd almost rather face a firing squad. The bitter contempt I have for this vial corrupt system makes me want to have it out right now. You can't imagine and I can't explain the torrent of emotions as I open the courtroom door for my mother.

Siler comes over and ushers us back out into the halls. After a quick intro and exchange of pleasantries we get right to it.

He says, "You're a little late. Thought you might not be coming."

I reply, "It wasn't easy to come down here, man."

Siler says, "No, I imagine not."

I say, "You look a little rattled counselor. What's wrong?"

Siler says, "I haven't told you this, but I've got my own troubles."

I reply, "What's goin' on man?"

Siler says, "Well, I've been charged with conspiracy."

I reply, "What the fuck is you talkin' 'bout man?"

Siler says, "Yeah, they set me up real good. A client of mine rolled over and accused me of federal drug offenses."

I understand why he chose not to tell me before today. When a person is accused, guilt is irrelevant. People tend to look at you as tainted. If the gaze belongs to someone you know it's painful so much so you become sensitive to the shameful blame in their eyes.

I say, "Not you counselor!"

Siler says, "Yeah, me. In fact, I don't know if they will even allow me to stand up with you today."

I reply, "Goddamn man! So what, burning your office down didn't scare you off, so they decide to set you up?"

Siler says, "Looks that way."

I reply, "You didn't think they'd just let that multi-million dollar lawsuit slide, did you?"

Siler says, "They were trying to get me for some time now. I just never thought they'd do it."

I say, "Come on counselor, you know better than I do how evil these crazy crackers down here are. If you knew they were head hunting you, why'd you stick around? You should've been gone."

Siler says, "Well, my daughters are here. My life is here. Plus, I figured if I didn't give them anything, they wouldn't have anything. In hindsight, that was a bit naive."

I reply, "Yeah man, you ain't got to be wrong for them to be right."

He tells me how they've spread the mustard on real thick. All types of fowl rumors and going out of their way to discredit him. Generally making life for him and his family as fucked up as possible which in a small town like this ain't difficult. The woman he was in love with left him; she couldn't take the talk and he found out she was using him for his money.

I say, "Well damn man, you didn't want or need no bitch like that no way."

Siler says, "No, but that doesn't stop the hurt."

I reply, "Yeah man. I can dig that."

He broke several of his vertebrae while in law school and he still managed to graduate. Now he's facing disbarment and federal prison time. Siler's situation is so diabolical I forgot the reason I'm here, even if just for a moment. He tells me the judge will say a few words and then I'll be taken into custody.

I gave my wallet, watch and keys to my mother. They won't get a second chance to steal my shit. I have no anxiety about returning to this jail. There's nothing unknown to me. I've got a stash of weed on me for medicinal purposes. Just like the first time, I intend to do absolutely no penance. Most people have no idea how much work and thinking it takes to keep from thinking and working. They've succeeded in incarcerating my body, but they're incapable of incarcerating my mind. All I can think about in this moment are the countless lives that have been irrevocably damaged and destroyed by this process and these people.

The judge shuffles a few papers and I'm officially a ward of the court. I shake Siler's hand and turn to hug my mother, but a bailiff stops me. The look in my mother's eyes makes me glad she's not armed. I wave goodbye before they take me behind the courtroom. The same two deputies that transported me that fateful night are standing on the other side of the door. As they place the cuffs on me, the door to the courtroom opens momentarily. I hear the judge call Siler's name and watch him respond, "Yes your honor." The judge reads the charges of conspiracy against my attorney, but his real crime is being a nigger lover. I get booked in, a CO removes the cuffs and a door from an adjacent cell opens.

There's a part of the booking process when they ask you about any identifying marks - scars, tattoos and the like. I have both. One tattoo and one scar. After making sure the tat isn't gang related, the CO asks about the scar, "Surgical, I donated a kidney." There happens to be a cop standing next to the CO and he asks, "How much do you get for something like that?" Fucking pig automatically assumes I'm in here for drugs, so I must've sold my kidney. Weed doesn't make you go to any extremes. If you ain't got no weed, you just ain't got no weed. But because his chosen occupation keeps him wallowing in the muck and mire of human shit, that's all he can see. I reply, "It was for my brother man!" It was clear from his expression, the thought never occurred. He's a hopeless pessimist and he's paid to walk around with a night stick and a loaded gun.

This place is full of nostalgia for me – the black "my

brother's keeper" cop and the dreaded orange suit. There's nothing more personal and degrading than being issued County underwear. In prison, we're all the same. The burglar is the same as the rapist, the drug dealer is the same as the wife abuser, and the murderer is the same as the addict. We must co-mingle and cohabitate. Society believes it's teaching us a lesson by locking us up, but the human psyche is far more complex. To spite our captives and those whom they represent, we offer each other the benefits of learning our respective disreputable skills. This is M.I.T. for the criminally inclined. Come here, get an education and make some connections. The conservatives are foolish enough to believe locking up criminals will in turn keep them safe and keeps them believing incarceration makes us want to repent. It's quite the contrary. Most convicts become more vindictive, more versatile and more determined.

It's Monday morning in this building they call the Annex and the population is as light as it gets. The tanks are encased in walls that are Plexiglas from the waist up; the duel cells are along the back wall and a day room in the center. The showers and toilets are located in the far corner. No more than eight people can fit in this tank. For now, I get a cell to myself. The door slams behind me with a heavy iron clank from which the colloquialism is derived. I make an effort not to let it get to me. I don't know why and I'm not asking, but the corner cell is open. I take it because it's furthest from the bathroom and I can see the TV from the bunk. I throw my bed roll on the steel bunk and settle in. As soon as I get set up, it's time to escape. Like a hotel, in jail there's always a Bible. These happen to be pocket-size. I'm not looking for Jesus, but the thin paper will serve as paraphernalia. I twist toilet paper and make a wick; I pop the socket and I'm smoking'. I've made no social moves, so my cellmates don't know what to make of me. They smell, but don't inquire. In addition to weed, this time I have a few hundred dollars on my books, so there's no need to socialize.

I'm lying on my bunk high as the Cliff's of Dover and it isn't long before my thoughts find their way back to Babygirl. When I left her house, I didn't shower. I want to smell her as long as I can, so I close my eyes, take a deep breath and there she is. Some might find this strange, but knowing I won't get close to a woman for Lord knows how long I figure I need all the help I can get. It's backfiring. Her scent makes the memory so strong it's painful. Still I can't bring myself to wash her off me. Lunch is coming. I've got the munchies and prison food is far from good, but it will do right now. I heard in passing the commissary lady just came on Saturday, so I have to wait until next week to get groceries.

There are no books to read in this tank except the Bible and most in here are missing pages. Besides, I already know how that book ends. The fact I actually want for a book is still a new experience. On the outside, I had no time for books. I was too busy living life. What I wouldn't do for a book right now. It's just before four in the afternoon and they're bringing dinner around. It's more of the same Chef Boyardee. Right now, I would commit a violent crime for a can of beefaroni. I've been locked up for a day and I'm already fantasizing about snacks.

Lights out is one of a myriad of not so subtle reminders of my absolute lack of control. Each one descends upon the psyche like the Attila and his Huns. The only logical recourse is to not care. It's no small matter to invest no mental or emotional effort in things of which you have no control. Most people never even attempt to develop the ability to influence their own mind which is why desire, jealousy, envy, greed, love, and hate hold so much sway. Right now, I desire not to be here and I hate those who put me here. I'm putting forth considerable effort to combat these feelings because they hold no benefit. These two emotions are parasitic. They have a tendency to devour from the inside. Hate will often times blow up at the wrong time and place due to the lack of opportunity to attack the intended target. This is the principal catalyst for the rampant violence in jail. It's why I'm spending my first incarcerated evening attempting to come to terms with my reality.

It's late Tuesday morning and in come six new cell mates. One of them picks the bunk on top of mine. He seems polite enough, but we don't talk too much. We're feeling each other out; he knows most of the men in here except for me. He's curious but cautious, "Where you from nigga?" "Cali." "Damn nigga, how you end up off in dis muthafucka?" "Weed." "Is dat right?" He turns to his belongings and pulls out a pound of the green. I sit straight up. I've made very little effort to hide the smell of my smoke. Fuck these guards. If they bust in, I'll just swallow what I've got left. The size of my eyes must have clued him in to my concerns, "Yeah man I know. It's a gang of shit. My homeboy was gettin' out, so he gave it to me. What you wanna do?" "Well you got it now, so fuck it." This may not seem the logical thing to do. I have few choices and snitching is not an option. Telling him to get the fuck out will probably result in a fight and will bring the guards which is the last thing any of us wants. The rest of the cells are now full, so I can't move. The only thing left is for us to go about out-smarting our jailers. He's already got a leg up on that, "Got da hookup wit a couple of COs I went to school with. Said they'd let me know if dey comin'." We go about stashing it all over the tank just in case. I show him my little stash. "Yeah nigga, knew I smelt it. Dat's why I showed yuh my shit. One thang fo' sho'e, we gonna stay high." I don't know if it's the weed, but I like this dude. Sam's his name. Having someone to talk shit with makes time go by a little faster. Sam has some store – I'm grateful. Being hungry and locked up will make the clock stop.

There's a white boy in here that looks familiar. I can't place him, so I assume it's from my previous stint. He's looking at me like he knows me. While we eat dinner he says, "You don't remember me?" I reply, "Yeah man, but I can't place the face." He says, "Remember Rockmon?" I reply, "Oh, shit! Now I got it." He responds, "What you doin' back in here?" I reply, "Same shit. What about you?" "He says, "Fuck man, I'm always in 'n' out o' this bitch." I respond, "Shit, you sound like you like it." He says, "Hail no. It just seems to kinda work out like that." I ask, "You heard from Rockmon?" He replies, "No, but I heard he's still down there." I ask, "How long did he get?" He replies, "Don't know, but they don't expect 'em back no time soon. Siler's your lawyer?" I reply, "Yeah." He says, "You heard what happen to 'em?" I reply, "Yeah, I heard. Fucked up. They got 'em good." He says, "I know the dude who turned on 'em." I reply, "Word?" He states, "Yep. They promised to drop all the shit they had on 'em if he flipped." I ask, "What'd he say Siler did?" He responds, "Said he paid 'em with weed." I said, "That's all it took? Some muthafucka saying he did somethin'?" He responds, "Well they got a couple other people to co-sign." I reply, "Siler's too square for shit like that." He says, "Yeah I know. Had 'em mu'self one time. He ain't have no idea 'bout nuthin'. I mean he didn't know nuthin' bout the drug game." I say, "Yeah, I got the same impression." He says, "But all that don't matter none now. Way I hear tell, he's all but done. Shame too cause he's bout the best we had." Sam has a gang of questions about all this. Something tells me to keep the specifics on the down low. I don't want the particulars to be common gossip. I make a head motion to Sam and we head to our cell.

Sam asks how I got here, so I break it down. I leave out little things like names and dates just in case he knows Homegirl. When I get through regaling he says, "Shit like that happens all the time around here. Ain't nothin' new." I reply, "Shit's new to me." Sam's nonchalance allows for a natural segue into a welcomed change in subject. I ask, "You born and raise around here?" He says, "All my life." I reply, "Don't know how anyone could do that. I'm a military kid. I gotta go, see and do." He says, "That's how you got yo' ass up in here, ain't' it?" I respond, "Maybe, but what's your excuse?" He says, "Got a point." He asks where I've been; I talk for hours.

We've had a steady stream of inmate rotation this week. One in particular is a mess. He's fucked up. I don't know what he's on, but he took too much. He can't stand up or sit down. He's sloppy and incoherent. It isn't alcohol or meth. From what we can get out of him, in between laughing and making fun, he's a truck driver. He crashed into an overpass. He finally found his way to a bunk and fell asleep for a couple hours. It's still early and most have gone back to sleep. In his semi unconscious state, he gets up out of his bunk, walks out of his cell and right into the wrong cell to take a shit. The two brothas asleep in the cell wake to the sound of a flushing toilet, "What the fuck is you doin'? Dis muthafucka done lost his mind! Get the fuck up and stink up yo' own cell." We're sick with laughter until one of the brothas hits dude upside his head, "Come on man, you know he ain't right in the head." "Fuck you! You say dat cause you didn't wake up to dis stank ass muthafucka on yo' toilet." He stumbles back to his bunk. I'm not sure he feels the knot on his head. When dinner comes around the fucked-up truck driver is coming around, but the brothas are still hot. They knock his tray on to the floor. He's a little upset, but there's nothing he can do unless he wants more lumps. I feel kind of bad for the old dude. He obviously doesn't mean any harm, but all things considered he got off light. He just as easily could be battered, bruised and bleeding to go along with his detox.

The next day, the truck driver is giving intimate details about molesting his farm animals, "Had this old heifer. Anytime she'd see me comin', she'd turn around and raise her tail." He did it so often he had her trained, "She'd back right on up to the fence. I'd just climb up on the fence, grab a hold t' them hip bones and go to town." Three white boys sitting at a table are laughing about how sheep pussy looks and feels just like a woman's. As bad as this sound, I know it's much worse. This is what they freely admit to which makes me to wonder what they aren't saying. What else have they tried to stick their dick in? After all, these are the people who made bestiality infamous. The sight of them is making me physically sick.

It's Monday morning and I'm being moved to the main jail. Just as I'm packing up, the commissary lady is making her way down the hall. I missed her by that much. Sam says, "Don't worry dog, I'll take good care of yo' shit." In truth, I don't mind Sam getting my store. I must've smoked twice as much worth of weed. Plus he was a real cool celly. The forced march across the street is a welcome bit of daylight. It's cold so the sun feels that much better. The high thin clouds are blowing across the crystal cobalt sky. The distant sight of the horizon is a welcome reprieve from my reality. There's about ten of us making our way to our new home. No one is speaking, not even in a whisper. Each pair of eyes is cast to the distance. There's a reverence for the loss of free will. Our faces are expressionless and peaceful.

I'm back behind bars forced to deal with foul smells and lost souls. I prayed like hell to the Creator never to have to see this place again. Still here I am, cast down in the house of the wretched. I'm being unfair to the almighty, but to be locked up for something I didn't do is a cold piece of irony. This tank holds 50 men, so I find a spot in the far corner providing the most cover possible. It's also far from the toilets and urinals.

The preliminary report on this tank seems pretty good given the circumstances. There's a definite established hierarchy. The alpha is a large, bald headed, middle aged brotha who's full of the Holy Ghost. They call him Bear. A few brothas who are schooled in the art of jailhouse politics run the day-to-day; two bunk next to me. Everyone here is damn near all black. There are only three white boys, two Mexicans and few youth. They seem to keep the bullshit to a minimum and amongst themselves. There's even another brotha from Cali - Oakland to be exact.

This tank is a well-oiled machine. The way the tricks of the trades are discussed, diagnosed and disseminated is done with almost deliberate professionalism. There are 6 men encircling the bunk next to mine. A guy named Trey is giving a seminar on the best way to run a surveillance system on a crack house. The problem being security cameras are an automatic conspiracy charge, but not to have them is foolishly dangerous. They can give you a leg up not only on the cops, but rivals as well. If done right, it will provide enough time to flush, fight or flee. His solution was to rent the house next to or across the street from a trap (a colloquialism for drug house) and set cameras up facing the trap. He explains how this serves as protection. If there's a raid, the cops won't find the cameras. A young inmate speaks up, "I ain't gonna waste no money on no extra house. Fuck dat!" To which Trey responded, "It ain't no waste if it's the difference between 5 years and 25 to life." Trey is intelligent, very street wise and hard, but he's not an asshole about it. Trey is of a different variety. He's battle hardened and has the scars to prove it. He was shot in his face and he's still alive and kicking'. In the street, that's tantamount to a full bird colonel. Tray's got a co-pilot named Ricky. They're kindred spirits. He's short in stature and easy going, but not someone to fool with. He's the kind of dude, if he's angry enough to fight, then you had that beating coming.

I just found out the commissary lady won't be back this way until next Monday. Damn, damn, damn! I bet Sam is knee deep in my store. He probably has crumbs everywhere, lips shinning and greazin' his gut while I'm forced to sustain myself on putrid rations which is the first obstacle in my path to an existence of ease in this place. I could get a line of credit, but the interest is 100%. One box of cookies for two. Being in debt is no way to begin so I'll have to go back into business for myself by selling swine.

I've been watching one white boy closely. He's got a swastika tattooed on the nape of his neck right below the collar line. They call him Bull. He's a rodeo cowboy. When I first saw his tatt, I figured I knew all about him. Upon closer inspection my initial assessment was a bit shallow. Watching his interactions with not only the brothas, but the two Mexicans has shown me some things. I've seen far more racial intolerance from whites without Nazi tattoos; the kind of bigotry most white people don't even know they're exhibiting. The brothas have no problems interacting with him either. This red neck isn't a racist; his rebel nature wants to be associated with bad ass white boys. Bull is a troubled young man, but I like him. For the second night in a row he's sent to segregation. The guards try to assert some authority over him. He will not budge. Rather than shutting up, he bucks. He keeps on bucking well past the mandatory 8 seconds, so the guards threaten him with seg, "Fuck you! Take me to seg. I ain't scared bitch. Are you?" The first night this happened I thought he was stupid. Now I see the rhyme in his reason. If they know they can't intimidate someone, they won't even try.

The book cart has finally arrived. It's a dusty old wooden library cart with squeaky wheels pushed around by an old white man with arthritis. He's slowly pushing it from tank to tank handing out his brand of escapism. Books allow us to fly free, not only to escape, but to get far away from this place. I choose two books I'm surprised to find behind bars - one about Genghis Khan and another entitled *Shaitan* which means satan in Arabic. This old white man has the best dope on the block.

I'm told the DA has 60 days to transfer me from the county jail to the penitentiary which means I'll most likely be here closer to 90. I'm hoping for an uneventful stint so I can finish these books. I have no idea what *Shaitan* is about, but I'm eager to find out. I know a lot about the infamous Khan and no doubt the great general still has much to teach me. This new-found pleasure in books makes me, for the first time, a willing student.

It's late and most of us are asleep until someone dropped a small plastic cup in one of the toilets. Without removing the cup, a young brotha flushed the toilet causing excrement to spray three bunks from top to bottom. Everyone is howling with laughter except the victims who are mortified and disgusted. Worse, the perpetrator is petrified because he's about to be stomped by six hostile and slightly soggy ruffians. He's in luck. The lateness of the hour has given him a respite; no one is awake enough to fight, so they huff, puff, cuss and threaten. They change sheets, wash up and go back to sleep. One nasty bastard rolled over and went back to sleep drenched in sewage. The manner of men with which I'm forced to share facilities with is disgusting. The rampant rashes, festering infections and perpetual filth are disturbing. For a jail cell, the one I'm in is kept as clean as possible considering the circumstances. The other tank I was in stayed filthy. Where I'm going is bound to be damn near medieval. I don't want to think about it.

Tray starts in on a tale from his previous stint in west Texas. He says the winters were particularly brutal due to the fact the windows were always busted out. They're made of Plexiglas which is the quickest way for an inmate to get his hands on a shank. For any prisoner, self-preservation is a survival mechanism. Imagine having to kill a man because he doesn't like you. There's no other manner of settling disputes. A white boy asks, "Why don't the guards try and stop it?" Ricky says, "Shit man, the guards ain't nothin' but instigators. They bet on us like a muthafuckin cock fight." I swear I heard someone in the next cell call a familiar name.

I ask, "Say Ricky, is that Littlewood over there?"

Ricky replies, "Yeah, you know him?"

I respond, "I did three months with him across the hall about four years ago."

Ricky asks, "Which Littlewood? You know there are two."

I say, "Big Littlewood."

Ricky responds, "Well, that's little Littlewood over there."

I say, "I don't know him."

Then Ricky tells me something I find hard to believe, "You know Littlewood's snitchin'?"

I reply, "You bullshittin'!"

Ricky says, "Nope, said he told it on some muthafucka."

I say, "Don't sound like the Littlewood I know."

Ricky replies, "That's what they say."

I don't ask for details because it's clear Ricky is working from hearsay, but I don't want to believe it. Still, every man has his breaking point. If it's true, they must've put the screws to him.

Speaking of snitching, one of the biggest dealers in town just caught a Fed case; he got 35 years to life. He was snitched on by one of his homeboys trying to save his own ass. This snitches name is printed in the local newspaper. Word on the street is the Feds have been on his ass for years. Everyone is shaken up. This man employed a fair number of people in this town. He had many legit business interests. He seems to have been a very affable boss and now he's down the hall. One deeply concerned dude in this tank is Rugman; I don't like him. He's brazen with his stupidity. He says the now downtrodden kingpin was his supplier and entrusted him with $60,000 to hold. This isn't uncommon. Rugman says he did what was asked. He hid it. The dumb fuck that he is, he hid it in his own house. A couple of days later the Feds show up to his house asking all kinds of questions. At this point any thinking man would know the jig is up, but because the Feds don't arrest him he thought he got away with something. Now he's in jail for a variety of unrelated offenses. Nothing is going as his lawyer says, so he's in legal limbo. Now that his boss is down the hall he's concerned the Feds may have shit on him as well. He asks Tray and Ricky if they think this could have something to do with that. Tray and Ricky, not liking Rugman too much, shrug and say, "I don't know man." Oakland looks at me with obvious irritation as if to say, "Is he that stupid?" I just smile and look away. Oakland comes around to my bunk and says, "That's a dumb ass nigga. He shoulda been gone when the Feds showed up to his house. Now he sittin' in here wonderin'." I say,"No man, he knows. He just don't wanna know." *Shaitan* is damn good so far. It's about a man-eating leopard in turn of the century India. The Muslim population gave him the name of the devil and so far he's living up to the name.

Bear, the OG in this tank, has a business proposition for me.

He has a son with a birthday coming up and I happen to be wearing a pair of brand new FUBUs. His son happens to wear my size. They won't allow me to wear these shoes to the pen and they will more than likely end up in the trash, so I sell them to Bear. To be able to get his boy a present despite being locked up will make Bear feel better about missing his boy's big day. He's a good man and I'm glad I can help. He asks, "What you want fo'e 'em?" I reply, "What you got? You know my lock box stay full." We make a deal for $20 of store and $20 worth of weed. Just in time, too. My pork proceeds are meager at best not to mention I've been sober for damn near a week. Being a church going man, he has no weed, but he does have influence which he uses to hook up a side deal with Tray. In doing so, Bear has facilitated future transactions.

This tank isn't constructed like the last one I was in. This one is 180 degrees of bars requiring a different weed smoking strategy. I've been instructed to rub grape jelly on the rolling paper which is supposed to smell like black licorice. I'll be damned if it don't smell like licorice! I hear Bear say, "A'ight Cali. Come on outta dere!" It seems I didn't use enough jelly. This tank is well managed. We won't see SRT run in here every other day. The brothas on the board are mature enough to think first and so far it's been relatively peaceful. We got a few new cellies early Monday morning. One is a white boy from Humboldt County. He's a tattoo artist and as soon as he makes mention of the fact, he's booked solid for the next week. It's strange to me how almost everyone wants the same kinds of tatts - crucifix, praying hands and rosaries. I don't understand why anyone would want a rubber-stamped tattoo. I was thinking of getting another tatt. Like my first, it will be an original. In here, he must be sanitary in the extreme; infection in this place is a real threat, so while these fools rush in, I'll watch how he gets down.

Tray and Ricky are making a spread. I'm still skeptical, but I'm interested. Sooner or later I'll have to get acquainted with jail house cuisine. The commissary lady has made me a wealthy man. My box is filled to its limits. Not only that, she's going to reimburse what Sam intercepted last week giving me more than I know what to do with. All of this behooves me to learn some new recipes. I'll be eating this shit for a while, so I ask for a taste. Ricky breaks me off a few bites. It's actually good. It's not five star, but it's far better than the shit the county calls food. I ask them to teach me how to make it. They show me a couple different combinations, each is better than the last. Tuna base, chili base. My favorite is the beef summer sausage.

I wake in the morning to a loud voice coming from the next cell. The voice is calling for Tray. This sort of inter-cell communication is vital to the system of organized crime that flourishes behind bars. Anything you can pay for, you can get. Tray is being entrusted with a cell phone. Dude got word the SRT is planning a raid, so the most valuable of contraband is passed to trusted cohorts in connecting tanks. Tray met a dude in that west Texas prison. He called him a "booty bandit." He was known to knock people out cold, and then rape them. He prefers young white boys. As sick as the idea is, all I can think is how deep the psychosis goes.

The CO on guard tells me I have a visitor. My lawyer would like to see me. As I walk past the guards they whisper, "That's him. He's his lawyer." They stare at me as if they know all my sins. The word out on Siler must be bad. It always amazes me how those living in glass houses just can't wait to throw the biggest stones they can find. There's more debauchery and corruption in this house of justice than there are bars. Siler has merely been accused. They're treating him like the unforgiven.

Siler is waiting for me in an empty single cell. He has the look of a man with the world on his shoulders. The guard is standing just out of sight, but in ear shot.

I say, "What's happenin' counselor?"

Siler replies, "I just came to check on you. How are you doing?"

I say, "Feel like I should be askin' you that. After that last day in court I thought you might end up in here with me."

Siler says, "I managed to hold them off for a while."

I say, "You know I got the low down on you in here."

Siler says, "Figured you would".

I say, "You know the dude I got it from."

Siler asks, "Oh yeah?"

I say, "He's an old client of yours. He doesn't believe it either. Too bad all your character witnesses have no character, at least not officially."

Siler says, "That wouldn't help me now anyway. Too far gone."

I say, "Hate to see bad shit happen to a man like you."

We talked for a while. I told him how I came to write that letter requesting his services. How all the inmates were singing his praises about the statistic improbability of any lawyer being so well-liked by inmates no less. I want him to know how he's loved and how all he did wasn't in vain. Maybe it will bring him some inner peace.

I'm in a deep and melancholy mood as I return to the tank. The CO opens the bars with a knowing and accusatory grin. I shoot him one back momentarily removing the grin from his gaze. I don't even get back to my bunk before I'm called to the bars again. They intended to strip search me before I got back in the tank assuming Siler may have slipped me something. The CO was too busy reveling in my sad mood.

Everyone wants to know what's up with Siler. He's got lots of friends in low places and he's doing as well as can be expected. He doesn't want to talk about it, but they keep pushing me for information. I tell them about him standing in front of the judge right after me. They mull that over and mumble how fucked up it is. The thought of Siler in these county blues is hard to take. The field day the DA must be having with Siler. The hate is hard to swallow when you've spent your life looking for justice. Right and wrong don't enter the equation.

I'm shootin' the shit with Oakland. It's good to talk to someone from home. His memories help mine come into focus. As he talks I remember the simple things I've forgotten like Roscoe's, KBLX, the smell of eucalyptus and the sun slipping into the Pacific. As we're talking, I hear a voice from the past. I can't place it, but the familiarity is unmistakable; loud and coming from down the hall. Whoever it is, they're very popular. He's carrying on conversations with several groups of people in different tanks. Someone calls his name and I smile. As Tweety approaches the bars I ask if he remembers me.

Tweety says, "Yeah nigga, I 'member. What the fuck is you doin' back in dis muthafacka?"

I say, "Same shit. Trial didn't go good."

Tweety says, "Word?"

I say, "Yeah man, I'm goin' where you've just been."

Tweety says, "What'd they give yuh?"

I reply, "Fo'e years."

Tweety says, "Shit nigga, you be out in 2. Don't trip. You be a'ight."

A CO ushers him along. His reassuring words of encouragement hit their mark. The last time I saw him was the night he went to the pen. I remember what he said when asked how he felt about going, "A little nervous, a little scared like any man." His brave honesty is helpful now as it was then.

A month has passed and I've had a chance to observe Chris, the tattoo artist, ply his trade. He's damn good and he's clean. He makes everyone create their own needle and inkwell under his direct supervision. He cleans his gun with boiling water and rubbing alcohol. We use sharpened paper clips and staples for the needles. Ink is made of soot from burning baby oil or hair grease and then it's combined with liquid soap. He made the gun from an old pair of hair clippers all done under the guard's nose which is always half the fun. I've decided to give Chris my business. I came up with a unique Black Muslim tattoo that I think represents me – an ace of spades symbol with a crescent moon and 5-point star in the center. He starts tomorrow.

We're having a small economics issue in our tank. An old school brother named Willy has come up on a large sum of weed. He's decided to flood the market. 20% lower price and 50% more product. This has caused a bit of a problem because it puts a couple of inmate's right out of the free market competition. They aren't happy. Willy is a veteran who's been in and out of prison for most of his life so he does what he wants. I like Willy. He's a cool old dude who has no problem dispensing his particular brand of wisdom. He's on his way back to the pen, but for him it's nothing but something to do. We smoke and talk a while. I can't ask too many question or act too surprised at the things he says, no matter how outlandish.

Ricky is on the chain tonight. As the departing line up at the gate, there's a mix up down the hall. An inmate is protesting profusely, "But I ain't supposed to go. That's what I'm trying to tell you." "Your name is on the list. That's enough for me." "But I'm gettin' out in two months man." The CO goes and gets his boss. This man is perfect for his job. He's big, stupid and does what he's told. This automaton comes lumbering down the hall huffing and puffing about keeping his schedule. "I'm tryin' to tell yo man here, I ain't supposed to be on that list." "The judge says you go, so you go! Now get your ass up and come on." 30 minutes later dude comes bounding back up the halls, "See, I told y'all I ain't supposed to go'." He's grinning from ear to ear and damn near skipping. Good for him! Inside, down deep, I'm praying when it comes my time to go, I come across such a clerical error.

I finished *Shaitan*. It's a damn good book, but the ending was predictable. The great white hunter finally shoots the nearly 200 pound leopard, but not before it kills and eats a record number of people, in the most savage and horrifying ways possible. Tonight, I begin reading about Genghis Khan. The Mongols are the reason the Great Wall was built. Battle strategies and tactics are to me of great interest. This dude whipped more ass than Sugar Ray Robinson and he subdued damn near the whole world and never lost a single battle. Who better to learn such things from than the most successful general in all human history?

I keep hearing stories about something called the hoe squad; the chain gang without the chain. I'm getting up before the sun to go work in the fields under the direct supervision of a straw hat wearing CO and his shotgun on horseback just like an overseer. There's no way I'll be a field nigga for the state of Texas. Lock me up, turn me into a convicted felon, but you will not turn me into a field slave. There isn't a black man in America who should be subjected to anything remotely resembling slavery. I don't give a damn if they catch a nigga killin' a house full of white women. I don't care if the nigga was behind the grassy knoll, but not indentured servitude. These crackers go out of their way to make sure it looks, feels, smells, sounds and tastes just like slavery. These country negroes say nothing can be done because there's no getting around it. If you can walk, you'll go to the fields.

I'm getting a haircut today something I'm not looking

forward to. I took my cornrows down last night; my foot-long afro is fascinating to Bull and the other white boys. The white COs are gathering at the bars while I try in vain to dismiss them. Still, there they stand dumbfounded and goofy looking. Tray has braids too. The look on his face is full of dreaded anticipation. Rugman says my hair made me look mixed. Oakland is doing the honors. I tell him just take it to the slab. As the clumps tumble away, I can hear the last vestiges of my freedom shatter as each strand tumbles to the cement floor. "Now you look civilized," Rugman says. I look him dead in his eyes, "Why the fuck would I want to look civilized?!" Non-conformity is completely inconceivable to this man. He rebels exactly as told. No wonder we don't get along.

Its 3 am and breakfast is being served. Tray and Willy are talking about Homegirl and her sisters. Her husband is big in this little pond. He moves a lot of weight. Tray is telling us how he's fucking all of them including the one I was so enamored with. She was the reason Homegirl couldn't take anymore. Had I known this she wouldn't have interested me in the slightest. I'm disappointed in myself for thinking so highly of her in the first place.

Bear is conducting a Holy Ghost meeting. A jail cell may sound like a strange place for Sunday school, but who else is in need of saving more than the damned. The most incorrigible are the most attentive who are in search of some measure of redemption with no intention of sticking to the straight and narrow. Despite what they may have done, for the most part, these are not evil men. The human animal is far more complex than just inherently good or evil. Yes, he may sell crack. Most of the profit goes to is mother's hospital bills. He may beat his wife, but the same man is working two jobs to put his baby sister through school. I knew a 3rd grade teacher who spent her own money on books and school supplies for the children in her classes. She can't do this on a teacher's salary, so she sells the best weed in all of west Dallas. I know cops who risk life and limb on a daily in some of the deadliest hoods on the planet to protect and serve, but they're also shaking down prostitutes and dealers for a percentage. The Assistant DA who has a puritanical intolerance for drug offenders supports a $1,500 a week coke habit. The judge has a record of maximum sentences for child molesters, yet his favorite whore house specializes in 13 year old girls. This is the human animal in all its wondrous glory.

It's been two months and no sign of those SRT sons of bitches. They've run in on other tanks, but not us. Watching them stampede down the hall is quite comical. The immense and futile efforts put into being fierce and intimidating, yet barely managing to achieve the annoyance of a gnat. I suppose the effort must be made if only to give the appearance of vigilance. Still, it must be difficult to deal with such constant ineptitude. It's one thing to suck. It's another to work, train and still suck. Not having them swarm up in here is a blessing and a perk of having schooled crooks running shit. There's a dude by the name of Ben in this tank that works in the chow hall. He's the kind of dude so in shape you can see the muscle definition in his bald cranial cap. He's quiet and solitary. The word is he's in for murder. I've been conversating with him slowly and from what I can gather he killed a few white boys. He's in for 20 to life. He must suffer from unmanageable levels of bitterness. He seems to handle it all with the dignity and grace of a Shaolin monk. It's taken me a while to gather any amount of info. He's still fighting his case. Unlike me, he has to do so from the inside. Behind bars for at least 20 years while simultaneously in open, mortal and futile combat with this most foul and corrupt judicial system.

Old school Willy is fuckin' with a little Mexican dude. He's 5'2" and 100 pounds soaking wet with 10 pounds boots on. This vato looks 14 years old. Willy's giving him a hard time, "Come here you lil' pretty muthafucka you, sit next to Daddy. Don't be afraid of love. You gonna gimme some'uh dat tonight?" He's been fuckin' with him since he got here two days ago. He won't do anything to the little dude and strangely enough he's actually lookin' out for El Lito. He's helping him get his mind around what he's sure to have to face in earnest, sooner rather than later and he's forcing him to answer questions about himself. There's a freedom lost in a place such as this. I don't speak of the obvious physical limitations. I'm talking about a freedom of the spirit. I gallivanted up and down the California coast for 20 years doing things most people don't even have the imagination to fantasize about.

Most of which requires a foolish brand of courage; the kind that comes with the invincibility of youth. I simply took for granted nothing could happen to me. Regardless of how many times I danced with the devil, no more. I'm confronted with so many real life reasons and ways someone's existence could so easily be shattered sitting in the cell. Fault or blame is as irrelevant as guilt or innocence. Some may call it chickening out. Some call it, growing up. Call it what you will, the fact remains, I no longer feel that reckless abandon brand of freedom. I no longer take breathing for granted.

Genghis Khan is a damn good read. The book starts with his early relationship with his parents and a world of a captured rival tribe's woman and those responsible for her abduction and captivity. What a way to begin a life. It was said he came out of the birth canal with his right hand dripping in blood. Now I'm not a man who believes in omens, but damn! The young Khan grew into a boy who killed his older brother. He refused to live under even his oppression. We're all products of our environment. Young Temujin is a Khan from the womb, refusing even as a child to be acted upon; choosing instead to act, a mark of a true pack leader.

There's a fight brewing. Tray and Rugman are enthralled in a disagreement. There was a conversation about his girl. I don't know what Rugman said, but he obviously went too far. Voices are now raised. Threats are being adamantly spoken. Bear makes an obligatory, if half-hearted attempt to intervene offering a few fatherly words of restrain. Rugman is afraid. This fact is not lost on the audience. Rugman is out matched and he knows it. Tray however is unmoved. Barring any further agitation, he seems willing to let it go at an argument. When Tray approaches, Rugman starts politicking and acquiescing which culminates with an apology. Tray let it go with a warning. Rugman's unpopularity is almost unanimous. The consensus is people wanted to see Tray beat the dog shit out of him. Some are walking by his bunk telling him so. They go so far as to discuss Rug's medical weaknesses. He has a faulty sternum. The real reason for all those push-ups is over compensation. This isn't information he would want to become public knowledge. It goes to show ain't no secrets in a small town. I've seen him slap boxing. He uses a common street defense designed to protect the face. His elbows are wide leaving his chest exposed. Gathering tactical data on any potential adversaries is necessary. Contemplating a strategic plan of attack is prudent.

There are 10 tanks in this jail and guess who finds his way into this particular one? Sam. I'm happy to see my old celly. We grin and shake hands, "You just gettin' out of the holdin' tanks man?" "Yeah. Startin' to thank they forgot about me." "I know you ain't want for no food." "Man Cali yo' store was right on time. Ate good for almost a month." "I know you did." "They gave it all back to yuh didn't they?" "Oh yeah, goddamn right. I ain't wanted for shit since." "You manage to bootleg any of that smoke over here with yuh?" "Naw man, had to dump most of that shit." "Oh know that hurt." "Shit yeah." "Well I got a little somethin' to smoke on, so it's all good." Tray and Oakland want to know, "how you two niggas know each other?" "We spent a week in a cell gettin' high together." "Oh, y'all was in the Annex together?" "Yeah." Oakland and I almost come to fisticuffs over something as stupid as a spades game which is a byproduct of these confines. I was willing to let it go at that. Then I find out he's been talking' shit because my box stays full and he has nothing. I've been generous and now I find out he's been mistaking my kindness for weakness. I should've known. During our conversations, he let me know he and his family don't get along. He had another falling out with his mother. He never got along with his siblings, so he's doing his time alone. His own family has no love for him. Now I can see why. I was just happy to converse with someone from home. I didn't like to see him suffer. A lesson learned.

In prison, something as simple as this can easily cost a man his life. Ricky tells me a story about a white boy who gave a young brotha soup with the promise of returning it when he got his store the next week. Time came for brotha to give back, but he told the white boy to go fuck himself. Now he's got to fight. If he doesn't he becomes a target. For two months on sight he goes toe to toe with the young brotha. Some he won, most he lost. He's in and out of solitary and the infirmary. All of this aggravation over a simple act of kindness over a 25-cent soup.

Old school Willy is on the chain tonight. This combined

with the arrival of Sam means no sleep. We're smoking and drinking the night into the morning. As Willy is packing up in preparation for a return trip to prison, I fight off a somber mood stemming from the constant reminder of how soon my turn is coming. It's been almost 3 months now I can expect the word to come any day. The sight of another man going before me does nothing for my insomnia. To keep my mind in motion, Sam and I keep the stories flowing. They flow 'til we fall asleep.

I'm up early in the morning to close out Khan. I almost hate for the book to end. I've enjoyed all that I've learned. Genghis Khan is unmatched in the practical application of battlefield tactics and political prowess. He was wise enough to incorporate the best of all he conquered. To this day, Genghis Kahn is reputed to be the fiercest and most blood-thirsty of all the conquerors. This too was employed as a battlefield tactic. His terrifying reputation insured many battles were over before even beginning. Khan never pushed a religious agenda. His free thinking introduced the world to itself. The trade routes he established facilitated not only the exchange of goods, but information, bringing many nations out of their long and self-imposed darkness. What then could stop the best Calvary lead army ever? The ill-fated decision to turn themselves into a navy. Even then it took a Kamikaze, a "divine wind" of a typhoon to sink them just off the Japanese coast. When I finish a book as good as this I can't help but wonder what I've been denying myself. Wonder what I've missed.

I'm on the chain tonight. It's 11 pm now and I won't leave until 3 am which is plenty of time to sauté in anticipation. All five of my senses are on overload; I'm trying not to let it show which isn't easy. This day has been on the horizon for a long time. Now that the moment has arrived I feel an emotion I didn't expect − fuck it! Let's do the damn thing. The sooner it starts, the sooner it's over. I'm trying to work it into some deliberate determination. There's a thing in most men, a curiosity about his internal fortitude. How will he handle himself in the midst of anarchy and chaos? Like a soldier before his first battle. There's no way to know until bullets are flying. I heard Counselor Siler is down the hall. They gave him

15 years fed time. Corruption can ill afford an honest man.

Sam and I are conversing. I'm telling him about the SR 71 Blackbird Spy Plane, but I have other things on my mind tonight. I'm going to smoke most of my weed before they tell me it's time to go. I'll eat what's left before we leave. I enjoy the irony of being high on a prison bus and maybe the weed will take the edge off my nerves. Truth is I'm afraid. I hear the call, "Hennington roll it up!" and I'm overcome with a strange combination of apprehension and excitement. I give most of my stuff to Sam and a few things to Tray. I give daps all around and I make a special point of shaking Bear's hand.

The CO is opening the gate and there she is – a Bluebird retrofitted school bus. In California, we call it the "Grey Goose" - dark blue with a lead painted white iron caged interior. The bars on the windows aren't enough; they're reinforced with an iron grate. I'm forced up the steps of the bus and prodded past the drivers' seat by a shotgun wielding hillbilly. I have the bus to myself, but not for long. I take a seat in the back, so I don't have to deal with new inmates we pick up along the way. We've stopped at four different county jails, so the bus is almost at capacity. How did it come to this? I'm on a Texas prison bus with 50 of the foulest individuals the state has to offer who are dead silent. I count myself amongst them.

The man sitting next to me stinks to high heaven. He's got that dirty white boy smell like a wet dog. I'm not the only one who's noticed. Three or four brothas crack their windows. I'm enjoying the simple pleasure of cold predawn air while I can. The steady rumble and constant bumping of the bus has taken its toll on my high. Now that I'm almost sober the full measure of my circumstances is settling squarely on my shoulders. Despite all the overwhelming evidence, I'm still finding it difficult to believe.

The sun is coming up as I'm staring through iron grate, watching vast, and countless seas of dew drenched Texas prairies stream by. I wonder how many more water towers and pecan groves to go until we get to where we're going. My contemplation is heavy. There's a threshold most people never approach, let alone cross. I'm approaching it right now. No telling what I might have to do to keep my life or my manhood. The time has come for me to make a decision. Whatever it takes for me to come out alive is what I have to do. This isn't the first time I've gone to prison. The first was long ago. I was 11 years old. I was at school, but I didn't want to be, so I called my mom and played sick. She yelled, "Shit boy. I ain't got time to be messin' with you today. I'm already late. You just gonna have to come to work with me." Work? That's last thing I wanted to do. She worked at the prison in Vacaville. I just wanted to go home and watch Mighty Mouse and Foghorn Leghorn. My plan had backfired.

The prison in Vacaville is no ordinary penitentiary. It's a medical facility. One must be deemed criminally insane by a physician to be admitted. Charles Manson barely qualified. He tried to play that crazy shit with the Mexican inmates and they pulled his card. He told those vatos he was Jesus Christ. He failed to factor in he wasn't dealing with silly little acid trippin' hippie white girls. Them vatos weren't havin' it. They dowsed him in alcohol, set his ass on fire and told him to prove it by resurrecting himself from the fire. The guards put out the flames and promptly sent his singed hide off to San Quentin. Charles Manson didn't make the grade, but they have 5,000 men who do.

When you walk through the prison in Vacaville, they constantly tell you, "This is an all-male facility. Every inmate you see in here is male." Before long it's clear why they find it necessary to reiterate that statement. The men have had stunning sex changes. In the officer's dining hall where mom worked, it got real interesting. All the prisoners doted on me like I was their own which made me nervous. I didn't know it at the time, but I couldn't have been safer in my mother's womb. A prisoner who harms a child has no place to hide. The inmates cooked me the biggest burger I'd ever seen, a plate full of fries and a towering chocolate shake. They sat me down and began telling me what everyone was in for, "See that dude right there? Killed his wife and 2 of her friends because they walked in on him fuckin' some man. Then killed the man. Him, he kidnapped and killed his ex-girlfriend. Kept her body in his basement. That dude raped and killed his own mother." I wondered what he did to get here. I didn't ask for fear he just might tell me. He tells me they just got off lockdown. Someone hung himself in his cell, "Why'd he do that? "Cuz they were gonna send him to Texas." "What's wrong with that?" "You don't want to do no time in Texas. He's better off dead."

We've arrived at a Texas prison called Gurney.

9

Rolling back the 40 foot high chain link gate, shotgun toting guards are going through their security procedures while sharp shooters are looking down from their towers. I'm unafraid. I thought my knees would be shaking. I thought it would be difficult to stand. I was certain my fear would betray me. Instead I'm overcome with a strangely steeled resolve. I don't know where it came from, but it's here. I'm herded off the bus into an adjacent building. All 50 of us standing butt naked for all to see. I wonder how many times I'll have to suffer this indignity. "Lift up your nut sack. Turn around and bend over. Spread your butt cheeks." All their yelling, barking of orders in an attempt at intimidation is to me but background noise. Having random men and women stare up my asshole is something I could do without. I have the misfortune of standing next to a nervous little man. He feels compelled to talk as instructions are being spewed at us. He tells me how he's been through this before. If so, I'm wondering why he doesn't know to shut the fuck up. Before I could finish the thought, he's singled out and chastised severely. He's made to answer "yesser, noser, yesser" in rapid succession. Upon the conclusion of his humiliation this fool leans over to me and says, "See, I told you." Out of the 50 men, the man standing directly to my right is the only one suffering from diarrhea of the mouth. One would think the lack of any response on my part would clue him in. If only it were that simple. I'm anticipating the saving grace of being separated by procedure.

Standing in three separate lines to receive part of our prison issue, of all the things I must consider and calculate at this moment, I'm calculating my separation from this fool standing next to me. The guards corralled us into three different 15 x 20 chain link cages with 20 men in each. There's a white boy in here who's quite adapt at story telling. All of his stories involve the many penitentiaries in his not-so distant past, "After the riot, they stripped me and put me in solitary. Bout' 20 minutes later, here they come. Fo' of'em in full riot gear. Come to beat me 'til I talk. I said man you can kick me, you can beat me. I don't give a fuck. Just don't beat me necked! Come on man, just don't beat me necked. That's awl I ask! So, what'd they do?" Almost everyone in this cage simultaneously says, "beat you necked." We laugh long and hard so much so the CO has to hit the cage with his night stick to shut us up. I haven't been in prison for more than an hour and I have a stomach ache from laughter. After about another hour or so our numbers have been whittled down to just three. We await the barber chair. Just like the military, everybody gets a buzz cut. It's my turn, but there ain't much to cut. Next, a shower. This is the first time I've had to shower in public. There are three showers against the back wall and 15 men and women. I'm feeling vulnerable and exposed. This place is infamous for its strip search process. We call it "Butt Naked Gurney."

I'm handed a tiny sliver of pink soap about 1/4 the size of hotel soap. The first rule of showering in prison is don't drop the soap. I dropped the soap, but I didn't pick it up. I left it where it lay. I'm issued state clothing, sheets and a mattress. I'm told to go sit on steel benches in the far corner. I can't set my stuff down before the fool comes buddying up to me. I thought about dismissing him, but a fool may come in handy. I'm keeping this dude at a stiff arm's length. The immediate price to pay is I must hear him run his mouth, but I'm not listening. My mind is somewhere else.

We're being ushered off to a different waiting room. There seems to be some order to this process. We're assigned different rooms. I lose one fool and gain an entire room full of fools. This is like after-school detention when the teacher leaves the room. There are 15 of us in here. It was quiet at first which lasted all of three minutes. I get summoned down the hall where I sit in front of a nice white lady and her computer. She's asking me all manner of personal history questions, "Ever been in trouble with the law before? Anyone in your family? Any friends? Ever been to prison before? After about 100 more questions of this manner and 100 no answers, she stops and looks at me with one more question in her eyes, "What are you doing in here?" "I got drafted." "Well it's obvious you don't belong, so just do your time and get out." "That's the plan." We have a nice, lengthy conversation about everything from the history of world religions to the current political climate. I was in no rush to get locked up. She didn't seem all that eager to get back to her mundane existence, so I keep her intrigued and entertained for a while longer.

This place is laid out like a military base. It's one of these newfangled prisons. There are pods instead of cell blocks; five pods with 4 to 65 man tanks a piece. Each controlled by a central electronic security control booth. 12 of us are shuffled into a pod. I'm the only one selected for this tank. Standing here with everything I don't own under my arm and a bed roll on my shoulder, I hear the metal door clank closed and locked behind me.

I'm officially in prison.

As soon as I put my stuff on the assigned bunk I see a familiar face - Old school Willy. I give him a pound and he, in turn, gives me the low down. He tells me it takes two weeks for money to hit your books which means I'll have nothing for a while, not even shower shoes. Everyone uses rubber sandals to keep from having to make actual contact with the shower stall. I'm issued a few toiletries, a couple slivers of soap, small tube of toothpaste and a 3 inch tooth brush. This keeps us from filing it down into a shank. They think of everything. Willy says I can use his shower shoes until my money hits. I don't know what I would've done if he wasn't here. I suppose I would've avoided the shower for two weeks. I'm glad it won't come to that. Having nothing makes every little thing big.

It's time for lunch and the entire prison population is in motion. I see why they call this place "Butt Naked Gurney." Guards are randomly pulling inmates out of line and strip searching them on the spot. This practice has almost eliminated the traffic and trading of contraband, but no amount of police presence will stop an entire population of crooks from being crooks. There are things to be had, but both the prices and the risks are high. Crooks being what they are, this just makes it more interesting.

We're huddled around stainless-steel tables that seat four; fanning flies with one hand and stabbing something they've given the name of "pork steak" in the other. Willy tells me to ask for a pork free tray. Upon request, I'm handed a tray with a spoonful of veggie mush and a slice of government cheese. I wouldn't eat that pork steak even if I ate pork. It's a hardly recognizable ¼ inch thick slab of fatty under cooked swine flesh. Willy says most of the food is prison grown, harvested or slaughtered by inmates. You can't imagine how appetizing that thought is, so I fight the flies, eat my slice of cheese and shut up. Willy says the food grown here is intended to subsidize the cost of feeding us. Since the amount of production is controlled and calculated by the prison, the food budget can be manipulated to the financial advantage of the administration. The prison administrators tell the public how the prisoners are learning the value of an honest hard day's work while they rape, pillage, plunder and gorge themselves on untold and ill-gotten gains. This sounds similar to the pre-civil war situation. Granted, my ancestors were never convicted. Before I can finish my slice of cheese a CO taps his knuckles on the table indicating it's time to move on. We're walking and eating at the same time trying to finish before we get to the garbage can. The minimum caloric intake minus the skim leaves a lot to be desired. Now I know why the inmates take the risks inherent with smuggling food.

Willy tells me breakfast is served at 3 am. He lends me his shower shoes so I can put some soap on my entire body this time. Showering and simultaneously watching to make sure I'm not being watched is a bit unsettling. It's pancakes today.

I'll have to find a way to get two trays of food. Not an easy undertaking. The rotations of the ins and outs are separated by a good 200 feet, not to mention the CO factor. These guards are on steroids. Everyone's busy trying to set an example. I haven't seen it done yet. We're served good sized pancakes, apple sauce and powdered eggs. On each table is a pitcher of what is alleged to be powdered milk. It looks like cloudy water to me. Appears they've found more than one way to skim the milk. My plate is almost clean before I sit down. Then Willy gives me the signal, so I create a diversion. I picked a table in the corner next to the incoming door. He got one on the other side of the dining hall. As I get up a dude seated next to me places my tray under his. At the same time, Willy drops his tray with a loud crash. In one sweeping motion, I lift my legs over the iron rail and step to the wall. Four inmates obscure my presence. There's an unspoken cohesion amongst the inmates. There's a unanimous sense of "fuck them." It's what made this possible. I'm full, but I'm gonna eat a second tray of pancakes anyway.

I'm going to sleep and I plan on staying asleep until lunch tomorrow. I plan to keep to myself and out of trouble. We'll see how long that lasts. Boredom has a way of corrupting a man. This is the wrong place to be looking for something to get into because more than likely you'll find it or it will find you. I asked Willy to wake me for lunch. Other than that you will find me in this bunk. As for tonight, that's all he wrote.

Willy wakes me up in time for lunch. I look out the door and see the hoe squad coming back from the fields. All prison issued clothes are white. You wouldn't know it by the dirt covering their clothing. These men are exhausted. They're the spitting image of a field hand draggin' ass back into their tank. 300 of them have to get into 4 shower stalls before they call for chow. After being in the fields since before the sun, they must be as hungry as a hostage. I just got out of bed and I'm wondering if I should risk another double play. The sight of those sorry bastards reminds me to connive a medical, so I fill out a form for a "sick call", a note to see the doctor. I haven't figured out what excuse I'll give but it'll have to be good.

Goddamn, the flies around here are possessed! I've seen garbage dumps with fewer flies. The warden has the nerve to put up a few strips of fly paper; every last one is far exceeding their maximum capacity. I wonder what it's like in the kitchen. Despite my best efforts, I'm choking this shit called food down my throat and hoping it's larva free. The flies and guards conspire to ensure we don't enjoy this brief reprieve.

Walking back into the pod I'm forced to step aside as a celly is taken out on a stretcher. The medics are working on him. I don't know what happened, but the sight of this man begging for his next breath reinforces the fact I sleep in harm's way. Being locked behind bars with the unsavory element for months now has desensitized me to the inherent dangers. All I've had to complain about is bad food and flies. Don't get it twisted, this is my intent. I want my stay here as uneventful as possible. Most of the people in here did what they did intending to get away with it. Most of the inmates give me no real cause for concern. There are two men that make me sleep real light; the kind of men with one look in their eyes and you know they don't give a fuck about getting caught. Despite my best efforts the words of that Assistant District Attorney were prophetic. I'm stuck in here thinking about what I didn't do. When I was fighting this on appeal, I got a call from one of my dirt doing' homeboys in California. He heard about my troubles and couldn't resist a few words of admonishment, "I heard you got caught up down there fuckin' wit that yellow meat. I told you about bein' nice to them bitches!" All of this came to pass because that bitch new she could call me and I would be nice to her. She needed help and knew I would help her. I've always had a weakness for women. From time to time it has proved inconvenient. This time it's proved to be considerately more than inconvenient. My brother once told me helping is costly. While I hope to learn from this experience, I also hope I'm not changed by it. Is that contradictory?

I sit down to write my mother a letter. I don't want to but I know she's worried sick. Having worked in corrections she doesn't have to wonder what goes on in here, so I keep it light. I let her know I'm ok and tell her a few things so she doesn't think I'm holding out. I do my best to keep her from worrying about what I'm not telling' her. I can't tell you how difficult it is for me to write this letter. This is the first letter I've ever written in my life. I never had a need for written correspondence. My aversion to the written word made sure I found an alternate form of communication. Writing my first letter to my mother from prison is almost more than I can bear, but what can I do.

I'm in the infirmary waiting to see the doctor. I need to figure out a way to keep my black ass off the hoe squad, so I go with the old standby football injury, "Yeah doc, injured my shoulder and back." "What? Oh, linebacker." Works like a charm. He starts going into stories about his high school gridiron glory days. I listen intently offering just enough input to keep him talking. Before long he's telling me about his injuries. We segway into a whole other conversation about ice packs, Ben Gay and Ace Bandages. A few minutes later I got what I came for – "light duty restriction."

As I'm walking back in the tank an older brother over hears Willy talking shit about his weed selling exploits in the county. He asks me to co-sign his assertions. "Cali, tell these niggas how we smoked all day, eerie day in da county." "Sho'e nuff. Spent very few sober days in that jail. "What county y'all fall out uh?" "Bowie." "Y'all from Texarkana?" "I'm from Cali, but he is. "Oh yeah? I'm from T-town too." "Is that right? My folks are from down there." "Who yo' people?" This brother knows all my relatives. He used to play basketball with my uncles. He even had a crush on one of my aunts and had many a meal at Big Mama's table.

I spend the next couple hours being regaled with stories about my aunts and uncles as adolescents. I hear the good shit. The catalysts and the real reasons why. All the things conveniently left out of the stories I've been hearing all my life. That six degrees of separation shit has the most confounded timing. This man with so many keys to the locked doors of my lineage is on the chain tonight. I've been issued a prison I.D. I can't do, go or get anything in prison without it. Along with the card every prisoner gets a number. I've been advised to commit this number to memory because I'll be made to recite it everywhere I go. Every time I think they're finished indoctrinating me they come up with one more way. I wonder how long it will take me to forget this prison identification number. The prison issues a stainless-steel neck chain with the

ID. It looks like silver bees strung together like the ones issued with military dog tags. The chain itself is a safety measure. It'll break if someone attempts to strangle you with it. I wonder how many people were strangled before this safety measure was implemented.

The longest last two weeks have passed and I'm finally standing in the store line. $60 is the limit and my list is exactly $60. I thought about selling my pork allotment, but I'm not comfortable enough in my surroundings to conduct business. I'm still trying to maintain some anonymity. Now that my money has hit, I don't even have to go to chow if I don't want. With the spread making skills I picked up in the county, I have more recipes than Emeril. Right now, I'm greazin' my gut with 2 pints of ice cream. I gave another to Willy for the use of his shower shoes. We sit, eat and play dominoes. The absence of hunger makes a John Grisham book so much better; we continue to play spades, dominoes and chess. This ever so slight bit of comfort is immeasurable. Being surrounded by the same four walls and the same 65 men 24 hours a day is unnatural to say the least. The only break in the monotony is the three daily outings to the chow hall. Going down there dodging the guards and swatting the flies for a slice of cheese is unfulfilling. This place doesn't need any help multiplying the misery, and yeah, I over did it. My stomach is upset and I don't give a fat fiddler's fuck.

Willy's on the chain. This prison is known as a transfer facility. Everyone here is waiting to be sent somewhere else. They never tell us where, but we find out. Willy's on his way to Huntsville. He's been there before. He tells me I'll be moving on in another couple of weeks. I'm glad he was here when I got here. He did his best to ease my transition and did so without me having to ask. He's a career criminal. To me he's just a cool old dude who looked out for me. He never asked for anything in return. In a place like this such behavior is all but unheard of. He offered a bit of familiarity amidst all this unfamiliar. For this I give him a pound and wish him well. "Much obliged old man." Another week has passed. I finished Grisham and started Patterson. There's nothing else to do except watch 4 channels of reruns, read a book or get into trouble. Willy gave me the run down on the weed. He said it can be had, but that the game is real foul. There's a lot of snitching to keep the COs content and the pipeline flowing. I've decided the smoke can wait. I'm not that good.

Today we got another influx of inmates. One gets the bunk next to me. As he's unpacking I notice a Holy Qur'an. "As-salāmu 'alaykum. Glad to see a fellow Muslim." "Likewise." We launch directly into a deep and diverse conversation, both of us grateful to have some commonality. The last dude who slept in that bunk was a white boy with a tendency to have violent bouts of rancid flatulence while sleeping. It was so foul it would wake me up. Talking with Malik, I can tell he's got some sense and some education. To be able to talk with someone about something other than the street is almost as freeing as a good book. From the length and enthusiasm of our conversation, I gather he's thinking the same.

We talk for hours. The subject of our respective offenses never comes up. There's an unspoken understanding. Though we each have the capacity, we choose not to relate to one another on a criminal level because it's impossible to forget where we are. My limited Spanish has earned me a few Latino friends. I've been watching and admiring how La Raza gets down in here. I see in them things that used to be true of my people. A brotherhood and cohesion we no longer possess something for which I have a great respect. I made mention of this to Malik. Before I could get it out of my mouth he says, "Shame we don't treat each other like that anymore. We used to because we had no choice." "Yeah, now some of us have more contempt for and mistrust of our own than for white folk. Just one example of the residual and collateral damage from the civil rights movement we don't talk about." "Yeah, and that's part of the problem. We were so determined to integrate; we didn't bother to consider the cost or consequences." We go into another deep sociological discussion. It's like we're playing mental chess - both on the same side of the board.

No sooner than I get through admiring and praising my border brothers, two vatos are getting into a fight. One is highly upset. He's cussing far too fast for me to comprehend, but it's clear he feels disrespected. Out pops his shank. The other dude has no intention on fighting. This is the 3rd fight this week. This amigo is affable in the extreme. Everyone knows he wouldn't swat a mosquito which is why the other dude is picking a fight with him. The amigo goes straight to the door and calls for a CO and gets an immediate transfer to a different tank. The combatant figures he'll gain some measure of fear or respect. It hasn't worked out that way. The entire tank has turned their backs on him. Malik phrased it for us the best, "He knows he wrong. The other dude was as friendly as a box of puppies."

Prison is reputed to be a place without mercy, understanding or pity, ruled by the lawlessness of anarchy and chaos. Prisons and prisoners are microcosms of the communities from which they are extracted. Inside just as out, the strong fight for the right to rule the weak. From time to time when the strong go too far, the public turns against them like when the police shoot or beat the wrong person for the wrong reason. Where the combatant made his mistake was overdoing his show of anger for a man who never angered anyone. This has branded him a bully and a coward. No one likes either. The penitentiary and the streets have been likened to the jungle and the untamed, unconquered lands. Wild, violent and lawless. This assertion maintains life and death hold less value and meaning outside civilized society. This is a belief held only by the ignorant. While there are obvious similarities, it's ignorant to assume either the jungle or the streets are lawless. They both have very old laws - about 650 billion years. These laws are both time tested and honored. They're just not written down anywhere. While it may be true they lack the sensibilities and sentimentality of civilized law, there can be no doubt of their effectiveness. Only the strong survive may be brutal by society's standards. Never on this planet has life ever been precious. Check your human history. The greatest threat to human life is that there's too much human life. The laws of nature have worked unchanged for longer than man has occupied this planet and will continue to work long after civilized man and his laws have rendered this planet uninhabitable. I heard an old Native American say, "The earth is alive and she will defend herself." Long after civilized man has worn out his welcome, nature and her laws will continue to thrive. But this is all abstract and theoretical.

In the "wild" there are but two reasons to kill -to eat or to keep from being eaten. Civilized man has many reasons to justify killing. Jealousy, hate, fear, rage, revenge, insanity, the list goes on. But the most diabolical reason is greed and money. When a poor black kid from the concrete jungle brings a gun to school it's for one of two reasons. To take someone's $200 pair of Jordans or to keep his from being taken. He shoots one motherfucker and everyone gets the point. When a white boy from civilized suburbia brings a gun to school it's for any number of reasons. And he kills indiscriminately. The lunch lady, bus driver, teachers, two classmates and that cute little co-ed who wouldn't give him none. Everyone from school counselors to child psychologists to the news media tries in vain to figure out why for a couple of months anyway. Such is the fruit of civilization.

Mail call is the only quiet time behind bars. There's no surer way to circumvent incarceration than with a letter from family and friends. The hope and anticipation in every inmate's eyes is like the family dog at the dinner table. Luckily for me, I was given a couple of bones. I received a letter from Mom and one from my friend Jen in the L.A. hills. I figured I wouldn't want to hear from anyone while locked up; I told people not to write. I was wrong. News from the outside is almost as good as oxygen. Nothing I could've said would stop Mom from writing. I knew not to try. I'm so glad Jen didn't listen to me. Mom is full of family news which is always good to hear. Jen is full of questions and concerns. She's naturally worried about her friend.

I'm leaving on the midnight chain. I'm on my way to a place up north called Bonham. I hear it's 10 minutes from the Oklahoma border. I pack up all of my stuff in 2 fishnet laundry sacks I got from store. I'm not sure how I'm going to tote all this shit, but all of it's coming with me. I've heard Bonham is another transfer facility with two kinds of inmates. Where I'm going sounds a little wilder than this place I'm in now.

I'm back on the bus and handcuffed to an unnamed inmate. This is a new low. Being handcuffed is dehumanizing. Being handcuffed to lord knows who is something else entirely. I don't know this motherfucker yet we're conjoined at the wrist like we come from the island of Siam. If he loses it and tries something, I have 2 choices - lose it with him or immobilize him. I can hear that fuckin' cop bullshit in my head as the cuffs click tight - "This is for your own safety." I don't think I'll have any trouble out of this dude. He's courteous and polite, and more worried about me than I am about him. The bus is kind of empty. There are only 20 of us and we're as spread out as we can be while handcuffed together. Looks like I'm in for another long, bumpy yet scenic ride through the country side. The ride is quiet and uneventful so most of us sleep. Given all our confines and constraints this is no easy undertaking by any means.

The view from a prison bus is priceless and I don't know how many more picturesque prairie sunrises I'll be forced to watch through a cage. Any will be too many. For me, the oceans of grasslands covered in a cold blanket of early morning due, dancing with the dawn breeze and iridescent in the golden luminescence of day break holds no beauty. It's no secret my feelings for this land of the lone star. There's a saying, "Don't mess with Texas. Come on vacation. Leave on probation." Truer words were never spoken.

We arrive moving slowly through the last in a long line of these 2 mule towns. This one is a real hillbilly haven. There isn't a house in town without wheels. No sidewalks and no stop lights; just compacted gravel and one stop sign in the middle of town. I caught a glimpse of a few outhouses which makes me feel as if we've fallen through a wormhole in the space time continuum. If the scenery hasn't changed, neither has the mentality. The last place was in the middle of nowhere, but at least it was integrated and paved. The only integration in this place is on this bus. Makes me wonder how hard these crackers had to work to keep it this lily white.

There's a special kind of stupidity to Texas racism. It comes from the pride they derive from having cheated and stolen this land. Not only from Mexico, but the Comanche's as well. Two hard won fights in rapid succession which gives them a sense of entitlement. "This is ours! We stole it fair and square!" The proof is in their violence and belligerence anytime they feel threatened.

10

Off the bus and off with the cuffs. I'm thankful for every little bit of freedom right now. We're spared the pleasure of another strip search. Not until this moment do I realize I got out of Butt Naked Gurney without being stripped butt naked. This place is nothing but a game of musical cages. Every time another cage door crashes closed and locked, I practice my "I don't give a fuck." Nothing could be farther from the truth. This is not the environment to exhibit the slightest emotional instability. It will be used against you by inmates and guards alike. A lesson this poor white boy who is obviously out of his element has yet to learn. He asked to go to the bathroom. A rookie mistake. After being on the bus for 6 hours all of us have to piss. He's the only one foolish enough to expect an actual toilet. "Boy you better hang your little pecker out the fence and do what you gotta do. No boy! Not over there. On the downhill side so y'all ain't stand in and smellin' yo' own piss."

Another intake interview with the same little white lady asking the same probing questions. I give the same "no" answers and she has the same perplexed look in her eyes. "What are you doing here?" "I received an invitation." This time I've no inclination to engage in small talk. I want get to a bunk and fall out. Since I fit none of her stereotypes she's got to know how I ended up in prison, "Well ma'am, I happen to not be guilty." "Oh come on. Everybody says that. Don't you think that's kinda strange?" I'm tired and she just insulted me, "The arrogance with which you make that ignorant statement is astounding." "What do you mean?" "Do you believe the judge, the DA, the police department and everyone employed by the justice system walks on water?" "No, of course not. I know they're human." Here sits before you a victim of their humanity." When I leave she is nowhere near as confident in the infallibility of the prison system. Coming in here I had no intention of getting into a discussion about the absence of justice in the justice system. It seems her audacious insolence was all it took to get me started. I still don't quite understand how damn near every prison employee has absolute faith in a system in which they themselves have absolutely no faith. When it comes to inmates, the system is always right. When it comes to employees, the system ain't ever right.

The layout here is like a continuation school; two rows of parallel single level aluminum and tin buildings extending about half a mile. The campus is quiet. There are few people in motion, guards or inmates. The setup is the same - 4 pods with 65 men in a tank. As I'm sitting on my bunk, I see a heavily tattooed Mexican with malice in his eyes. This motherfucker wants to test my testicles. I bend down at the waist and put my stuff down with a diversionary "sigh." As he pushes up out of the bunk, I launch a side kick into his sternum. He collapses into the fetal position on the floor grasping his chest and gasping for breath. For effect, I loom over him as he writhes at my feet. Because of his tats I know he's gang related, so I look around the pod. I see two more Mexicans walk my way; from their body language I can tell they don't want none. They just came to get their carnal off the floor. Goddamn! All I wanted to do was come in here and lay it down. Now I have to sit with my back to the wall. I'm watching everyone and everyone's watching me. Four of us are new to this tank, yet no one else had to fight for his bunk and because this motherfucker chose this bunk, I have to grow eyes in the back of my head. I hoped to enjoy a bit of anonymity, but instead I'm mean mugging' trying to ward off evil spirits.

Every nigga in this tank is talking about that one kick, "Big nigga quick wit dem feet ain't he?" By chow time it'll be all over the pen. Every ese in lockup is now a potential mortal enemy. El Placa, (the tattooed one) has recovered. Despite his best efforts it's obvious he doesn't want anymore. If he did it would've happened by now, but now I must concern myself with his homeboys. I don't know what they may have planned, but I'm not too worried. There are at least three of them in this tank, so a sneak attack is just as unlikely.

Chow rollin'! I hang out in the back just to keep everyone in front, particularly the three amigos. We're made to walk with our hands behind our backs as if we are cuffed. The guards at Gurney are assholes, but something in their behavior told me they're instructed to be harsh. While I have no doubt these guards are likewise instructed, there is a pernicious pleasure in their actions. The kind of people who wouldn't dare kick a man until he's down. I walk slow and do my best not to acknowledge their existence, keeping my eyes cast skyward, paying close attention to my peripherals. This chow hall is about half the size of the previous and has half the flies. As I'm eating, I'm scanning the hall for the three caballos. I have to make sure not to lose sight of them. All's well back in the tank and I see no slightest hint of a get back. Still I have my back to the wall. No sleep tonight.

For some reason six men are called to the door by a CO. El Placa and one of his carnales are included in the group. They're being moved. Has the Creator smiled on this old crook once again? As I watch these men pack up and move out, I think of all the times and ways grace has saved my hide. Yet another timely example of me not being abandoned. It's never anything overt or grandiose. No giant hand of the All Mighty descending from the clouds. No big booming voice to guide me from my wayward path; though it's always prompt and effective, and just enough to dilute the imminent danger to a manageable consistence. I'll remain mindful of the rest of the gang, but not tonight.

It's early in the morning and I've been summoned to a meeting. The administration is assigning jobs to the new inmates. So far, everyone is stuck with a hoe squad assignment. I hate it for them. Poor bastards. Wonder what kind of occupational opportunities light duty restriction will hold. "Hoe squad? No man, I have light duty restrictions." "Well, we'll put you on the light duty hoe squad." The smirk on his face lets me know he's enjoying this. I say nothing more. He's the kind of man who thinks prisons are too soft. He thinks it's his job is to make sure inmates suffer because being locked up 24 hours a day in an insane asylum ain't bad enough. Truth is he's all too aware. His fear keeps two COs standing guard in his office. His nightmares let him know he wouldn't last 10 minutes in one of these soft prisons, so the only thing left is for me to go around this frightened little man. On the way out of the admin building I grab a sick call slip. I'm getting medical restrictions one way or another.

Walking back to the tank, I'm angling. What the fuck am I going to say to the doctor this time? When I get back to the tank there's another surprise. Lalo wants to talk. He says no hard feelings and says dude had it comin', always fuckin' with people tryin' to prove how hard he is. When you was standin' over him I thought you was gonna stomp him." "Naw man, the point was made." "Yeah that's what I told him. He wanted to get you back. I told him you could've fucked him up real bad, but you didn't. Me and Javier told him to leave it alone. He wanted all 3 of us to jump you, but we wasn't tryin' to hear that." "Why's that?" "Because he had it comin' and you didn't kick him when he was already down. You made your point and let it go, so we told him to let it go." Prison etiquette.

It's NBA playoff time and the brothas got the TV on lock. The wagering is high. Everything from store to pushups to chest punches. Emotions, tempers and voices are high. These negroes are behaving as if their parole depends on this game's outcome. I like basketball. I have my favorite team. I like a fast break and a two-handed rim rocker as much as the next brotha, but I'm in prison. Never has the outcome of a pro-sporting event been so irrelevant. Lately I don't give a fuck about who wins any game. I don't understand and I'm irritated by all the going concern over something so frivolous. There will be more than one fight over this game tonight and even though the game will go way past lights out, the TV will stay on until the game is over. The guards don't want to deal with the fall out that will come from turning the game off.

There's a good ol' boy that does tattoos in here. The ink in mine has slightly faded. I ask him to touch it up. He's a bit taken aback. A black man trusting him? He's uncertain but excepts. The brothas are looking at me like I'm crazy. Why would I let this obviously racist white man anywhere near me with a needle? I've seen his work. I know artists. An artist's pride in his work goes far deeper than any pride he may have in something he had nothing to do with like the color of his skin. I can tell he's curious about me. I see the questions in his eyes with that "you ain't like the rest of them" look. As he begins to work, the conversation turns to black/white relations. He explains how we aren't that different. How he really doesn't care about a man's skin tone and how he's got a black brother-in-law. While he's trying to convince me how bigoted he isn't, he's letting me know exactly how much he is. There isn't anything unusual about a bigoted white boy in Texas. The more this one talks the more I can see just how conflicted he is about his convictions. Some of the things he's been taught have been proven false, so he has reason to doubt the rest. The environment from which he hails is not conducive to positive growth or change of any kind. I applaud his efforts and his craftsmanship.

I'm reading a book on the Native American Chiefs Pontiac and Tucumpsa. I have an affinity for the Natives and a need to know all I can about them. I'm learning things no scholastic education will teach. It's a way of looking at the world, a philosophy of life, a new and different wrench in my old tool box. It makes adjusting the carburetor of life a little easier. So much of one's outlook depends on perspective which is why I'm always looking for and find it in the strangest of places. Tucumpsa, Pontiac and their people had beautiful perspectives in the midst of all their so-called savagery. They believe everything in this life is a gift and lived accordingly. It's been my experience civilized man has no problem believing, but seems to have the greatest of difficulty living.

It's well before sunrise and I'm being awakened to go to the fields. I should be hearing from the doctor soon, so for now I make sure they can't see they've gotten to me. There are 200 of us out here in the dark. The COs separated us into four squads. I notice the other inmates are tucking their pant legs in their socks. I don't ask why, I just follow suit. For some reason one of the guys says "Fuck it. I ain't tuckin' mine in." I got a feeling that's not the move. I don't know why he's so adamant, but dudes are looking at him and shaking their heads. They know something that he doesn't. He's either too proud or too ignorant to fall in line. Guess he's asserting his individuality.

Another scenic sunrise over the Texas plains and a tractor pulling a trailer full of garden hoes is pulling up. The hoe squad bosses are on horseback, wearing straw cowboy hats and toting shotguns. The only thing missing are the whips. They're all sporting a cocky grin of satisfaction as if to say, "Now this is the way it's supposed to be." We're told to pick up a hoe and walk to the fields. Are you fuckin' kidding me? Fuckin' blood hounds! Off in the distance I can see and hear a kennel. That distinctive blood hound bark breaking the morning silence like a simultaneous exclamation of blissful pleasure and an exaltation of tormented anguish. All the movies I've seen, all the stories I've heard concerning runaway slaves and the hounds hot on their asses are now on constant playback. With every howling bark another one of these stories plays on my mental projector. This prison system has gone to great lengths to make this experience just like slavery. They derive immense and untold amounts of sadistic satisfaction from doing so and all directed at a 85% black inmate workforce. Am I the only person to whom all this seems psychologically cruel and unusual? Some things you just don't do.

We're hacking weeds in a crop of peas. I'm using all my cunning and conniving skills to ensure I do as little as possible. Suddenly someone yells out loud, panicked and fearful. It's the dude who didn't tuck his pant legs in. He's screaming and squeezing his left thigh with both hands at the same time. Blood is running down all over his boot when a bloody rat drops dead from under his pant leg cuff. Hobbled and limping while grasping his thigh, he's obviously suffering from a bite. My sympathetic pangs stem from thinking what might've happened if he wasn't so quick. Couple more inches and the bite would've been infinitely more painful and damaging. After a few minutes a tractor carries him back to the prison. We haven't been out here an hour and I've seen all kinds of little varmints scurrying through these fields. It didn't take me but a minute to figure out why we tucked our pant legs in our socks. It hit me like an epiphany. This man has taken a great risk to secure his exodus from these fields. Brilliant. What I mistook for brazen stupidity has turned out to be daring and ingenious. We're done with the hoes and now we're picking berries. I don't care if it's berries, sugar cane, tobacco or cotton, this shit is wrong on so many levels. It's not yet 9 am and the sun has me dripping dirty brown sweat into my eyes as I cast them out over the endless acres of Texas agriculture. I'm standing in the very soil my tormented forefathers tilled and toiled. It's the same soil from which they would have tried to escape. This is the light duty hoe squad. We're headed back in and I'm glad. This type of work isn't for me. Blister and all, it isn't the work that fucks with me, it's the ambiance.

When I return to the tank I receive the sick call I've been waiting for. I need to come up with something more substantial than my initial assertions. These crackers enjoy this massa-slave relationship they've cultivated here far too much to relinquish it for a run of the mill excuse. I feel a responsibility to my ancestors especially the ones that attempted escape. Whether or not they succeeded is irrelevant; they had the nuts to try. I like to think if I were in their shoes I would've tried, too. Today I was closer than I would've ever thought possible. That's why whatever I have do while I'm here is just what I have to do. That's why dude had to let himself get bit. Rabies is preferable to the hoe squad. "Well Doc, when I donated a kidney to my brother the incision didn't heal properly. Consequently, I suffer from extreme muscle spasms. The repetitive motion of swinging that hoe is just too much. It's got me doubled over in pain. Can you do something or give me something for it?" It's a risky move suggesting a prescription. I'm betting the price of pain pills and the prospect of legal narcotics in their prison will be avoided at all costs. Doc asks to see my scar and that's all it took. I can see he's writing more work restrictions. No walking on uneven surfaces, no lifting overhead, no repetitive bending and no lifting over 20 pounds. "That should take care of it. Do you need anything for the pain? No Doc, that's cool. I'll just stand in a hot shower for a while." "Ok, let me know if you need any more work restrictions." "Thanks Doc, this ought to do it." I thought about milking it for a prescription. An inmate can name his own price for pain pills, but the doctor operated in good faith and he didn't make me jump through any hoops. Plus, I don't want to make it tougher on the next guy. Every one of the rules in this place comes from some dumb inmate fucking it up for the rest of us, so I leave well enough alone. A thousand pardons for impugning the most excellent work performed by the surgical team and staff at UCSF Medical Center.

A couple of days have past and I've acclimated myself to my new surroundings. I wake up in the morning just to watch the poor bastards on the hoe squad fall out then I go back to sleep. Sleeping helps me endure the stifling boredom that permeates any captive existence, a not so subtle reminder I could be bored or I could be out in them fuckin' fields. To a lot of these country negroes working in the fields is just what they do without the shotgun toting cracker on horseback. I'm not from the country which is why most of the time I keep to myself. I have a few brief conversations with Tony the tat man and Lalo the pachuco, but that's it. I don't feel the need to make new acquaintances. The irritation of my incarceration is beginning to weigh on me, so I immerse myself in learning more about Chief Pontiac. The brothas in this tank think I'm strange because I keep to myself, I don't watch basketball and my face is always in a book.

The days are growing hotter and the humidity is from another world. Being locked in a tin shed with 65 men is unspeakable during the hot months. I thought when I got outside the fresh air would be better. A slight miscalculation - ain't no fresh, ain't no air. Inside or out, it's thick and muggy. As I'm standing in the store line, I see a white-haired inmate on the ground at the other end of the walkway. What are they doing? Why are the guards walking around taking their sweet time? Why are they just standing around him gawking? Get the man some help! After a good 5 minutes the guards bring a wheel chair. The inmate is 65 to 70 years old, 6'4" and 230 pounds. He collapsed and is unconscious. Why the fuck would they bring a wheel chair? After fumbling and failing to get the man in the chair, one of them has the brilliant, albeit late idea of getting a gurney and some nurses. It takes six guards to get him onto the stretcher. I can't help but think this man's time has come. Not from his illness, but from the ineptitude of the COs. The nurses saved his life.

I got my groceries and I'm heading back to the tank so I can eat my ice cream before I end up having to drink it. Another game is on tonight and the inmate sports analysts are cussing statistical facts of games past while casting dispersions - both personal and professional - upon the opponent's players and swearing prophetic predictions before the pregame show. There was a time when I enjoyed such shit debates. Now they annoy me to no end. In prison, any opinion pertaining to sporting contests and/or athletes is of no consequence other than whatever has been put on the line. I'm not a betting man. All this shit talking is done in the hope of being correct so they can say I told you. This way the next time they talk shit their voice will contain some validity.

Word is going around a man died. The preliminary reports are not of any foul play and it turns out he died in his sleep. Cellmates couldn't wake him up is the story I heard. I have a feeling it's the old man who fell out the other day. I've seen death up close and the old man didn't look like he would survive. Prison must be the worst place to meet your maker. This place is for short timers. I hope someone pours out a little liquor for the old brotha. What a foul prospect it must be to be notified a loved one has passed away while behind bars.

I'm being moved to a tank for kitchen workers. It's the same tank where the old man died. I'm not a superstitious man, but I hope I'm not assigned his bunk. Who says death ain't contagious? This tank has a chain link cage from floor to ceiling encircling the day room. It looks like WWF cages with the bunks lined around the walls. Imagine a cage inside a cage. The bunks are separated like 4-man cubicles. This bunk isn't the old man's and I'm glad. Out of the four of us in here, I'm the only brother. At least it'll be relatively quiet.

There are two Muslim brothers in here. One is a corn-fed country ghetto brotha from two-mule Texas and the other is from Baghdad. Corn-fed's name is Rahim. I saw him reading the Qur'an, so I inquired. Khan saw my tattoo, so he inquired.

They've convinced me to check out the Muslim community in here, but I'm not a man for organized religion. I prefer a personal and individual relationship with the Almighty, but I'm curious to see how my Muslim brothers get down. This tank is diverse. There's even a couple of Asians, both are called Chino despite being from two different Asian countries. No one around here knows the difference or gives a fuck for that matter. Two of the three white men I bunk next to keep to their own kind. The third one, named Tim, keeps to himself. He's an educated man who's out of his comfort zone. I saw him trying not to be noticed listening to my conversations with Khan and Rahim. He's got questions, but he's also got apprehensions. I have questions as well. I wonder how such a man ends up on the inside. What this place must be like for him! He's timid and meek, yet he is cunningly skillful at staying under the radar. Most men in his position, especially white would seek to make alliances to insure his safety – a rookie mistake. Tim's method of survival is far superior. No one acknowledges or bothers him. His method requires character which explains why it's the road less traveled. I like him.

They've seen fit to put me on the lunch line; my job is to scoop vegetables onto trays - work that requires no work. I have nothing against work. I do however take issue with working in them fuckin' fields for these crackers and no pay. Right away I'm questioned by the other inmates, "How'd you get this gig? Most nigga's gotta be on the hoe squad fo' years befo' gettin' in the kitchen." "I ain't most niggas." "Oh, you thank you somethin' don't you?" "But I is." A CO calls me by name to the office, "Hennington!" One of my co-workers says, "Green Cadillac?" "That's Grandpah." "Then you is somethin'. Yo' granddaddy was a damn good man. Did a lot fo' folk where I come from." "You from Texarkana?" "No, Linden. He got a lot of love down there." "So I'm told." "You from Texarkana?" "Hell no, Cali. I did fall out of Bowie County though." "What was yo' California ass doin' down in T-town?" "Gettin' caught up."

Grandpa Hennington had been retired for more than 30 years, dead more than 10. Yet his good deeds have earned his last grandson a measure of respect 40 years removed and 400 miles way down deep in a territorial prison. Seems there's no telling how far a man's good deeds will travel. Life being what it is the same must be said for the bad. In the office I'm issued a hair net, hat and an apron. Then told what is expected of me. They have Rahim show me around the kitchen; he just happens to be standing around the door to the office as we come out. While he's showing me where everything is he also shows me how to get my smuggle on. I'm told who does what and when.

The baker is a Muslim, his name is Mustafa. He's got the hook up on ground beef. He cooks it in the ovens right along with the cakes and cookies. When they serve pork, we eat hamburger. Fuck them and their slice of cheese now! All of this has to be done covertly which makes it taste better. Dave, the man who knew my grandfather, is working the line with me. All the time we're slinging' slop he's regaling me with stories of Grandpa. Most of these stories I've heard. I listen anyway as if I'm hearing them for the first time. During the winter, Grandpa would get to school at 5 am every morning to light wood stoves so the children would have warm classrooms. He knew each child, their parents and siblings by their first names and if a student missed school he was at their house that night asking parents why. At a time when teenage pregnancy was not tolerated, he let the girls go to school until they couldn't hide it any longer. This may not seem like much, but in east Texas during the 40s, 50s and 60s this was unheard of. You couldn't even say the word "pregnant." You had to say "with child" or "expecting." I hear the honest appreciation and prideful admiration for my grandfather in this man's voice. You'd think he was talking about his own grandfather. In a way I guess he was. Grandpa had that kind of effect on people. He was more than an educator. I've heard that same appreciation and admiration for him before as a child. In Texarkana, everyone knew who my brothers and I were. We heard, "them's Fessa Hennington's grandbabies" or "that's Ol' Prof's grandchild" on a regular basis including when it came to scolding me, "Boy, yo' granddaddy know you down here messin' up my garden, eatin' up all my yellow meat? No he don't know. If he did, he'd skin yo' little ass alive!" As I recall there were seven children in that garden that day, but I was the only one who was called by last name.

After serving the inmates it's time for us to eat. Rahim, Mustafa and I are all larger than average men. We get a table in the far corner and sit with our backs to the guards. We eat big. We have more food than all three us could possibly finish. This doesn't stop us from giving it our best shot. Everyone else eats highly suspect pork link sausage while we dine on Mustafa's mom's recipe for brown sugar meatloaf. We have meatloaf, cookies and cake stashed all over the dining hall. We have to clean up the kitchen before we can go. For me this means wiping down the steam table. I make sure it's spotless. After the CO inspects my work, I stash the contraband food under and behind the stainless steel. I'm told 5 minutes before we leave that depending on the on duty CO, we may be stripped searched or patted down. Just before the door is unlocked we pack ourselves from socks to hat. My first day on the job and I'm an effective embezzler.

It's Friday and I've decided to go to Muslim services. Besides the all-white inmate clothing, you would never know this is a prison Muslim community. There's a genuine brotherhood here. The Imam is white; he's the only white face in the crowd. Belial is his name. First thing that comes to my mind is all the ignorant shit he must have to deal with on the day to day. He's obviously respected in here as he should be. He holds an elected office. One of his responsibilities is to represent and speak for the Muslims to the prison administration. I can only imagine the hell these Appalachian-Americans put him through. In spite of this he's doing a damn good job.

This is a good size community. It's well organized and managed. Every brother respects the mosque without having to be reminded. He even managed to get us an air-conditioned room. There's an older brother who holds a secretarial position in the community by the name of Rafeeq. He and I hit it off right away. He's a self-educated man. We launch directly into a world history conversation as seen through the eyes of Islam. Each surprising the other with our respective intellectual insights. In prison as in society most of the population is uneducated. For a person of some cerebral agility the opportunity for an analytical discussion is highly coveted.

Before we know it, we've captivated an audience. I'm by no means formally educated. It's more accurate to say I'm formally uneducated. For reasons unknown to me, I suffer from an insatiable thirst for knowledge and a disdain for the scholastic. To compensate for this contradictory affliction, it's my belief I've been blessed with a Hover Dam like ability to retain information – a mixed blessing. For me the written word is nowhere near as easily retained as the audible, so I listen.

I'm listening to Belial give the Khutbah. That's the equivalent of Sunday sermon. The khutbah is far more difficult. In a church, the preacher interprets the Bible for his congregation. In Islam it's incumbent upon every Muslim to interpret the Qur'an for himself. In Islam every person is responsible for their own soul. Consequently, an Imam can't get away with any mistakes, deviations or loose interpretations. He must know his stuff. Belial is up to the task. He's knowledgeable and fluent, but lacks fire in his speech. Most of these Muslims are reverts, but raised Southern Baptist. No man on this earth has more fire in his speech than a Southern Baptist preacher. Belial's lack of theatrics is more in line with Islamic protocol which is one of the things that attracted me to Islam. After the khutbah and Jummah Salaat, that's Friday prayer, we congregate and discuss the khutbah. Khan, Rafeeq and I approach Belial with comments and questions which quickly turns into an open discussion; I'm enjoying this thoroughly. A group conversation with men of intellect is intoxicating by cognition. There's an old Islamic saying, "Allah has created nothing better than rationale." All praise be to Allah.

On the way back to the tank, I thank Rahim and Khan for suggesting I attend Jummah. Khan is gracious, but Rahim gives me a bunch of "I told you so!" We laugh and joke all the way back to the tank. We've managed to have a good time in prison so much so our joy is irritating the guards. A few of them feel compelled to chastise us for being happy, but that's not the reason they gave us. They give the excuse about being too loud and not walking in line. Khan and I hardly take note, but Rahim is hostile. I can't stop smiling. Khan and I thank them for their reproach and usher Rahim through the door. As the door closes I look through the security glass and see that the guards are angry - sulking, cussing and kicking. My smile will not leave my face for a long time.

The cheer and good will I feel is extended to Tim. When I speak to him, he's surprised and stutters his response, "I...I...I'm fine. How are you?" I ask about the book he's reading. It's a book on aeronautics. He served in the Air Force. I tell him I'm an Air Force brat and the conversational flood gates open. He was an officer who worked in military intelligence; he even got his wings. I tell him my father was a flight engineer on C-130's and C-5's, and retired from Travis. We talk about where we've been stationed and what parts of the world we've seen. We talk about Okinawa for hours.

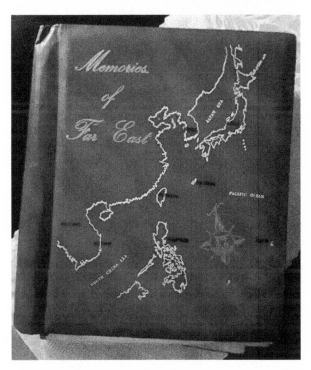

Family photo album from our time in Japan

Papa-san, Mama-san & me

Samurai in downtown Tokyo, Japan.

11

It's Monday and I'm back in the kitchen slinging' slop. It's another day and another stream of hungry men all clad in white. I've got it as good as any inmate could hope - a cake walk job in the kitchen, a steady supply of contraband, my store stays full and I found my Muslim brothers. In a lousy place like prison with crooks, con men and hustlers on both sides of the bars, I've managed to do alright for myself.

Tony the tatt man limps in to the chow hall and he doesn't look good. "Damn man, what the fuck happened to you?" I ask. "I didn't thank you'd tawlk tuh me" he replies. I ask, "Why's that?" "You ain't heard?" He replied. "Naw, what happened Tony?" I ask. "I fell." He replies. "Well take it easy man." Tony is real fucked up. He's on crutches with a cast on his right leg and one on his left arm. His face is severely lumped, discolored and scarred. He's missing two of his upper left front teeth. One of his homeboys has to carry his tray for him. One of my kitchen co-workers asks, "You know that white boy?" I reply, "Yeah, I know him. He did some tat work for me. Why?" My co-worker says, "He's a racist. Got to talkin' that white supremacy shit to my homeboy Ray. Ray wasn't havin' it. Took his ass back in the showers and beat the white off'm. Ray had him in there beggin' to stop. Bet he ain't gonna talk that white power shit no mo'e." I reply, "No shit? Fuh sho'e. When did this happen?" He replies, "Last night." Looks like Tony failed to come to terms with his contradictory convictions. It looks like brotha Ray did his damnedest to help him out with that. I wonder if it did any good.

It's another Friday and we just finished salat. Rafeeq asked to speak to me alone. He tells me he and Belial want me to be the assistant Imam; "I don't know what to say man. I'm honored that you would even think of me, but this ain't really my thang. I've always been wary of organized religion. Besides, I ain't all that devout." Rafeeq says, "So what? You are knowledgeable and well spoken. Plus ain't none of us all that devout. If we were we wouldn't be here. Besides, Belial needs help. He and I agreed. We think it should be you. He couldn't be here today or he'd ask you himself." I reply, "Well, man what would I have to do?" Rafeeq replies, "Just make the khutbahs when Belial ain't here, maybe a taleem or two. I don't think you'd ever have to deal with the Warden and even if you did, you could handle it." "I don't know man. This is more than I signed up for. Gonna have to let me think about it", I said. "That's cool. We meet next Wednesday. Let us know by then?" "Cool." While I'm flattered they want me, I don't know if I want to get that involved. I have all I need and I hoped to do my time in the background.

When we return to the tank, Khan senses my concerns. Normally I wouldn't talk about things of this nature because it could easily be misconstrued as weakness. What I know of Khan, he doesn't think like that. Plus it's been my experience people from different cultures always have a different perspective. We have a frank discussion. I tell him I'm uncertain about the problems that could arise. He gives me a very Islamic response, "No one can ever know. Allah knows. Trust in Allah." This is a man born and raised without the influences of modern Christianity. For such a Muslim, the answer is clear. It is written. Whether there be smooth sailing or troubled waters in one's forecast, only Allah knows. Good or bad, man is not qualified to judge. Therefore, trust in Allah.

Failure to do so is un-Islamic. This is an idea I've recently come to comprehend. What I thought were bad times in my life turned out to be the best thing for me. Allah is the best of planners. I thank Khan for his clarifying perspective.

I've got a visitor. It must be my mother. My feelings are mixed. I want to see her, but I don't want her to see her baby like this. The pain and disappointment in her eyes will grieve my soul which is one reason why I want to do my time by myself. Having people I care about see me in prison won't make the endless long, slow, lonely and quiet nights any easier. I can't tell my mother not to visit although I wish I could. I don't know if seeing me like this will do either of us any good. As they strip search me I realize my mother has to submit to a search as well. She's no shrinking violet by any means. Still, one more thing I've put her through. She's squeezing tight, sniffling and starting to cry. I have to stop her before she gets started and before I start to cry. We sit down and I have to stop her again. It's hard to look at her, but I know I must let her see in my eyes that I'm okay. My Uncle Rasheed is with her. Though there's awkward silence between us, I have no problem looking at him. It's hard to find something worthwhile to say under these circumstances and small talk doesn't seem appropriate. I ask about the latest in family news and goings on. This allows my mother to talk for damn near the entire hour. Plus, it's an excellent diversionary topic. A CO says our time is up. I stop her from crying again. I give my mother a hug, my Uncle Rasheed a pound and we say our goodbyes. I exit in a hurry. This was more difficult than I thought.

It's Monday morning and I'm sitting in a prison classroom. Without testing any of us, the prison administrators have decided we're in need of remedial education. I'm talking 6th grade level. Most of the men in here could benefit from this class. The only problem – they're grown men. Education is not something that can be forced on a grown man. A room full of ignorant country criminals? You can hang it up. Not only do they not want to learn, they don't think school has anything to teach them. Oh, how wrong they are. Our teacher is a little old white lady and as nice as can be. She's so nice that despite my classmates being who they are, they show her respect. This class is nowhere near as rowdy as one might think. I'm an authority on remedial education classrooms. I've seen my share of special education teachers. This is the first time I've seen the nice and sweet routine work so well on these demographics. She has my admiration. Being back in a grade school classroom again is perturbing in the extreme. Most of my special ed teachers talked to me as if I was fucking stupid which is one more reason for me to abhor academics. A few of them new damn well I wasn't stupid. This little white lady is nice, but she's patronizing. Due to the lack of responses to her questions, the teacher switches up her teaching style to a lecture. She's going on about the founding fathers and the ideals this country was founded upon. I interject with a scoffing chuckle. "What is it Mr. Hennington?" "I'm sitting here considering the hypocrisy of it all." "I see. Yes, well of course you're right." She backs off this topic before subtlety moving on to the civil war. I hoped for a request to clarify or to expound, but I can tell by the way she tip-toed away from the subject she agreed but didn't care to discuss the matter.

It's Friday and it's my turn to give the Khutbah. Rafeeq tells me the brothers are eagerly anticipating what I have to say, "You know man, they like the way you talk." "No, I didn't know, but thanks for tellin' me." I have no idea what to say. Public speaking has never been my forte, but the brothers don't know that. I watched and listened to a lot of Malcolm X when I was younger, so I will draw from him and give it to them right between the eyes. After we make salaat, I'm pleasantly surprised at the number of brothers who approach me with smiles on their faces and accolades on their lips. Rafeeq says "See, told you you'd be good." Since I had no idea what I was doing I ask him, Rahim and Khan for specific examples of what they liked and disliked. As I was speaking, I tried to gauge the crowd. It was obvious I had their undivided attention, but that's all I could see. I'm pleased and relieved to hear the feedback my brothers are giving me, but I hope they don't ask me to do this again.

The prison is having a heat issue. There are two exhaust fans at the rear of the tank, but now that the temperature is constantly in the 100s the guards refuse to turn them on during the day except of course when they come in for count time. They have no problem turning them on at night when there's no need or desire for a fan. A perfect example of the administration's belief prisoners don't suffer enough. We have it too easy, so they take it in upon themselves to increase our torment whenever possible. 65 men in a tin shed under the Texas sun is like nothing I've experienced before. A shed in which one man I know of has already died. These sick sons of bitches have to send someone to check the temperature which is 115 to 120, never mind the humidity and stench. We are forced to act out just to get them to turn the fans on during the day rather than at night. You would think we were asking the prison officials to import prostitutes. The guards would say "Oh come on! It ain't that hot." "Then why do you turn the fans on at count time?" "Because it stinks in here." "Don't you think we know that? That's one of the reasons for the exhaust fans." This argument has gone on for weeks now. The fans will have absolutely no effect on them and still it's taken them weeks to send a man with a lazar thermometer to confirm the obvious. The fans are finally on.

Rahim had a problem with a homosexual in the kitchen. He's hostile at this dude for a reason I have yet to ascertain. He's more upset at the fact he had to deal with a gay man; he's calling him every name. Our conversation moves to gay Muslims, "You know they tryin' to open a gay mosque in Canada?" "Yeah, I heard that. So what? That's between them and Allah." "Fuck that! If I see some shit like that, I'll burn that muthafucka down." "Wait a minute Akee. It's not your place to interfere with any man's attempt to practice his faith." "Fuck that! It's an abomination. I don't want them prayin' next to me." "How are you gonna judge somebody else's sins? Don't you got enough of your own sins to answer for? I know I do." "Yeah, but I don't suck dick or fuck another man in the ass." "Preachin' to the choir, but what they do ain't got shit to do with you or me, so why do you give a damn what they do?" "Because it's an abomination." Yes, but brotha you sell crack!" He's got no retort for that, but he's refusing to concede. "Guess you got no problem with gays in the military either?" "Since I ain't gonna join the military, I really don't give a fuck. But since you asked my opinion, I refer to history. Both Caesar and Alexander were gay. There ain't a military commander alive or dead who wouldn't cut off his left nut to count either one of them amongst their generals. Come to think of it, some samurai were gay. "Fuck that and fuck history!" I end the discussion right there.

There's a fight brewing. A scrawny young man is going out of his way to pick a fight with a very large man. The man has given the boy more than one chance to shut the fuck up. He simply refuses to stop talking shit. The big man has reached his limit. It's count time now and while the guards are counting, he's lacing his boots. He's not saying a word. The boy hasn't stopped talking. Tim wants to know if the boy is crazy. "No, he's just a young man who thinks he has something to prove." "Is he trying to prove how stupid he is?" "That's just a by-product." The guards are off counting another tank and the bell has sounded. The boy is standing there with his fists balled up and his gums are still bumpin'. Big Man gets up out of his bunk and walks directly toward the boy with intent in every step. The moment he's within striking distance he lets loose a straight right followed with a quick left. The boy is covering and back peddling. He hasn't thrown a shot yet and the Big Man is relentless in his pursuit. He backed the duckin' and dodgin' boy up into our cubicle. The white boy in the bunk under me has been forcibly ejected. After a few minutes of scuffling, Big Man grows tired of this one-sided fight. He leaves the boy balled up on the bunk – he's still talking shit. He had his chance and didn't throw a shot and he's talking about how he was outweighed by 150 pounds and he's still standing omitting the fact he spent the whole fight in retreat, rolled up in a ball. He's got the whole tank shakin' their heads in disbelief. Tim asks, "What's wrong with the boy?" "He thinks he's proven something, and he has. Not what he thinks. He's proven he's unworthy of any effort to be taught." The boy's fellow gang members are chastising him for acting so foolishly and running off at the mouth as if he has something to brag about. This is fascinating to Tim, "I thought they'd all ganged up on the big dude." "Naw man, that's not how gangs operate. The point of any gang is safety in numbers. This little stupid bastard went looking for trouble and found it. He made something out of nothing. They all watched him make an ass out of himself and brag about it. His gang ain't gonna co-sign that bullshit. He's on his own." "I didn't know gangs have codes of conduct." "What? Did you think anarchy ruled?" "Actually yes." "It's quite the contrary. Every gang in history was formed for the express purposes of protection. The bad behavior is merely a side effect when any number of angry and ill-behaved adolescents congregate for any length of time. Truth is all gangs have strict rules and regulations. It just so happens none of them are designed to benefit society." With work every day, class three times a week and my religious activities twice a week, the days are moving right along.

It's been more than two months now and things are going pretty good. So far anyway. I manage to keep my lock box full and my mind occupied. The men in this tank just want to do their time, but one doesn't have to look far for trouble. It's never out of arms reach. Most prisoners keep a razor blade where he can get to it which is why cooler heads prevail. Fist fights are common, but that ain't nothin' but bravado and entertainment. The more of them I see the less entertaining they become. The threat of violence is a bore.

Another Friday and I'm asked to give another Khutbah. This will be the 4th for me and with each my confidence has grown. The brothers really seem to enjoy what I have to say. From the school house to the kitchen, brothers approach questioning and requesting, "When you gonna give another Khutbah?" It fills me with a quiet satisfaction to know they look forward to my public speaking. I thought I'd suck at it and then they wouldn't ask me to do it again. They think I'm good and I'm doing my best to remain humble. The discovery of a new personal ability is no small affair for me especially one to which I had so long ago conceded defeat.

I've been enrolled in yet another class - machine shop using computers to construct, lathe and cut metal. This one may turn out to be instructive. I'm good with my hands; I've always had an aptitude for the creative. Maybe I'll get the opportunity to make a prison souvenir like the chess sets in the teacher's display case. They use a computer to make board and pieces out of stainless steel and brass. The instructor is an aging white man who works in the field. My classmates are a good mix of the same kind of person. Grown versions of high school shop kids. One might think 30 convicts in a room with all this heavy and sharp metal lying around would be cause for concern. I know I did. The men in this class seem to be interested in learning. Who'duh thunk it?

We're on lockdown for a week. I forgot it was happening. The prison administrators have gone to great lengths to keep this lockdown covert without any success. The COs go from tank to tank and search for contraband. The inmates and all our belongings are shuffled outside for a group strip search and inspection. I'm standing out on the yard butt ass naked while some ignorant and evil cracker looks searches everywhere including my rectum. Since the COs won't find anything we don't want them to, this entire undertaking is an exercise in futility. The only tangible effect is, for the next week, time will cease to be perpetual.

In preparation of lockdown I stocked up. My lock box is full and I have three new books to read- sci-fi, espionage and a Louis L'amour. I figured I'd need some light entertainment. Boredom is a villainous nemesis which requires constant vigilance. Self- constraint and discipline aren't popular characteristics in prison or in society. Most people never make an honest effort to manage their desires. I'm no exception. I have few vices, women and weed neither of which can be had nor enjoyed anytime soon. Mischief and mayhem for me no longer hold much allure. Problem is neither does boredom.

Three days have come and gone since this lockdown started. We're eating Johnny sack lunches again - a glob of oily peanut butter and jelly mashed in the center of oil soggy white bread served in an oil stained brown paper sack. We eat it for lack of anything else to do. Because I've got the provisions, I've become quite skilled in the art of prison cuisine. Khan, Rahim and Tim have all chipped in. If our lock boxes are empty, we steal what we want. Tonight I'm making a mean tuna salad – tuna, onion, celery and dried herbs and spices. I even managed to get my hands on ranch dressing from the Officer's Dining Room (ODR). You didn't think I was working for free did you? As we eat dinner, the conversation turns to the hoe squad. I ask Rahim how the brothas around here can let these crackers enjoy our pain like they do, "Ain't nothin' we can do." "Bullshit. Y'all could shut this muthafucka down or riot like we do in Cali." Khan says, "Since I've been in this country the black people in California have rioted 3 times." I reply, "That's right. Did you see the palm trees on fire in Oakland when the Raiders lost the Super bowl? They looked like 200 feet torches. Think what would've happened if they'd won. And do I have to mention Rodney King?" Tim says, "That's something I never understood. Why did they burn down their own community?" I like the fact Tim feels uninhibited enough to join our discussions, but he picked the wrong subject. I say, "Of course, you don't understand. You're not a man of color. You have no reason to hate the police. Oh, you may have reason to dislike the police. I'm talking about all you've ever known for them is a contemptuous disdainful hate. We're talking' about the gang capital of the world. The biggest gang in Los Angeles is the LAPD and they have carte blanche to murder, rape, torture, and terrorize at will. That's just what they do for fun. What they do for money, you wouldn't believe if I told you. They finally caught some of them muthafuckas red handed. Elbow deep in the cookie jar and crumbs all around their mouths. On video with the whole world watching. Still we waited for the verdict. When that finally came the outrage ignited. Every person of color instantly understood we can't let this slide. If we did the police would lose their only reason for constraint. Open season on niggas so for 6 days we burned and looted everything in sight. We made the police afraid to do their job and showed them for the cowards they really are. To answer your question Tim, as angry as we were, we ain't stupid. If hostile people of color were to attempt the sacking of Beverly Hills the National Guard would be called out. No such courtesy would be extended to the inner city. The fight was not with the National Guard. It was and is with the LAPD." Tim asks, "Yeah but what'd get you?" I reply, "Consideration. Remember after the O.J. trial? They were forced to consider whether or not we would riot. Had that seemingly insignificant consideration been considered, those cops would've never been acquitted. Tim says, "Don't tell me you think O.J. was innocent." I say, "No, I'm tellin' you I don't give a fuck about O.J. or that white bitch and her friend. Did you see the video of the verdict with the two audiences, one white, one black? Did you notice the polar opposite reactions? White folks seething with anger and disbelief over this miscarriage of justice; black folks ecstatic and elated. Something most white people in America could never understand. They think we were happy simply because he's black. If you notice Tim I didn't include you in that stereotypical category. That's because I figure you just might be able to comprehend what I'm about to say. That spontaneous and unanimous outpouring of jubilance was the sweet sound of revenge served on ice. Not too long ago, if a black man so much as looked at a white woman the wrong way he'd be dead before the sun came up. This is every American black person's personal family history. Now here's a black man acquitted of killing two white people. To us this represented a watershed moment of monumental progress. Proof this country is slowly outgrowing it's racism. Now, if a nigga has enough money even he can buy himself some American justice. Not to mention he did it on TV so the entire world could see. As for the victims, charge them to the game. Charge them to the thousands of untold and unnamed black people who fell victim to the city, county, state, and federal sanctioned oppression for 150 years after slavery in this country. The price one pays for progress. Now these same white people want and expect us to show some concern for two dead white people? And Tim, if what I've said offends you in any way ask yourself a question. How does it feel?" Tim says, "No I'm not offended at all. It actually makes sense. And you're right; I never would've figured it like that. Not saying I agree, but I do understand." Rahim steps in, "See Tim, that's why we let you hang with us." I wasn't too sure if he could handle the truth but he asked. The COs are herding us outside to the rec yard basketball courts. This is the first time I've been out here. The yard is encased in a 20 foot chain link fence rimmed with razor wire and a tin roof. I have no wish to be locked up outside.

We're on lockdown, but before it's over they turn the water and electricity back on for tanks that have been searched. I asked a CO why they find it necessary to turn off the water. He said they didn't want us to flush any contraband. "That's bullshit. Just as easy to throw it away." "We search the trash." "So, what? The trash is anonymous." "True, but it'll give us an idea of what's bein' smuggled in." "That might be the case if you could keep the lockdown a secret." "Oh, you'd be surprised what we find." "No, I wouldn't." "Maybe you wouldn't. Surprises the hail outta me. Don't know how y'all get some uh that stuff in here." "Yes, you do. Your coworkers are crooked." He was overcome with a disheveled expression before walking away.

From our many conversations, Tim thinks I'm a pessimist, "I'm of the opinion I'm a realist, a pragmatist. I don't know where you got all this faith in your fellow man." "I'd like to think people are basically good." "Exactly man, you would like to think. You see things as they should be or how you'd like them to be. I see them as they are. People are only as good as they have to be and as bad as they think they can get away with. Are you not familiar with your Bible?" "That's not always true. I know a lot of good people. My father was a good man through and through, and everybody knew it." "What did your father do?" "Sold and serviced antique model trains. People would come from 400 miles away to do business with him." "You've just proven my point." "How do you figure?" "Why do you suppose people would travel so far to do business with your father?" "Because they knew he would be fair and equitable." "That's right. One honest business man is worth traveling 400 miles for. That's how rare they are." "I'll frame it in your Christian religion for you. Preachers don't teach their congregations to do the right thing because it's the right thing to do. They bribe and threaten. Do righteous deeds that they may attain ever-lasting life in heaven. Do the Devil's deeds and thou shall spend eternity in the Hellfire? It's starts as a child. Be good or Santa won't bring you any presents. Despite their obvious and overwhelming differences most world religions operate on a similar principle; Buddhist karma and Hindu reincarnation, for example. Yes, even Islam." "Just where did you get this pragmatic view of the world?" "I watched, listened and learned to see reality regardless of the camouflage. I learned to listen for the truth irrespective of what was said."

They've moved Mustafa in with us; this is a good thing. Now nothing in the kitchen is safe. We'll corner the market with Mustafa's access. Today was one of the rare times we had chicken. Mustafa brought the whole barn yard with him. We're having Aa post lockdown celebration with chicken salad sandwiches tonight. My prison-made salsa is a big hit. I smuggled jalapenos and habaneros from my old cellmate Lalo who's still working in the fields. I add bell pepper, onion, tomato, garlic, dried herbs, salt, pepper, pickled jalapenos and three different kinds of hot sauce from the store. This isn't for tender mouthed motherfuckers. There aren't many people in Texas who can't stand the heat that we've stolen out of the kitchen. Even if they couldn't, they wouldn't admit it like the young white boy who bunks under me. He's sweating and talking about how good it is. Mustafa took one look at him and fell out laughing. Khan compliments my cooking as we eat and I begin asking questions about his homeland. I ask him about what's really going on over there. We discuss the current events as they unfold by watching the news. It's fascinating to hear him explain the difference between what's reported and what the facts are.

We're in the kitchen and the smuggling is rampant. Everyone is forced to restock after the lockdown. The cooperating subterfuge and coordinated diversionary tactics are seamless and timely like the gears in a Swiss watch. The conniving is so cunning you would think it's rehearsed. I find myself almost pitying these poor COs. Some of them actually take their jobs seriously. We find joy to pilfer, misappropriate and down-right plunder right under their noses. Most of these inmates take what they can to supplement their survival. The pleasure is just a byproduct. I do it out of contempt.

Slinging slop day after day is how I mark the passage of time. I see Tony the Tatt Man. His scabs and bruises have all but healed and he's down to one cast and one crutch. As slowly as time is passing for me, I can't imagine how slow it must be for him. Dave wants to know why I still speak and act civil to a racist white person, "I've dealt with this man on more than one occasion. He doesn't have a racial problem with me, so I don't find it necessary to have a racial problem with him." I didn't tell Dave the whole truth. I have respect for this man. Yes, he has bigoted tendencies - he's a white man from the backwoods of Texas. I expect that. What strikes me about him is he's taken issue with everything he's learned. Racism is taught - Mom, dad, aunts, uncles, grandma and grandpa, friends and acquaintances. This is the river in which he's attempting to swim upstream. It's uncharacteristic for any such person as he to fight that current. Though he obviously ain't winning the fight, he did lace up and get in the ring. That makes him different. Where he's from different is tantamount to liberalism, in other words mutinous treason. Most people will never know the courage this requires.

Tim's got trouble. Someone was fucking with him in the shower. There's a misunderstanding about a shower head and who's turn it was to use it. He was threatened with physical violence which is exactly what he's working so hard to avoid. Tim can't fight, so he never shows the slightest bit of aggression to anyone. Against my better judgment I ask who it was. It's not my business and prison protocol is to stay out of it, but somebody picking on this man who goes out of his way to avoid confrontation bothers me. Tim tells me it's was Chino, the one remaining Asian in this tank. I shower at the same time as Tim for a while to make sure he doesn't get fucked with. Chino is intelligent and has a good sense of humor. He's familiar with the elevated level of ignorance around these parts so he was able to get out of doing something he didn't want to do assigned to him by the COs. In his best Mexican accent, he tells the CO, "No habla ingles." Fooled and frustrated, the CO gives up. When I stopped laughing I had to let him know, "That shit was funny as hell, Chino!" "You liked that huh?" Now the situation may dictate I make him an enemy. The next day at jummah Belial says Tim told him his troubles. He asked me if I knew the dude and to look out for him, "Don't trip akhi. Already on it." This is why I didn't want to get too involved. I don't want to have to look out for someone else. It's not a big deal - yet. I've had no further trouble from Chino, but it could've just as easily been enough to start a riot.

Rahim, Khan and Mustafa approach my bunk to ask me if I've heard of Tim's problem, "Yeah man, I've been watching." Tim overhears and is astonished and perplexed, "You guys would do that for me?" Overcome with emotion he bursts into tears. He tries and fails to contain himself, "Ah Jesus guys don't know how to thank you." Khan replies, "No thanks necessary. It's the right thing to do." Now he's really blubberin' and blowin' snot. "I, I, uh, don't know what to say." Rahim says, "Don't say nothin' man. It's all good. You don't bother nobody, so nobody should bother you." "I, I, would've never

thought, I mean no one's ever stood up for me like this."
Mustafa says, "Yeah, well don't worry about it. As long as
you're in the right, we got your back." From time to time I
think about the more diminutive and docile people in this
world who end up in places like prison. Being picked on and
taken advantage of will turn anyone into prey. When people
are always fuckin' with you, you stay livin' in fear of dark
people and dark places. Every day this poor man hopes he
doesn't have anything anybody else might want. Not even a
shower stall.

I got in a little trouble. Because of the lockdown they
bypassed our tank's turn to go to store and I've gone through
damn near all my loot. Now they skipped my turn and expect
me to do without. As I left the kitchen, I noticed the line in
front of the store. I decide to smuggle my store bags in my
pants on the way to shop class. On the way back, I tip toe my
way into the store line. As big as I am, I shouldn't be trying to
sneak anywhere. I'm almost getting away with it. Everything is
regulated, so I'm forced to show my prison ID. When I show
them my ID they'll know I'm not supposed to be in line, but I
gotta shoot my shot. I talk my way past the guard at the
window. I gave him a sob story about not having the
opportunity to go because of the lockdown. It's the truth but to
procure the necessary sympathy, I had to get my Academy
Award on. I get all the way back to the tank and wouldn't you
know it, I run into a stickler. I have to fuss and fight with this
jack off and his supervisor for half an hour. I get to keep my
store, but I got written up; they call it an "out of place case."
It's no big deal. It's like a demerit. The punishment is extra
clean up duty. I won't do it. I'm the only one in this tank who
has any store; I'll just pay a less fortunate inmate to do the
duty for me. I'm not doing any penance.

I'm being moved to a different tank which means I must
get reacquainted and reorganized, again. Not only that, they've
seen fit to take me out of the machine class just when I was
actually starting to learn something. So here I go with my
mattress rolled up on my shoulder and my rations in two net
grocery bags. It's early morning so the sun isn't homicidal, but
it's always hot and sticky.

This tank is damn near all white boys – the first time I've

seen this. No wonder, it's the administrative tank. These inmates work in one of the offices doing paper work or in maintenance. The white boys get these jobs. "Rafeeq! Thought I was alone in this Clorox factory." "Naw man, but it is kinda bright in here ain't it? Me and Jay were the only brothas until now." "I got a couple of eses and they're cool." "This is a quiet tank." "We like it like that." "So do I." "You play chess Akee?" "You damn Skippy." "Cool, lost my last opponent two days ago. I play Jay from time to time, but he ain't no fun. He beats me every time." "Oh' you think I'm an easy way huh?" "I hope not. I would like to get beat in a different way."

I'm in a bunk in the back next to the exhaust fans. I might wake up in the morning without all the condensation. This tank is 10 degrees cooler because there's no chain link cage in the middle of the tank so there's less steel radiating heat. The administration has no problem running the fans for the white boys in here.

My thoughts go to Tim and how much better he would fair in a tank such as this; not out of danger by any means, but there's opportunity to keep out of danger. Over a game of chess, Rafeeq and I get down to business. I need to know who does what and how. As he's breaking it down, it occurs to me the primary commodity traded on this exchange is information. These guys have access to the word. This and every prison puts forth a concerted effort to keep the inmates in the dark. They call it a security measure, but prison administrators are too greedy to pay for security. They can't see paying people to shuffle their paperwork when there's a steady pool of slave labor. It cuts too deep into the skim. That's money they could be stealing. They tell the public they're saving the tax payer's money – the first clue the tax payers are being robbed blind. These inmates are the muted witnesses to the systematic plunder. What the paper shufflers don't see, the maintenance workers overhear. They're always crawling under a desk or following a wire in the ceiling which is one of the reasons why the lockdowns are never a secret. As I'm calculating all the possible profitable ramifications, Rafeeq sneaks a knight past my bishop and lucks up on a check mate. But I couldn't let that slide. In the rematch, I smash him in quick 8 moves.

I'm making a spread to keep Rafeeq from killing' my salsa. "Damn Akee, this is good. Better than anything I've had in the world. How you make this?" "One part skill, two parts conniving." "You gonna have to hook me up with the recipe." "Ain't got no recipe. Just anything I can get my hands on." As I'm mulling over the peculiarity of this conversation, a gang fight breaks out. A white boy rumble. 8 or 9 cowboys and they're going at it. Looks like the bar fight in the movie "Shane." Behind bars and I'm enjoying an evening out. Dinner and a show. Couple of them are bleeders, but they got heart. Damn, in come the COs, "I thought you said this is a quiet tank?" "It usually is. They've been dancing' around that fight for two weeks. The one who got his nose broke needed it broke. Almost did it myself." First thing in the morning we get replacements. Eight white and one Mexican.

I'm being transferred in the morning; I'm going to a place called Edinburg. I'm told its way down in the toe cheese of Texas - 20 minutes from the Gulf and Mexico. I won't get official word until the morning, but I'm packing and saying my goodbyes. While arraigning my belongings and discarding the inessentials, I can't help but wonder about all the unknowns. Rafeeq, who gathered some reconnaissance info for me says it's a transfer facility and pre-release unit and it's set up just like this one except larger. It's in the desert, just in time for July, but at least it's air conditioned. The preliminary report sounds good.

On the way out, I see Rahim walking back to his tank. We say our goodbyes. I'll miss my new-found friends; they made my stay bearable. I'm off to another great unknown. I'm back on the Blue Bird; hand-cuffed to an inmate I don't know. The first time I got on this bus I was afraid and angry. Now it's a bore and a bother. I don't care if I ever see the Texas country side again.

The rumble on the bus is that were pulling into Huntsville. I'm to spend the weekend at a place called The Walls. This prison has fifty feet high red brick walls that look like they're all about to come tumbling down like Joshua and his boys have been here. There's not a right angle to be found. The old prison rodeo stadium walls are made of red brick. They're sunken and leaning into the sun baked red clay. We pull around back and the view doesn't change. More red brick. More red clay. More incessant red dust. We're looking out the windows for some clue or indication of what's about to happen to us. As the bus comes to a stop, I can see a small chain link cage. The kind one might expect to contain dogs. We get off the bus, off with the cuffs, and in the cage we go. Corralled in a kennel with guards circling and surveying forces a man to have a firm grip on his humanity. The taking of our freedom simply won't suffice. They must have our humanity as well. Looking in the faces of my comrades in chains, I wonder if I'm the only one who's so adversely affected by this. It's improper prison protocol to allow such emotions to show. This is a pit stop and I don't know how long we'll be here.

We're being marched into the main building when something catches my eye. It's a wooden plaque carved by inmates that hangs over the entry way. "Est. 1849" which means it was most likely built by slaves. Below the sign there's an iron cross. The same one Hitler wore around his neck. To be fair the iron cross has its origins in the Kingdom of Prussia. Something tells me these Texans are not identifying themselves with Prussia. I doubt any of these real Americans have ever even heard of Prussia. This prison is six stories high with four tiers of cells and a sky light ceiling infested with nesting pigeons. It looks like this used to be the gymnasium and it's clear it hasn't been used for that purpose in a while. There are 10 portable chain link cages evenly distributed throughout. After that extended bus ride we're draggin' ass tired. Now that there's conniving to be done, the vigor has returned. I've given my place in line to three different cons. They've got contraband hidden; we've all figured out which guards are derelict in their duties and luckily for me I've nothing to hide. It's a good idea to know which guards to stay away from. Plus, I prefer not to have this little bit of personal property finger fucked by an overzealous CO. Not too long ago pills we're at the bottom of a full peanut butter jar. Now toothpaste, deodorant, hair pomade, even mayonnaise and jelly jars are all violated in the most disgusting manner. For all their efforts the results are meager at best. Out of the 3 I helped, 2 came through unscathed. The other had minor casualties, but acceptable losses.

Now, this is prison!

Everything you've ever seen on screen or heard on the street manifested right before my eyes. They walk us in on the ground floor. 100 yards of 5 feet wide dilapidated two man cells along one wall down the entire length of this dank and dismal corridor. There's steel staircases at both ends, 4 tiers high. The opposite wall is made of windows, protected by a rust ridden chain link barrier. It overlooks the dungeon from where we've just come. This place looks feels, smells and sounds every bit of 150 years old. In each cell there's a single bald bulb for lighting. For some unknown reason the illumination does not extend beyond the bars which gives each cell a black hole effect. The gravitational forces of anguish and despair are so strong not even light escapes.

It's the 4th of July and hotter than the crack of Satan's ass. My cell is on the top tier. It's a hell of a view of hell down below. We're told to stand in front of our assigned cells until they open the bars. I got a cell to myself. The cell doors are controlled by a manual hand crank located at the end of the tier. The guards yell, "Doors rollin'!" and the sound of 50 chain driven iron gates simultaneously slam open. The bars make the same noise as they close except for the echoing reverb of the heavy iron latches clanking as the locks catch. These confines remind me of an old gas station bathroom. Is it me or is a conjoined sink and toilet just wrong? I set my bags against the wall, throw my bed roll up on the bunk, unroll the mattress pad and spread out the sheets.

The heat in this cell is not only alive but sentient. So much so, the store sells fans. I have no fan and no inmate will sell his fan either. I won't be here long enough to go to store, but I'm not without recourse. Khan told a story about this heat. In that story was a remedy. Strip down to nothing. Strip the sheets off the bed roll. Wet them all in the sink. Put the sheets back on the mattress pad. Put the wet underwear back on your ass. Lay down and be still. Be prepared to repeat in a few hours, as the water will return to room temp rather quickly.

As I lay here unmoving, I hope to catch a piece of a nonexistent breeze blowing across the bars. The walls in this cell are covered in varieties of graffiti including pen, pencil, marker, scratched, scraped and carved. There's profane,

155

pornographic, gossip, gang related, racial, religious, and plain bullshit. One specific epithet scraped into several layers of battleship gray paint is a full date which happens to be my birthday. Of all the prisons in Texas, all the cells in this particular prison, this can't be a coincidental accident. What are the statistical probabilities? What else could it be? Why would any of these guards take the time? I'm not of any consequence. Besides, the engraving is not new. There are overlapping inscriptions obviously put thereafter. This is super natural. I don't know what to make of this. I don't even know if there's anything to be made of this. The sight of my full birth date scratched on this prison cell wall like a damn welcome mat is detrimental to my psychological well-being.

We're on our way down to the chow hall. I figured they would bring the food around to us. Glad they didn't. I'm looking forward to getting out of this cell. It's only a few hours, but I can feel the onset of sensory deprivation. I want to walk more than three steps and see something other than gray bars. There are 400 convicts on the move. The traffic and trading are at a fever pitch. Contraband is flying in every direction. Times like this is when you broker your best deals and cut out the middle man.

To get to the chow hall, we walk outside and make our way through a courtyard. If it weren't for all the mold and moss, the masonry work would be admirable. The courtyard almost has the look of an ivy league campus. I've been here a few hours and I have a heightened appreciation for the little things. I can't imagine what 30 or 40 years does to a man. I'm grateful my stay here will only last the weekend. The chow hall is surprisingly modern and free of flies. Here they don't have a problem with a heaping spoonful of food which means I may not have to supplement my caloric intake tonight. Our Independence Day dinner includes smoked brisket and yellow meat watermelon. The irony of celebrating independence in prison doesn't escape me.

It's late and I'm disorientated. The only way I know night has fallen is due to the slight drop in temperature. By myself, here in this dark cell, it's as if time doesn't exist, let alone move. Time is all that exists. I've never heard such an eerie silence. Any noise at all, like the slow drip in the sink, has a hollow, baritone and reverberating acoustical effect. The boot heals of the COs sound like they're right outside the cell even when they're at the other end of the tier. The occasional flush of a toilet is strangely comforting.

When I first arrived, I noticed all the cons laying in their bunks with their heads at the bars. To me this appeared to be a safety violation. Anyone walking by could seriously fuck you up in any number of ways. From boiling water, to a boot, to a razor blade. One of the dudes in the cell on the other side is living a nightmare. The parole board has psychologically tortured this man. They told him he was going home. They gave him a release date and shipped him out. He got to the Walls after being dragged half way across the state of Texas. He's been here 4 days waiting to walk out the front gates. He got word the parole board made a mistake. After all this he's being sent back to from whence he came. His celly is telling him this type of shit happens more than one might think. He wrote his loved ones and made arrangements. He promised his girl he was going blow her back out, too. He has welcome home parties and people coming to pick him up and he most likely got rid of all his food and belongings. Now they're telling him he's going back.

After breakfast, we head to the showers. For this we must go outside, across the quad to a building adjacent to the chow hall in underwear and shower shoes with soap and shampoo in hand. This must be a bitch in winter. There are 200 men waiting to use 50 showers. I don't know if I'll ever get used to public nudity. This has been the longest weekend in the history of weekends.

We're back on the Blue Bird bus and Texas back roads. We still have a ways to go. Driving across Texas is no quick excursion. When I was a child, my family drove us from Dallas to San Francisco. One of the things that still sticks out in my mind about that trip is it took longer to drive from Dallas to El Paso than it took to drive from El Paso to California, so it comes as no surprise to find out we'll make one more overnight stop before reaching our final destination.

The mile marker said "San Antonio 45 miles" which brings to mind pleasant memories of my childhood years spent in the city of the Alamo and memories of swimming with the cottonmouths in Kelly Creek. The first time I ever saw a snakes' fangs was on the surface of that creek and they were swimming in my direction. I had one of those big, slow, southern white boys everybody called "Bubba" for a friend. Bubba liked the woods because the woods never called him stupid. In the woods, he wasn't stupid. He knew every bug and leaf, and every animal by its tracks. Every man can remember the joys of being a boy and building a fort in the woods. My first fort was a wrecked C-130 deep in the back of Kelly Woods. Bubba showed me. No wings or tail, just cockpit and fuselage being consumed by what seemed to me at the time to be carnivorous foliage. It was used for training military dogs. This is where a young boy hides all those things a mother doesn't want him to have. I kept my dirty magazines, pocket knife and slingshot in the compartment for the landing gear. I hung my hammock over the pilot and co-pilot's chairs. Bubba, over the engineer. I spent countless hours imagining what all those gauges, dials, buttons, knobs, and switches did. I remember being proud that not only did my father know exactly what they did but could fix them as well. I replayed the drunken Vietnam war stories I'd overheard him and his squadron buddies tell when I was supposed to be asleep. Bubba's dad worked in supply. He had no such stories. Some of my father's stories were too outlandish for Hollywood, but they weren't for two rusty butt, dirty faced little boys playing war in the woods. What kid doesn't think his father is Superman? Here I thought I had proof.

They call this prison Darrington. It's also known as Chocolate City. It's 90% black, both inmates and employees. This place is nowhere near as old as the Walls but it's filthy. There are less security measures. No cages, no strip searches. We go straight into a day room. I can already tell this place is wide open despite all the bars and locks. There are three tiers; I'm on the 2nd tier. This time I'm alone. My celly is a young brotha who's polite, courteous and he's settled in. He's a bit of a neat freak and he has a fan and a radio! Not only that, he has books. We don't say much. I just point at one of his books and he hands it to me. Before I can get up in this bunk, a trustee walks up to the cell door and asks, "What you need?" "What you got?" "Tobacco, weed, rock, blow, jack mag." "Nah man,

I'm cool." "A'ight den, let me know." Cool." The fan is on high, the radio is on an blues station and I'm stretched out on this bunk with book in hand. What a difference a few amenities make. This book is a good one. Iceberg Slim is the author, an ex pimp turned writer. I don't want to get too far into this book though. I won't be able to finish it in two days. It's doing the trick though.

It's dinner time which is served to us in our cells. Trays of food are slid through a gap located under the bars. The roaches know it's dinner time as well. They're marching out like the Japanese out of the caves of Iwo. My celly tells me they employ Kamikaze tactics. "Look out Celli. The roaches crawl along the ceiling and drop into your food." "You bullshitin'?" "Nah man, I had to learn the hard way. You got some medicated talcum power?" "Yeah." "Sprinkle some on your belongings. Keeps them from crawlin' all in yo' shit." "What about the rats?" "They don't fuck wit yuh. They eat the trash." Cool." "If you don't mind, I'm gonna put powder all over this muthafucka." "Nah man, shake that shit everywhere. I'duh did it but I'm out." As I lay here, I'm moderately comforted by the belief my celly isn't insane.

Early in the morning and I'm made aware of yet another reason for lying with one's head at the bars of the cell. My celly is on the toilet. If I were to lay the other way my head would be a foot and a half away from the toilet. It's bad enough being eight feet away. The prison bathroom rule is simple - plop, flush, plop, flush. Celly is good with prison etiquette. I'm standing at the bars with my back to him. The most privacy men in our predicament could hope to have. I'm packing up and getting ready to roll out. I'm happy to be leaving this vermin infested disease trap, but I'm not looking forward to getting back on that bus. I'm headed to the southernmost point in Texas. Way down low in more ways than one. I'm told the place we're going is a prerelease unit. Maybe I won't have to get back on this bus anymore. Having to relocate is a bitch. Seems just as I get set up and settled in, get my mojo workin', I'm on the move again. Let us see what this place holds in store.

Pop & his planes

12

Dry south Texas desert heat is like nothing else in this world. The dirt is never-ending - sandy, granulated, dusty, wind-tossed and sun bleached. The grounds at this prison are well-manicured. The insects down here are predatory. Squinting is a requirement. Along with the variety of flies, mosquitoes and locusts, there's a gnat like insect that targets the moisture in our eyes. I swear the state bird should be the mosquito. The yellow rose of Texas is a fucking cactus. Let's not forget the June Bugs - dime sized bronze beetles that don't come out until June and are gone by July. I had to find out the hard way what a chigger was. I took a lovely young lady out for a midnight moon light escapade in a wooded suburban park down by a wooden bridge over the manmade lake. We laid out a big satin comforter and we had our way with each other. We woke up the next morning and found out we weren't the only ones. The little bastards had burrowed into our skin in the most unfortunate and inconvenient of places. Now I'm down here in a prison dug right out of the middle of the insect's natural habitat. I'm told besides the snakes, scorpions and stink bugs, I must be wary of the Brown Recluse, an infamous spider of ill repute that, with one bite, leaves ballooned limbs and golf ball size open, festering wounds. Another reason to hate Texas.

This place is more spread out. The COs have fifty of us standing around in the heat swatting gnats. We're waiting to go through another intake interview. There are more Mexicans in uniform down here than there were with Santa Anna outside the Alamo. I wonder how much collusion goes on around here. At first sight, the COs are far more spit 'n' polish than the last. None of it fools me. An honest prison official is like an honest politician, as rare as raw meat.

I'm getting real tired of these intake interviews. I have to deal with the same insulting questions and same befuddled look on the interviewer's face. Now I have to listen to her tell me how I don't belong here. "That's the same thing I told the judge and jury. We had a slight difference of opinion. I got a question for you ma'am. Why don't they get the answers to these questions from my file? This is the third time I've had to endure this inquisition. A bit redundant, don't you think?" She replies, "Have you seen parole yet?" "No, why?" "This is a prerelease unit. Maybe it'll be the last time you've gotta go through this." "One can hope." She's the first person to mention parole to me which puts me in a better mood.

I was moved to another tank and I watched my mood turn from positive to realistic. I'm not sure if I'm experiencing depression, but this is more than melancholy. At least the A/C works well in this prison. The general disposition in here is as cool as the air coming out of the vents. Most of these guys are short timers which could be a contributing factor. I have a top bunk in the middle of the room and an old cantankerous crook for a bunkmate beneath me. Usually I'd make an effort to get along with him. I like cantankerous old men, but right now I don't give a fuck.

I discovered a book on the great Chiricahua and Cochise, Geronimo's chief. I haven't put the book down which has caused some of my cellmates to think I'm a bit weird. Because of this, they leave me alone which is fine by me. I'm supposed to be working in the kitchen, but I haven't been called for duty yet. I've been stewing in my own mirthless misery for a week and a new inmate finally snaps me out of it. His right leg is cut off at the hip and 3rd degree burns cover 70% of the remainder of his body. I listened as this man answered inmate questions. He's an ex-Air Force man. He was involved in a jet crash at the end of the flight line. As the F-16 hit the ground, it exploded. One of its wings spewed inflamed jet fuel which severed and cauterized his leg and simultaneously set him ablaze. I don't know what this man is convicted of, but in my opinion this man has prepaid his debt to society in spades. Here I sit, hostile at the entire civilized world for all of its hyperactive hypocrisy and blatant bullshit, and I have no right to complain. This man was hacked to pieces and burned alive in the service of his country, yet Texas has a place for him in prison right next to me. I'm told there are prisons in Texas built specifically for the aged, infirmed and physically handicapped. As I watch this man apply epidermal medication and fine tune the fit of his false appendage, I thought I got a raw deal. I thought I had a reason to hate. This maimed and disfigured man has a light-hearted smile on his face and not one harsh word on his lips. You'd be hard pressed to find a single person who doesn't have a reason to hate. Granted, some more justifiable than others. The choice to hate is self-defeating. Not just the hypertension, stress and ulcers, but the philosophy of hate itself is parasitic in nature.

It's my first day on the job. I'm on the breakfast shift; up at 2 am so serving can begin by 3:30. I watch and learn the ropes. They're the same as the last joint. I'm studying the plundering protocol and procedures. This kitchen is run by independent contractors who are more like bottom line watchers. They're tight and stingy with the portions, but the good thing is the food isn't prison grown or raised. There are less COs around and old ladies similar to high school lunch ladies supervise us. I can't believe my eyes. They have Turkey sausage links, real milk in a carton and fresh fruit. What will they think of next? I'm told the work crew can eat all it wants which may seem generous on their part, but there's only so much of this flavorless fodder any of us can force down. We finish at 5 am after preparing and serving food to 3,000 inmates. Not bad, but these early morning hours will fuck up the rest of my day. I eat my fill so I can sleep through lunch which is 6 hours away. When I wake up, I'll have pancake wraps stuffed with turkey sausages and dripping with syrup. I got my stash spot worked out and I managed to get my hands on a few small trash bags out of the office. I'll cut off two corners of the bags and tie off syrup within. Then I'll prepare my breakfast burritos, wrap them tight in plastic and hide them in the steam table. Just in case they're on to that, I'll have an alternate stash on top of the 7 foot warming cabinets. After the strip search, I'll bootleg them back to the tank.

It's Friday and I've decided to see what my Muslim brothers are up to. When they call Muslim services, I hear the sounds of understanding from my cellmates, "Oh, shoulduh known. I knew that nigga was different." They couldn't figure out why I don't do what they do or why I keep to myself. Being a Muslim to them explains all that. It couldn't possibly be that form of passing time for me holds no entertainment value. That was fun when I was a teenager. The same old stories about who shot John, how much pussy you had and how much dope you sold or smoked doesn't cut it anymore, so I take myself to Masjid. For the second time, I'm pleasantly surprised. I'm welcomed with smiles and open arms. The Imam is a Colombian brotha, Akeem. His second in command is a brotha from the 5th ward in Houston, Akbar. Both men are knowledgeable and fluent in Arabic, something I've been petrified to even attempt to learn. I have enough trouble with my native alphabet. There's a Mexican Muslim here who doesn't speak any English which means I will flex my 30 word Spanish vocabulary.

I want to know more about Akeem, so I pull him aside after the service. I want to know how he ended up in America and Texas. Akeem tells me how he always wanted to come to America because of what he saw of African Americans on TV. He says the black people in Columbia are starved for anything black. Magazines, TV shows and movies with people that look like them are unheard of. "Man, I remember when New Jack City came on TV. It was an event. We all crowded around the TV in total silence. We could not believe what we were seeing. When I got to New York, I spoke no English. As I was learning a brotha told me I wasn't a real brotha. Man that hurt. I could not believe it. I tried so hard." "Well, you know he didn't know what he was talkin' about? His life experience has given him an extremely narrow view of what being black is." "Yeah, I know that now, but at that time I felt bad." As he's telling me this, I feel bad. It's one more reason to stoke the flames of my contempt under the boiling pot of ignorance. For the rest of our allotted time in the Masjid, I ask him questions about his homeland. He's all too happy to regale me with tails of his roots. I eat it up.

Akeem doesn't disappoint. I ask, "Have you ever been to the west coast?" "No, why?" "You've got to go. I want you to see all of America is not small minded. Out there, your being Colombian will be a commodity, not a liability." "What do you mean?" "Down here, diversity is an issue mainly because there isn't any. One religion, one perverted way of speaking the English language, one political party – that's it. They like it like that. Americans don't deal with change well at all especially change for the better. New York is diverse but they segregate themselves. Jew's live here, Italians over there, blacks up there, Puerto Ricans live next to them. Even the Asians separate themselves from each other. Not in Cali. Well, not on the coast. Perspectives seem to narrow incrementally as you travel inland. Why did you leave?" "I made a mistake. One I hope to rectify as soon as possible. You goin' home when you get out?" "No, I plan to see the world." "See that's what I mean. Most of the people down here rarely leave the county. Just talking to such a person is constricting, confining. It's why I asked you about Columbia. Speaking of which, tell me some more."

We have a new inmate in our tank, a Muslim from the Middle East. I've noticed and am not surprised he hangs with the Mexicans. I'm ashamed to admit it but they're the only ethnic group down here that would accept him out right, so I approach him and give him the greeting, As-salamu alaykum. Surprised, he reciprocates. His name is Jaleel and he's from Afghanistan. I begin asking him questions about the war much I like I did with my last cellmate who hailed from the same part of the world. He shares with me the horrors of war up close and personal, how his family members were part of the rebel freedom fighters, the Mujahedeen. He provides a firsthand report on how the U.S. runs its covert operations which is a stark contrast to what's being reported on CNN.

Right now the news is talking officials being kidnapped in Iraq. Jaleel tells me the seemingly good guys do a little kidnapping themselves. I heard similar stories from my father about his time fighting in the Vietnam War. The real reasons for wars are not what the troops are fighting and dying for which is the same story throughout the entire human history of armed conflict. This is how the street forms its opinions and points of view. We hear it from the not so innocent bystander who's had his innocence shattered by foreign policy and from the nurse with a big mouth and broken heart while on a weekend pass. We never hear the truth about war from the officials. Officials always have more reasons to lie than to tell the truth. The media and its reporters always have a story to sell. The street always knows what it's not supposed to know, always.

I'm close to finishing the book on Cochise. It's good. I always knew the Apache and the Chiricahua were super bad, but I had no idea to what extent. The Sioux pulled a Hannibal and annihilated Custer's entire command at the Little Big Horn in less the 30 minutes. Some years earlier, those same Sioux tried to take Apache land. It was said one could track the Sioux back to their Great Plains by following the trail of dead Sioux. Life on the Great Plains ain't no joke by any means, but having to survive in the desert for thousands of years made the Apache a motherfucker. Everyone knows how Geronimo and his band of 35 Chiricahua had the entire U.S. Army chasing their tail, repeatedly. He had a homeboy by the name of Victorio. This man won so many battles the Mexicans named him the Victorious One. The man who earned the right to call himself their chief was, as he should be the baddest of them all. He's the only chief to die by natural causes on his own land while at war with the Blue Coats. To this day, that land still holds his bones and bears his name, Cochise County AZ. I've seen these men portrayed in more than a few movies. Some are better than others, most notably Wes Studi's Geronimo. Damn if it still don't urk me no end to find out the book is better.

There's an amazing artist in the tank. I've been watching him work.

Artists are always well represented in prison. A weigh

station for the fringe of society. The creative often times see the world differently than most. It's not so easy for us to except the bullshit of civilization and just assimilate. I noticed this in all those resource classes. The ones the system called stupid, lazy, shiftless and incorrigible most of the time were the most creative with endless talent. My mother worked at a prison in Vacaville. She brought home all kinds of inmate artwork - paintings, drawings, jewelry, figurines and picture frames. The quality and craftsmanship was always second to none. In prison, a man's livelihood and life depends on his reputation. Word of mouth is the only thing that keeps business open. It's what keeps some prisoners alive.

When I saw Chewy with a steady clientele I took notice. He's mean with the pencil lead. A lot of artwork in the graphite medium tends to have a two dimensional appearance giving it a cartoon effect. Not Chewy's. His work has more of a photographic effect. Even the eyes in his portraits follow you.

I have a difficult task to ask of him.

I want him to draw a picture of me when my hair was still hanging on my shoulders. I have a photograph for him to work from, but it's a small. My head is a 1/2" square and I want him to blow it up to 12" x 18". I used to be pretty good with the lead myself, so I know what I'm asking for. It takes me a little while to talk Chewy into it. For him, it's an artistic challenge, but it's also a financial risk. If the portrait doesn't come out right it'll have a negative effect on his advertising budget. Three days after I submit my request he presents me with an impressive likeness.

I'm being moved to a different tank which means I won't be working in the kitchen anymore. I'll have even more time on my hands. I got the lowdown on this tank from one of my Muslim brothers, Shareef. He says it's jumpin' off up in here. Something is always going on. The noise hit me in my face as I walked in. The ambiance is a cross between a football locker room and an unsupervised special education classroom - loud, shit talkin' and trouble makin'. This isn't my scene, but for some reason I dig it. Shareef gave me a royal introduction, partly out of friendship, out of Islamic inclination and because of the two big bags of store I'm carrying.

A couple of inmates stick out right away. Enrique, a Puerto

Rican chivato from Brooklyn, who calls everyone kid or son and OG Leroy from East Oakland. "Aye, Leroy dis nigga from Cali, too." Right away he's asking me questions about home. As I'm putting away my belongings, I notice he's casing my stash, taking inventory of my store. It's wise to keep your eyes on a nigga from the town. It turns out he wants to do business. He works in the laundry and has the hook up on the brand new underwear. I need at least 4 pair. Any more than that gets difficult to conceal from the COs. He tries to sell me what's called "tight whites" - brand new crisp, white prison issue pants and shirts. A big seller. Prisoners starch clothing with either watered down powdered milk or sugar water. They press clothing using the flat on the steel bunk and under the mattress pad. After a day or two, shirts and pants will stand up by themselves. Most inmates keep them for visitations. They want their people to see them looking good. For me this is an impossibility. Ain't no lookin' good in prison. "You can keep them tight whites homes, just bring me the drawls." We make the deal for a couple of snack cakes and a few Raman soups. I look forward to getting my ass out of these public drawls. Anytime I'm issued a nearly new pair, I don't turn them in for laundry. I wash them in the sink myself.

In this tank there's a gay man who makes ends meet by doing laundry. He's got clothes hanging all over the bathroom. He's a real pro. He has contraband bleach and detergent, even fabric softener and starch. He works cheap, too. I'm not comfortable with the idea of him washing my clothes. I don't know if he'd derive pleasure from cleaning my drawls. It might sound perverse and judgmental, but that's the type of place this is.

Shareef and Enrique are arguing about something and want my two cents. This is sort of an indoctrination ceremony. I decline because I have no interest in active participation. I prefer the role of a voyeuristic commentator. It affords me a false sense of detachment which is one of the ways I keep from feeling like a convict. For me this is a temporary state of being. When it's over, I intend to leave it behind. If I ain't careful, being a convict can very easily become a permanent condition. Next thing I know I'll be wanting some tight whites. The long days and empty nights stretch out like a desolate desert road extending to the horizon. The closer I get to it, the further I have to go. My cohorts and I are talking about how much time we've done and how much time we have yet to do. 10, 15, 20 years are being tossed around like a Frisbee. I'm almost ashamed to mention my measly little 4 years, "Oh shit nigga, you just visitin'." I realize, in the grand scope of the relative context, I have little to complain about.

I wasted many years as a young man though at the time I didn't see it that way. I was busy learning the fine arts of the ill reputed trades and having fun doing so. Now, gray hairs are beginning to sprout and I hear the tick-tock of the clock. I spent 4 years trapped in Texas on bail, pending appeal. I'll do another two in here. If I'm lucky, two more tethered to the parole board. 8 years of my oh so precious prime is no longer mine to waste, but I feel it already is and in the most injurious and insidious manner conceivable. I could've avoided all this by simply pleading guilty. I watched people charged with similar crimes and far worse criminal records walk out of that court house with 10 years probation. I could've had probation transferred to my beloved California, far away from the Loan Star, but I had to fight no matter how futile.

Word is a lockdown is immanent sometime next week which means it's time to stock up - library tonight and store tomorrow. I need as many distractions to keep my eyes off these four walls and my mind off the ever more distant horizon. I think I'll pick fiction this time. I could use a little make believe. I'm grateful this lockdown will be air conditioned. I wonder how many prisoners had to die of heat stroke before they put in the swamp coolers. However many, I'm grateful to them.

It's recreation time, but I don't go out. I see no need to exchange one cage for another. At least this cage has A/C. When I go to chow or the Masjid, I keep my eyes squinted. The first time one of those kamikaze gnats targets your retina, you'll never forget it. You see them a split second before impact. Good luck flushing them little bastards. Outside, no thanks. Maybe this lockdown won't be that bad. Maybe the fiction will be good enough to grant me a furlough.

This lockdown has been relatively painless aside from the public sphincter inspection. The first few strip searches were severely dehumanizing. I've watched the COs perform their duty and I'm beginning to feel a little sorry for them. It's clear they take no pleasure in the strip searches. I've thought about the psychological impact such a vocation must have on my tormentors. They chose to be locked up in prison for 8 to 10 hours a day only to deal with some of the most fiendishly vial villains all while being paid slightly more than the minimum wage. Oh, and by the way, from time to time it will be necessary for you to personally examine 2,000 assholes. The uneducated and ignorant from small Texas towns don't have many employment options, so this is as good as it gets. Ain't life a bitch!

"Look man, I ain't got shit to say to you while you shittin'." Enrique thinks it's no big deal and why would he. 24 hours every day for years in close quarters brings about a certain amount of casual familiarity. I have no choice in the matter, but I can chose not to talk to a man while he's squattin' and squeezin'. Enrique doesn't want anything from me. He just wants to shoot the shit. We talk mostly about home sickness. The only thing we have in common is neither of us is from down here. Most people down here don't know anything else but down here. Brooklyn might as well be on the far side of the moon. I asked him how he ended up in the south. Enrique followed his family down here attempting to do what he used to do on the east coast. He was snitched on and landed in here. Akeem and Akbar asked me to speak at the next Jummah because the rest of the brothers should hear some what I have to say, "I don't know, Akeem. Some of the brothers ain't ready for some of the things I have to say." "Such as?" "Well, first and foremost, my complete and unyielding contempt for ignorance. Akbar chimes in, "Wait a minute man, we can't allow you to be beatin' up on the brothas." "See I told you." Akeem says, "Well, what do you mean?" "Akbar knows what I mean. One of the things that drew me to Islam was the incentive to learn and understand. The access to information, fertile ground for spiritual and intellectual expansion is more my style. "I can tell by the depths of y'alls understanding you feel me. So many of the brothers in this Masjid still think like colored folk." Akbar replies, "Yeah that's why you gotta go easy." "That's where you and I differ. I think it'll be good for them to get it right between the eyes. A few will get it and the rest ain't ever gonna get it." We decide I should speak at a taleem which translates to an exchange of information and ideals. The structure and guidelines are less rigid.

I was on a roll once I got started. Akbar didn't waste time with the admonishment, "Aight Malcolm!" I fall out, doubled over in uncontrollable howling laughter. A white collar brother named Malik can't stop laughing either. A few of the brothers are full of accolades and a few mean mugs from the others who took my truth personally. Malik's laughter tells me I hit my mark. Akeem doesn't say much. I didn't expect him to. This is a subject with which he has no firsthand experience. I discussed the black man's self-imposed problems and how the ignorance is fertile soil for all of our woes and how as Muslims, ignorant is the last thing we should be. Shaheed says, "Damn man, that was deep." "Thanks Akee."

Leroy, Enrique and Shaheed have decided to surround me and talk shit. I noticed my Mexican homies dropped off smuggled veggies from the fields and kitchen. They steal enough for me to make salsa for the tank. I chop and dice with a blade extracted from a disposable razor placed in the back of a disposable pen. Leroy and Shaheed want to know what a nigga is doing making salsa for Mexicans, "How in da fuck is you makin' salsa fo' dem Meskin's? Ain't enough you speak that Spanish shit, you cook it too?" Enrique doesn't say much, but he knows if these Tejanos are eating it, it's must be goood. I let them talk shit until I finish. "What, y'all nigga's ain't got shit to say now huh?" "Yeah Akee, it's hot." "It's supposed to be. It's salsa made for Mexicans. If it's too hot, stop eatin'." "Shit Ak', too good fo' dat."

My Mexican homeboys tell me they're having some internal conflicts. I hope they don't interfere with the importing of my veggies. From what I can gather some of them aren't following orders and their slippin'on their duties. They're speaking too fast so I catch every 3rd word or so. Enough to know bloodshed is eminent. The Mexican gang culture is far reaching, ancient and absolute. One's rank is not worn on the clothes but on the skin. Placas say who you are, what you are and where you come from. Get caught with the wrong tatt and they will cut or burn it off. Protocol will be obeyed. If you're Latino, you're expected to know.

I'm in the middle of interviewing a new produce employee when I receive news that's almost too good to be true. A CO tells me I'm to see someone in parole. This is the proverbial light at the end of the tunnel. For the first time in my life, I feel what could be called exultation. They gave me the 6 months I spent in the county and I've been in the pen almost 6 months now. If I had no access to a calendar you couldn't tell me it hadn't been years.

Parole is one lady in a small room with a computer. I'm a little disappointed. I was expecting a panel. I've been a model prisoner, I have no criminal history and the fact they've come to consider me quickly bodes well. I answer her questions as straight forward and honest as I can. We've hit a snag. I knew this question was coming. She asks if I regret what I've done. I know what she wants to hear - remorse and sorrow in my voice – but I can't do it. I know if I don't, all of this could go bad for me. Still, I can't do it. "Well ma'am, I know what I'm supposed to say. Unfortunately for me, I happen to not be guilty. I can't bring myself to tell you I'm sorry for something I didn't do." She doesn't say much for a while, just a low barely audible "I see." She shuffles files and sends me off with a "Thank you Mr. Hennington. We will let you know our decision in a few months." Until then, I'll wonder if my honesty cost me again.

It's Ramadan and Akeem and Akbar have out done themselves. The services were well organized and respected by the prison officials which is no small feat. The COs are pissed off about all the extra provisions that must be made. Last thing they want is more work. They must add two extra meals to be prepared before sunrise and after sunset just for the Muslims. For an entire month they have to supervise the kitchen crew and us while we eat. We're often threatened with, "We better not catch none uh y'all in here at regular chowtime. Ain't gonna have us doin' all this here fer nuthin'." We eat breakfast and dinner separately. I'm enjoying all the camaraderie and special treatment. Spending most of time with my brothas is a welcome change. The Muslim life is a relaxed and peaceful atmosphere which makes counting away the hours with religious discussions and introspection a benefit.

During Ramadan I sleep away the hunger during the

daylight hours by supplementing my caloric intake with midnight feedings. Shaheed and I sit around in the quiet hours stuffing our faces and regaling each other with tails of the free life, laughing and joking while trying to keep quiet. We tell stories of mischievous childhood days long gone. Things we got away with and things we had to take a beating for. A mutual appreciation for the lessons we've learned the hard way.

During this holy month the administrators are allowing us to spend most of the daylight hours in the Masjid. Akeem has open communication with the Muslim community in south Texas and was able to secure a steady stream of books, literature and videos. He even managed to have guest speakers from time to time. Today is such a time. My big brother used to visit several California prisons and speak to the Muslim inmates; I used to admire his sense of community and desire to give back. Still, there's no way you will catch me voluntarily walking into San Quintin. Back then you could've never told me I'd be sent to prison and that was at the height of my criminal activities. At his own expense, he brought more prayer rugs and books. I'm a man of very little faith in my fellow humans, but I'm pleased to shake this man's hand and thank him. For the Eid, the celebration at the end of Ramadan, Akeem pulled beef, chicken, lamb, and a plethora of veggies. We experienced genuine joy and good will in prison. Today we're allowed to spend a few hours virtually unsupervised. Alhamdulillah!

Another Thanksgiving behind bars. This season's penitentiary poultry leaves a lot to be desired. Half white half dark circular ¼" slice of what I hope is processed turkey. The dressing is under cooked and soggy like wet croutons. Times like this make it hard not to think of what my life was. I wonder if my family and friends are thinking of me. I get plenty of letters filled with news from home which are difficult to read. They're getting on with the business of living which is a painful reminder of being left out and left behind.

Still no word from parole. I fear I may have blown my chances of getting out of here early. Now and then my thoughts turn to Siler. I wonder how he's doing. I wonder where the feds sent him. I hope they sent him to one of those white collar fed pens.

He's not constituted for this shit. I think of his little girls. I hope they got out of that hillbilly haven.

There's some commotion in the corridor. A CO fight! What a rare treat and it's a good one. Two guards are going at it. One is well overdue for an ass whipping. He's bloody and being bounced off every wall in the hall. This is real entertainment. Usually when there's a fight, the crowd is loud and unruly. Not this time. Every man in attendance is silent and hoping the fight never ends. New Years is over and I'm on the chain again. I'm going to Mineral Wells. Fortune has smiled. I've heard nice things about this prison. It's like going from the dugout to being on deck. It's a place they send you before they release you. Convicts hope and pray to get sent there. The place is wide open, in more ways than one. Housed in old army barracks, prisoners are allowed to walk free range all over the post. There's free world clothes and pay phones in the hallways. I guess I didn't blow that parole interview after all.

13

No guard towers. No guards with high powered rifles or shotguns. No elaborate and overlapping security procedures. No overbearing COs if the two on the bus are any indication. Mineral Wells has one 8 foot chain link fence. From the front gate this place looks like every military base. We'll be housed in the old barracks. I can see air conditioning units in the windows which is a good sign. We aren't searched. Instead we're handed a blue jump suit. We're told we can have our folks send us some clothes or we can buy them from other inmates. I can't believe we're being instructed to traffic and trade in prison. We're issued sheets, blankets and a bed roll, given our housing assignment and sent on our way. The barracks look like the ones I used to sneak into when I was a teenager.

The cookie cutter military uniformity is how I first learned to get over on the system. My first experience was at 10 years old. I was locked out of my house because I lost my key after school in detention, so I figured a way to break in through the back door. As I was doing this, I noticed my neighbor's house was identical to mine, as are all the houses for miles in any direction. Even the ones that were different, such as the officers' quarters. I knew it wouldn't be too difficult to find my way in, so I did. I was in and out of houses all over the base - at home or on vacation, day or night. It didn't matter. The adrenaline rush, the wonderfully unusual sensations of being inside strange houses excited me. If they were home, even better. When I found a house that was vacant my friends and I had a ball. From spin the bottle to hide and go get it with the neighborhood girls. I learned every system is systematic. Once a weakness is exposed, it can be exploited over and over again. The key is not leaving any tracks or traces. Because of my difficulties with the written word and disdain for academics, I've been finding and exploiting weaknesses in school systems since the age of 5. That's how I came to lose my house key in detention that day.

This prison has a dorm environment. Before I can unpack, the black market merchants are soliciting. There's more to be had than at a corner store. I almost bought a radio, but I know I'll get a better price in a couple of days. All this is done out in the open. There's almost no attempt to conceal. There's no need. I haven't seen a guard for a minute and inmates are coming and going as they please.

"Say man close the door. Keep the noise out in the hallway." All the other barracks are divided into 4 man rooms. In here the walls have been removed. I room with 15 others which is still a far cry from the 65 cellmates in the last joint. Never mind the lockless doors and the relative freedom of mobility. I see I'll have to go out of my way to keep out of trouble here. I'm assigned a bottom bunk for the first time. I do my best to speak a little Spanish to the vato in the next bunk so that I can get the lowdown on this place. The vatos always have the inside on the inside. First question he's got for me is where did I learn to speak Spanish. I tell him I'm from California. The white boy in the bunk above me is overly accommodating. He's jumpy and full of nervous smiles. He's the kind of white boy who isn't comfortable around black people though he's trying his damnedest to hide the fact.

I finish unpacking and b-line it to the pay phone. FUCK! No one's home. I get a hold of my friend in Los Angeles. She's always been there for me, a true and loyal friend. She gives me comforting words of care and concern buried inside her million questions. She's afraid for me despite telling her not to worry. Her voice is soothing, providing me genuine feminine affection, pure and without the compulsion of obligation. Suddenly I understand and am apprehensive of the allure this phone holds. I can't talk to her long. It's getting too painful. We say our goodbyes and hang up. I have no desire to call anyone else.

I decide to do a little reconnaissance, so I go on a self-guided tour of the barracks. I'm not that interested at what I see because of being so tired from a long bus ride. Due to the time constraints, I'll have to limit my in depth investigation to the 2nd floor where I'm assigned. As far as poorly supervised inmates go, the ones on this floor are of a moderate variety. Count time is somewhat of an ordeal here. We're in the middle of a 3rd recount, a byproduct of all the personal liberties they give us. It's difficult to accurately account for each and every one of these free moving inmates and I heard sometimes the count can last for more than an hour. In other prisons count takes 15 to 20 minutes. The grumblings of pronounced impatience can be heard up and down the halls. I consider this a small price to pay for all these new found possibilities of mobility.

It's 7 am and I'm eating breakfast. I'm eating when I choose and while the sun is up no less. Today, I had pancakes and peanut butter, and traded sausage for another milk. It's so nice to eat in peace at my own pace. I can slow down and chew with no CO telling me it's time to go. I don't have to return directly back to my assigned quarters.

When I was a child I'd ride my bike around the perimeter of every base to which my father was stationed. I explored out by the flight line and beyond the restricted areas. Now as I walk this fence I can see what used to be this posts' housing. Quarters for the noncommissioned officers and their families, small, single level homes with a single car port; a modest home for modest living. I took for granted the simple things like not having to worry about poisoned Halloween candy and coming of age and growing to a point where we could leave the base unaccompanied. We'd raise hell with the girls and cause havoc amongst the boys in the outlying towns. When the heat got too hot or the opposition too numerous, we'd head back to the safety of the base. No police or rival could follow us. Knowing we had a safety net made us seem more brazen and brash to the others.

The only visible indication one has to know this is a prison is the barbed wire. From the looks, it could easily be a Y.M.C.A. Five full barracks, three large outdoor weight lifting areas, hand ball courts, horse shoes, even have a couple of rec rooms. From what I'm told, everything in here used to be a lot better like jobs that actually paid the inmates a wage. Inmates were allowed to work outside the gates and to leave for weekend furloughs. All it took was one stupid and sick convict to fuck all that up by raping some girl in town.

I just returned from a meeting with prison officials. They had me in a small room with 4 people whose job it is to tell new inmates what's to be expected. I was advised I'll be expected to clean the bathroom on my floor once a week. This I cannot and will not do. The thought of having to scrub public toilets gives me the willies. Having to use them has pushed me to my limits. Fortunately there's an inmate down the hall who's a bit of a neat freak who likes to clean the bathrooms to keep his lock box full.. He now has one more client.

I copped a radio, but it requires headphones. All the radios in this place do. There's a dude who's making me a speaker out of a plastic soda bottle, a magnet and a coil of wire. It cost me a couple of soups. Prison ingenuity still amazes me. Homeboy has radio parts and scrap electronics strewn all over his bunk area. He makes cigarette lighters out of a couple of 9 volt batteries and speaker wire. Tobacco is not allowed in this institution. Regardless of the fact, cigarettes are smoked openly and traded like currency. MacGyver doesn't smoke, but he's profiting from the rampant addiction to nicotine. Lighters are on back order from now until Judgement Day.

All these freedoms with which I've recently become reacquainted and I still find myself spending most of my time in this bunk. I'm either reading or listening to the radio. There's more freedom to be found in a good book or good song than can be had within this compound. Maybe the cold and rain has a little to do with it. Josh, the nervous little white boy in the bunk above me, is all too happy to lend me any of his literary collection. I got an antenna from Manny in the next bunk so now I can listen to the "Quiet Storm" smooth jazz station out of Dallas. I don't even have to go to chow. The day's menu can be delivered for a nominal shipping and handling fee. Manny has the hook up on a weed delivery, too. But he advises against it - the game is dirty because snitchin' is pandemic.

It's raining and I'm standing in the store line. The lax security restrictions allow for a few things like a full length toothbrush and a full bar of soap, Irish Spring no less. Back in TDCJ inmates would use hot water to mold a handful of state issued slivers of soap into a manageable bar. As soon as I get my rations I return to the barracks and turn my individual heater on high.

On the way back, crossing the bathroom, I see a young ese getting jumped into a gang. Standing spread legged and fist balled in a circle of 6 or so. They lay into him good. I walk on slowly so I hear what I can't see. It sounds painful. From the reaction on the lookout's face, El Chivato has survived his initiation. I never felt the need to count myself amongst the members of a group. To me it's indicative of a lack of intestinal fortitude. Manny says El Chivato had troubles with a brotha. That brotha happens to belong to a gang. Not wanting to be out numbered, he got himself some backup. Otherwise, there's little racial tension brewing around here. "Nah Manny, ain't no racial tension. It's gang tension." "Yeah, but there's no difference in prison." "What you gonna do if it jumps off?" "Ride with my crew." "What you gonna do?" "Roll solo like always." Manny looks at me with doubt in his eyes. He and I both know that isn't probable. If a riot does break out, a side will be chosen for me. I made a couple of casual connections to my Muslim brothers. If it gets real foul, I'll roll with them. My best bet is to keep out of the frivolous battles over ego. And I thought this place was a resort.

It's 1 am and I'm sitting on the toilet. I take the toilet in the far corner since I still have issues with the vulnerability factor. I hoped to finish my business by myself, but an older vato comes in and sits on the first toilet. Rule is plop-flush. Being an old con, he knows exactly what to do. Two seconds later he jumps straight up apparently not soon enough. His ass is dripping sewage, while his pants and underwear at his ankles fill with soggy toilet paper and all manner of human excrement. He looks at me with a horrified and disgusted expression. All I can do is reciprocate. He steps out of his clothes and throws them in the trash. I finish my business and stand up before flushing. As I leave the bathroom the thought hits me - his torment is not at an end. The showers are locked until 6 am. From what little I know of the man, he's a good old dude which begs the question, why do shitty things happen to good people? If I were him, I'd wash my ass in a sink, but I don't think I could get it clean enough.

Things are going pretty well. I got an extension cord plugged into the wire and still managing to stay under the radar. I come and go almost as I please. Anything I may need I have delivered. I'm so close to getting out, so the last thing I need is some accidental stupidity to spontaneously combust.

Outside the chow hall is a two-room building designated for disciplinary segregation. It's stays full. Most of these inmates have been expelled. A bus leaves here at least twice a week, taking them back to TDCJ. I'm no fool. Mo'e freedom is always mo'e better. To that end, I'm keeping a low profile. The desire to get out is a weakness that's often times turns into a liability.

Coming back from the Rec Room, I'm told to go see parole. "Where's parole?" "On the far end of the grounds just south of the main gate." I'm walking and trying to be cool. I have a bizarre mix of anticipation and anguish. l feel like I'm walking in buckets of water. A slight incline feels like Mt. Kilimanjaro.

Breathe man breathe.

I'm sweating and can't focus, visually or mentally. I don't know why I'm so worried. I don't have a criminal record. I've been a model prisoner. The Board doesn't have a justifiable reason to deny my parole, but then again justice didn't stop them from convicting me in the first place. "Have a seat Mr. Hennington. How are you? Glad to hear it. Well sir, I have some good news for you. Your parole has been granted. Yes that's correct. There is however a provision. You must complete a 6 month rehabilitation program. You are to be transferred back into TDCJ to complete this new program. Yes, unfortunately you do have to go back. But you have been granted parole. Isn't that good news?" "It's very good news sir, but it's tainted. I haven't been here two weeks and you're telling me I have to go back for a prison rehabilitation program. All that means to me is more constraints and constrictions, more loss of freedom." "Maybe, but at least you're getting out. " "Yeah, maybe."

I can't believe they're sending me back into a fucking Safe P. Program! A place called Hamilton for more of that "for your own good" bullshit where prison officials play psychologists with sad and pathetic attempts at reprogramming the mentality of inmates. It's an intensive overdose of structure and discipline. We're up at 6 am, make our bed to their specifications and then the programming begins. They make us sit around and listen to inmates chronicle their woes while they lie to themselves about how they ain't gonna do it no mo'e. I'm told one of the mandates of the program is forced snitching. A prison full of inmates all telling on each other. The Warden call this therapeutic. I will not be programmed. I will not allow any part time prison shrink access to my brain. The last thing I need are well meaning white folks from Texas fumbling around in my subconscious. I leave the day after tomorrow.

I'm back from store. I'm stocking up on all the things that can't be bought in TDCJ. If COs don't confiscate them, I can name my price. I'm trying to remember the security measures I'll have to circumvent, again. The thought is depressing. Knowing all of my new freedom will soon be forcibly denied me, again. I keep telling myself it's only for 6 months, a small comfort considering that's longer than I've spent in any of the other prisons. The time spent at each felt like years. Now, I have get my mind around the concepts of indoctrination.

I made the long bus ride back to the Walls. The last time I was in this cage I remember thinking that was the last time I'd ever be locked in a cage. I thought I was done with hillbillies fondling and finger fucking all my belongings. I never thought I'd see tight whites again.

So I thought.

14

We made it to Hamilton and more chain link, razor and barbed wire. The sun is high and the steel is glistening. Guards are barking orders for us to hurry up as if it's our fault they have yet to remove the cuffs. I've been cuffed to the same young Mexican dude since we left Mineral Wells. Right now he's being chastised for talking shit to the COs. I wouldn't condone such behavior, but at this moment I'm inclined to agree. I'm tired and pissed off, and I have no patience for COs and their bullshit. Against my better judgment I add my two cents, " If you could get your guards to do their job, we'd have no need for this conversation." All I get for my lip is a dirty look.

I'm told to wait in line to see the man in another building. A few minutes ago a white man with his number one "boy" walked into the building. His head bowed, two steps behind and repeating in quick succession, "Yesser Yesser." As they walk by, inmates are heard whispering "Warden, Warden." Inmates one at a time endure yet another intake process. This is my 5th, but the first time I've seen a warden show any interest in personally interviewing each new inmate. He's hands on with severe control issues. He believes in structure and discipline all the way.

The sun is relentless and my mood is getting darker. Something tells me this interview won't end well, "Mr. Hennington?" "Yes." "Yes sir?" "Oh yeah right, yes sir." "Have you ever been to Safe P. before?" "No." "No sir?" "Yeah, no sir." Warden's boy chimes in, "Don't I know you?" "No." "No sir?" "Yeah, no sir." "Yeah, I know you." "No you don't!" This house nigga is taken aback with my abrupt and direct tone. "You're arrogant. I don't thank you have what it takes to make it through my program. Where are you from?" "California." "Oh, well, that explains it." "That's right, eyes a free nigga." The silence is deafening. The Warden and his boy don't know what to make of me. The Warden's poker face cracked with a slight grin. "You definitely ain't gonna make it through my program. Well, Mr. Hennington, what do you do?" "I fix computers" "Is that right? Maybe we can find you a position in maintenance. Do you thank you can handle that?" "No doubt."

I'm uneasy about the job in maintenance. I've never seen a black maintenance worker. This makes me think the warden wants to keep an eye on me. That's all I need, a curious and inquisitive overseer. It could be argued a black inmate willfully asserting and defiantly declaring his freedom to a white southern warden and his chief CO is not necessarily a good idea. I've gone out of my way not to make an impression, positive or otherwise. I'm tired, irritated and dealing with hostility issues. Getting tag teamed by a totalitarian and his primary tyrant breached the limits of my forbearance. The warden is the dirtiest crook in the clank. This particular one has finagled a brand new prison with an opportunity to implement his rehab program. He has an aptitude for collusion and corruption just like most men in power.

Young Hector wants to know what the man said, "Same shit. Different prison." "Yeah, but I ain't never talked to a warden before." "Shit, me neither. What the fuck I got to say to a warden? Not a muthafuckin' thang. This dude is retentive." "What?" "A tight ass. He wants us to "sir" him all the goddamn time regardless if you mean it or not. He asked a couple yes/no questions and wanted to know if I'd ever been to Safe P. before. And he wanted to know what I did on the outside. He gave me a job in maintenance." Maintenance?!" "Yeah, that's what I said." "Chingale vato, how you swing that?" "No sey, that's what the man told me."

The tank I'm in is deceptively quiet. No noise but no doubt shit is happening. Nobody arguing in front of the TV or yelling across the tank. The crap games are quiet here, too. It's chowtime and I'm in line attempting to ascertain which of these kitchen workers will assist me in procuring fresh produce. I got my hands on dried herbs, spices, salt, pepper, onion, tomato, jalapenos, habaneras, and a clove of garlic. I'm making tamales and Spanish rice using V8 Juice. The vato in the next bunk is showing considerable interest in my aptitude for Mexican cuisine.

All of us are waiting on a spot into the rehab program on the other side of the unit. I check in with the Muslims and attend Jummah on Friday. The CO outside the mosque has me entranced. I can't stop looking at her. She's a beautiful caramel colored sista who looks exactly like a young Billie Holiday. The uniform is no turn on and we're in prison. Still, I can't take my eyes off of her. I'm enjoying her patting me down. I tried to purge myself of my feelings to no avail. The prayer has been called. Allah please forgive me. I'm taking a low key approach with my fellow Muslims. I don't want personal involvements to impede my parole. The atmosphere is relaxed and I don't sense the presence of any hot heads. Everyone here is a short timer which means stupidity will be at a minimum around here.

I'm not the only one who noticed the little Billie Holiday CO, "Say bruh, you see dat CO on the way in?" "Man, what you know 'bout?" "Oh man, pretty little thang ain't she?" "Sho'e is easy on the eye." "I cain't even look at her, hurts too much." "Know what you mean, but I cain't help it." Some of these men haven't had any female contact in 15 to 20 years. We walk past her in complete silence. Some inmates were gawking, some shaking their heads and some looking away. I was trying to envision her without that uniform.

Almost two weeks now and no word on that maintenance job, and another day of idol emptiness. More of the same nothing. I'm thinking about how much better it would've been if they'd left me back at Mineral Wells. Out of all the drug addicted horror stories in the prison system, I get chosen for a rehab program. Maybe it had to do with me declaring my innocence to that parole lady. I should've told her what she wanted to hear - a blubbering sob story full of remorse. Why do I give a fuck what she thinks? The moment the gavel fell my wrongful and unjust conviction became a moot point. Everything that's happened since reinforces just how moot. I still refuse to except that fact. I'm stubborn. It's all I have left. They win if I fold.

I think about those lying cops, pointing and laughing at me in open court. The pleasure in their eyes and sadistic satisfaction on their faces makes me sick including the female Assistant District Attorney high on cocaine in open court while accusing me of being a marijuana dealer. I remember hearing about the DA's son who was the biggest ecstasy dealer in his high school. I remember it all, most of all the rampant corruption.

I'm packed up and leaving again.

15

I'm headed to the program. As I'm exiting the tank I see Hector, "Damn man, I can't go nowhere without you vato!" "Sounds like you missed me." As we walk across the grounds he's asking me all kinds of question, "I ain't got no idea man. Something tells me we're about to find out." There are four different buildings with two to three tanks each. It looks like Hector and I are headed for the same building. I like this young vato. He's 19, but more sensible and intelligent than his years.

This tank has a lot of chaos and commotion. Inmates are hollering, talking shit and taking bets. Ah, the joy of eminent release. I expected it to be more sober and reserved. The prisons I've been to previously were mostly short timers. Maybe five years at the most. The men here have served severe sentences. Most are at the end of 30 year stretches. They're convicts in mind, body and soul. The state of Texas has decided to take the last 6 months to try and reprogram us to be productive citizens again. Now with the proverbial light emanating from the surface finally within sight, we've been rerouted to serve final months in a decompression chamber.

I'm issued a top bunk against the middle of the back wall. A young brotha from south Dallas is on the bottom bunk. Hector is in the front corner of the tank. True to form the eses welcomed him into the fold. The brothas are watching me. This being a rehab program the demographics are pretty much divided evenly. Surveying the room, surprisingly enough all seem to intermingle relatively well. I like my south Dallas celly already. After count time he vacates and give me some space to unpack. As I unpack, I'm watching my back but I don't see anything. My celly gave me the low down, "Say man, how long we gotta listen to rehab shit?" "Bout 3 hours every day." "You mean we gotta listen to grown men bitch and complain about their feelings for 3 hours every day for the next 6 months?" "Not every day. We don't program on the weekends." "When we go anywhere we have to walk with our hands behind our backs like we're handcuffed?" "Yeah, and when you talk to a CO gotta have your hands behind your back too. That ain't all. We have to march in step and sing out in cadences to the chow hall." "You bullshittin'?" "Naw man, no bullshit." I can see I'll be spending all my time trying to figure ways not to program.

It's 7 am and I have an old white lady who's obviously not pleased with how her own life has turned out, chastising me about my bunk not being made to her specifications. She has no idea I made it up improperly on purpose. I want to get a close look at her scrutinizing techniques. If I'm to endure this humiliation on a daily basis for the next 6 months I shall make it a game. While she's telling me how she expects it to be done, I'm taking note of what she is and isn't noticing. I realize it's easier to comply and conform, but fuck that. Fuck this batty old hag, fuck this bunk and fuck this motherfucking program!

After bunk inspection we're made to stand and pledge allegiance to the program, a bootleg prison version of the Serenity prayer. I didn't fall for the hand over heart and swearing an oath of undying loyalty to a flag that never in its existence showed me and mine the slightest bit of loyalty. I felt that way at the age of 6. Imagine how I feel about being told to commit to memory, recite in unison and on command first thing every morning a prescribed "just say no" positive motivation mantra designed to indoctrinate and self-inoculate. No, I think not. I'm barely moving my mouth.

Listening to tales of woe, one after the other is more

depressing than being in prison. A plump bald headed white man is talking about how he lost his multimillion dollar computer consulting business, $1.5 million home, wife and kids to his meth habit. He admitted that it was wrong to watch his life crumble, but the meth was more important. And now he's getting delinquent child support letters in prison. His wife and kids are living in her mother's basement and don't want anything to do with him. A self-reputed Mexican king pin said he had more than 200 men on the street selling product. He said he broke the first rule in dope sales - don't get high on your own supply, "I thought I was bad. I thought I could handle it. At the end I was so far gone I was in debt to my own dealers." This is why I've never fucked with coke or crack. I never wanted to get that fucked up. I never wanted to be that high.

Here I sit in a circle of 65 murderers, rapists and drug addicted dealers discussing their feelings. Not one has the slightest inclination of how to go about or even begin this process so we are being instructed and supervised by Mrs. Garrett. It's not hard to tell none of us are comfortable in the situation. Expressing emotions for most men is difficult. It's as painful as pulling teeth.

I'm seated next to two vatos putting forth the utmost care and effort into not getting caught not giving a fuck. From my many years in the back of classes honing my skills as a grade-A slacker, I can tell these dudes have done post graduate work on the subject. I stop myself from laughing at their conversation in English and Spanish. One of them is being deported upon his release. The other is from El Paso. I gave him a nudge when Mrs. Garrett was eyeballing them. Mrs. Garrett leaves the room and some inmates have chosen to continue toeing the company line. Within an hour to go we are unsupervised and still programming. What type of convicts are these? I take the opportunity to cast dispersions upon this skinny, big headed dude attempting to take over as master of ceremony. In my best Spanish I ask the vato from El Paso what's up with this egg headed dude. He's a bit shocked by my Spanish and laughs, "I don't know, but this dude is always like this." "Don't he know we only have to program when they're watching us? It's like he likes this programming shit." "Tonto." "Simone.

Donde vivas?" "Califas. Y tu?" "Matamoros." We talked about the origin of the name Matamoros. It was named by the invading Spanish to mark the occasion of liberating Spain from the Moors. Matamores translates to dead Moors. We go into an in depth discussion about the history and sociopolitics of this world until lunch time.

Programming isn't over. We're still required to march in cadence to the chow hall. I'm not alone in my discontent for this show of solidarity. I've watched soldiers marching and saluting since I was in diapers. The sight of free thinking men surrendering their individual identities never sat well with me. Not even as a child. Having to watch my father snap to and salute made me mad even before I knew why. That was the military. Now I'm subjected to prison counselors and officials telling me to fall in. I ain't gonna be able to do it.

There are no field workers at this prison, so I'm forced to smuggle produce from the kitchen myself. The middle man speaks Spanish, so when I place my order in Spanish, Parra (the vato from El Paso) classifies me as Cuban, "No Califas. Tu pinche Cubano." Navarez, the one who's waiting to be deported concurs, "Simone ese." They say I don't speak Spanish like an American and force me to defend my blackness, "I didn't learn Spanish in a classroom. I learned it on the street. No Cubano, no Boricua, no Columbiano, no Nicaragua. Yo total Africano." "Cayate pinche Cubano." Before we leave the chow hall I have a new nickname – Cuba.

Back in the tank and making salsa has solidified my new moniker. Parra and Navarez have gathered a few other vatos around to watch and make fun of me. For all the laughing they're doing, I knew all the laughing would stop as soon as they got a taste. Now every Mexican in the joint is calling me Cuba. My south Dallas celly is looking at me like I'm crazy, but it doesn't stop him from sampling the salsa.

Parra is the best artist I've seen in prison. He's so good he drew a picture of a woman in a bikini with coloring pencils that's so life like prisoners borrow it for the express purpose of jacking off. He's using ink, a most unforgiving medium. Watching him work is the best art instruction I've ever received. I don't know what crime this man is convicted of, but he should be somewhere else getting paid a lot for his talent.

He's working on 5 different pieces at once, moving back and forth between them to keep from getting bored. One of the portraits Parra is working on is of Navarez's father.

Our conversation moves from art and food to religion. Navarez wants to know why I've chosen to be a Muslim, "I had too many unanswerable questions about Christianity. The answers I got didn't fit. For me religion required too big a leap of faith not to mention the historical problems. I went looking for my own answers." "What do you mean historical problems?" "My people weren't Christian when those Christians herded them on those ships. My people being Christian was Massa's idea. Do you think he had our best interest at heart? Christians make for better slaves. Matter of fact that ain't too different from the way you became Catholic." "How do you figure?" "Well, you weren't Catholic when Cortez showed up on the coast. That required a sword in one hand, a Bible in the other and lest we not forget the small pox up his sleeve. In fact I bet the only reason you're Catholic is because your parents said you were Catholic." "Yeah, never thought of it like that. But why a Muslim?" "I studied a few of the world's religions. To me Islam is the most rational." As we're talking, Parra is repeatedly slapping me around a chess board. His skills are remarkable. Hector joins us in time to talk shit about Parra beating me at chess, again, "With all that shit you talkin' Hector, I see you keepin' yo ass on the sidelines. What's the matter? Afraid to suit up?" "Naw man, I don't play." "Ah, the safest place for one to talk shit." "Yep." "Now I can't call you a coward just an idiot. I'll teach you." "Naw, that's ok." "Why not? Ain't like you ain't got the time or you just wanna talk shit." "Yeah, it's more fun." "How do you know? You don't know how to play?" Navarez chimes in, "Leave him alone."

It's chowtime again and all kinds of bootlegging traffic and trading is going on. The COs open all tank doors simultaneously causing a flood of cons to collide in the corridor. There's no way they could hope to maintain any semblance of order in such a situation. The COs rely on hunger to direct the flow of traffic. All of this makes me suspicious. It smells like a set up.

After chow, on the way back in the tank the COs are out in front frisking at random. There's a not so small pile of contraband behind them. You should see them awash in smug satisfaction. They're all too pleased with their plunder as if they've done their good deed for the day. As if they're putting a dent in the smuggling.

It's lights out and Celly is asking how I learned to speak Spanish. What he really wants to know is have I compromised my blackness. He framed his question carefully so as not to offend me. I explain the similarities between our two cultures and the concept of the phrase "The enemy of my enemy is my friend." I purposely give it to him heavy and deep so he stops questioning me. Before I can finish I notice there are several other brothas who are ear hustling. A slick talkin' brotha from the Fifth Word in Houston named Ricky says, "Yeah nigga, fuck all dat. How you learn to speak dat shit?" "Well I got a thang for pinocha, so for me it became advantageous to learn Spanish." "Yeah nigga, knew you had some reason."

I've been here for two days. I'm half asleep and bored to tears. The empty routine of prison life has been replaced by someone else's idea of constructive time management. This is like being forced to watch TV infomercials for hours on end. While I fall in and out of what can only be described as an almost slobbering slumber, I hear something that snaps me to attention, "Now, the white South Africans have to give up their land and homes. Is that fair?" Hearing those words filled me with a seething caldron of boiling hate. "Fair? What the fuck is you talkin' bout fair? After 50 years of Apartheid and now you wanna talk about fair! Only white folks would say some stupid shit like that. Let me tell it, them Zulu's should've burned every last one of them crackas alive and then danced and pissed on their smoldering ashes! What the fuck is you talkin' bout fair? Fuck fair!" This is quickly followed by silence of shock and a few mumbles of "yeah he's right." I expect as much from people of color, but these are red neck white boys co-signing my Black Nationalist movement is too much.

My earlier outburst has aroused curiosity of a few white boys who want me to go further in our discussion about fair. I thought at first they were sizing me up. Then I thought my militancy made them afraid which is common for white people. My militancy began when I was 15. My very presence was unnerving to some and downright frightening to others, and that was California which is different than Texas white folks. Yet here they are, relating to and agreeing with this would be Nat Turner with genuine respect and honest curiosity. The more honest and direct I am with them, the more they seem to like it. In return, they earn some measure of respect from me. Just as I'm conjuring an exit strategy they announce over the intercom "Muslim services." "That's me guys. Gotta go." "Ohhh, you're a Muslim." I turn and shot him a look of confrontation, "That's right." After a long 10 seconds of tense silence "Well that's, I mean that's cool." Without losing eye contact I reply, "Glad you approve of my religion." "No, I didn't mean it like that." "Yeah, I know what you meant." Before I can get out of the tank, my celly shoots me a grin and says, "Stop scarrin' dem white boys like dat."

It's almost lights out. Ricky, Celly and I are fixing a spread and Dave, the one who made that ignorant ass statement about South Africa, has come over to apologize for his thoughtlessness. The fact he waited so long to plead his case makes him suspect. The fact that he came over by himself and interrupted three brothas to express his regret goes a long way toward his redemption. He tried too hard to convince me he wasn't a bigot. "A'ight man, you ain't gotta convince me. We can usually tell right away with whom we are dealing." He was surprised at how much I understood. To further bemuse him I fixed him a plate of food and handed it to him. He sat down with us and started eating. He cleaned his plate, compliments my cooking and talks a little shit with us.

Two weeks in now and it's more of the same nothing, but things are better than one might reasonably expect. My hook ups are in place and I have all the food and supplies I can fit in my box. I still need to figure a way to get out of this rehab program. If I stay vigilant an opportunity will present itself. The easy thing to do would be to do the program and get out, but my hostility issues won't let me. My issues are exacerbated by a warden who told me I wouldn't make it through his program. Shit, He's here for a visit and has the nerve to be smiling like everything is everything. He sees me and asks, "What's the matter with you?" "What do you mean what's the matter with me? I'm in prison." "It could be worse. At least you're here. Where were you before you came here?" "Mineral

Wells." "Oh, I see." He turns on his heels, gathers his entourage and walks away. He knew he couldn't sell that bullshit here about being fortunate to be in his program, but I made a mistake and tipped my hand by allowing him to see my hate. I must've subconsciously mean mugged the warden. He came directly over to me without speaking to anyone else. I'm not one of his happy darkies. I let that son of a bitch get my pressure up. Mike, the dude who lost his computer business to meth, is asking me why I'm so upset at the warden, "Because he's an evil, dirty muthafucka!" Mike says, "Why do yuh say that?" I ask, "What do you mean why? He's the warden. It is he who holds the office opposite Saint Peter and is the keeper of the gates of Hell. That makes him an evil and dirty muthafucka. He's a prison official and a politician which means he's the most corrupt person in prison." Mike asks, "Aren't you being a little hard on the man? He could just be doing his job." I say, "Yeah you would think some shit like that." Mike asks, "Why'd you say that?" I say, "Cause you ain't got no street." Mike asks, "What does that mean - no street?" I explain, "The fact you have to ask that question validates the statement. It means you ain't got no crust on your bread. You are failing to properly calculate the X factor that is the human equation. You think TDCJ gave him this brand new prison to implement his program based on merit because that's the way things are supposed to work. I know he lied, cheated, stole and conned to get what he wanted because that's the way it's always worked." "No, not always." I ask, "You seem to be an educated man. Answer a question for me. When in the entire history of human kind on this planet has love, peace, harmony, justice, equality and a sense of fair play ever been more than a punch line? Let me help you out. I can think of 3 separate occasions - Atlantis, Camelot and Shangri-La. A person with no street believes corruption is the exception. The warden has spent his entire adult life in prisons by choice! His whole life he's tried to one up on all the convicts. It takes a con to catch a con. It takes ambition to become a warden. Now ask yourself why anyone would work real hard to voluntarily spend forever in a prison? If you ask him, he'll probably give you that text book response about being a public servant. That same bullshit cops spew about protecting and serving. The truth is he knows there's ten ways from Sunday to rape and pillage the system. I gotta get the fuck out of Texas. Got nothin' but hate for this muthafucka!" Mike asks, "What's wrong with Texas? This is the best state in the country. I love it here." I say, "Of course you do. You're a conservative thinking white man with cracker tendencies. For you this place must be paradise on earth."

My conversation with Mike is interrupted by Navarez and Parra who call me over to the TV. "Ay, you came from Mineral Wells?" "Yeah, me and Hector." "Mira!" The local news is reporting that a race riot broke out at Mineral Wells. Blacks against the Mexicans. Twelve people life-flighted. I'm not surprised the gang conflict shit finally ignited. In a prison as wide open as that one, there's no telling all the weapons they had stashed around that place. Hector half-jokingly whispers a rhetorical question, "Who's side would you've been on?" "I would've just rolled with the Muslims. As a rule, we tend not to get involved in petty bullshit arguments. We behave amicably to avoid such foolishness. Islam does not advise the turning of the other cheek. The Qur'an contends in this life there are occasions when violence is not only justified, but necessary. The only people who attempted in earnest the practical application of non-violence were Jesus, Mahatma, Martin and Cesar. We know what happened to most them.

Every time I think I have a reason to complain or be hostile I get an adjustment. I thought it was unfortunate to have to leave Mineral Wells. I thought they were going out of their way to fuck with me. I really thought I was being taken from the Waldorf Astoria to be sold back up the Okavango into Angola. There seems to be glaring evidence to the contrary. I miss the relative freedoms and individuality afforded an inmate at Mineral Wells, but this place is comparatively not that bad. The atmosphere here is considerably more peaceable.

I'm in the infirmary waiting to see the doctor. I need sinus medicine. I'm next in line a few people behind a dude who suffers from explosive bowel syndrome. They open the door and call me just as he's leaving. I notice the nurses with pitying, mournful looks of sympathetic sorrow all over their faces. I overheard them talking about a wrecked rectum; the room filled with empathetic and sorrowful whispers of how terrible it must've been for him. Last week he had an incident in the toilet where his asshole sneezed all up in the bowl.

Dave, the South African sympathizer, has a co-pilot; a friendly white boy named Matt. They're thick as thieves and genuinely nice guys. They keep to themselves; they don't cotton to these other white boys. It's almost like they aren't from Texas. Both are fitness freaks, the kind that overdose on protein and creatine every day. Dave is an acquired taste and Matt is so cool he doesn't give a fuck. I've heard a few of their conversations. If this were high school they'd be nerds, Trekkies, Dungeons and Dragons weirdos. I like them both.

We got a new counselor today, a man this time who's better than the old women. He's relaxed and not such a stickler. He doesn't interfere unless we get too loud. Parra is still beating my ass all over the chess board again, but I finally got me one. I had to out sneak him. He got caught in a repetitive move between queens, back and forth. He'd thrust, I'd perry. On the 9th move I stopped short. He over perused. Got his bitch! A beautiful checkmate behind my rook and knight. And Parra was taking it easy on me.

Matt and I have found common ground. Both of us have a little more than a passing fancy for computers. He told me about a new processor that's water cooled, "No shit, a radiator?" Until this conversation I didn't realize how rapidly unused knowledge evaporates. I struggle to remember things I used to know in my sleep. Prison has a way of preserving the body and rotting the mind. It's as if I can feel the deterioration. My vocabulary, cognition and acuity have suffered in this environment. Conversely, instinct, intuitiveness and every base emotion are all acutely honed, chambered, locked and loaded. I hope this is just the brain temporarily compensating for my surroundings. Deep intellectual thought and philosophical contemplation in prison are about as useful as calculus to crocodile.

It's 7 am and we got word the counselors are running late. We're left to our own devices, so we congregate in a circle to placate the guards, That's all the programming they'll get out of us today. Several people are getting released at the end of this month, so the conversation turns to the free world. Everyone here is in the home stretch so the subject matter is no longer rude. Only joyous tales of "I can't wait 'till and the first thing I'm gonna do." New discoveries like, "You mean there are fast food restaurants in gas stations now?" "Internet on cell phones?" Some of these guys have been away a while. One man says he hasn't seen a knife or a fork in 17 years. Another says he hasn't had a piece of toast in 23 years, "I can't wait to be stuck in traffic or just roll over in bed without falling out." Oddly enough, I hear nothing of pussy, "I don't know about you Navarez man, but the first thang on my list is pussy with all the trimmings." "Simone, got a letter from mi hyna ayer." Parra has been in for 10 years. He did his entire bid, he didn't want to get out on parole. He was most likely denied parole. All he wants to do is go to the bathroom by himself.

Mr. B, the new counselor brought a guitar and a harmonica to class today. The man has skills. He went straight into John Lee Hooker's "Boom Boom, Boom Boom", quickly followed by Little Walter's "My Baby." Sanchez, the kingpin, is playing percussion and bass on the metal bunks. The joint is jumping. Ricky is stepping with Terry the dry cleaner and the whole tank is singing backup. The COs are outside looking in like they want to be in here with us. Elvis can't tell us shit about no Jailhouse Rock. A good time was had by all.

I pulled Mr. B to the side and asked him where he learned to pluck and blow like that, "Say Mr. B, didn't know you was that muddy. Where you learn to wobble like that?" "I'll never tell." "Is that right like dat dere huh? What, you from the black bottom or somethin'?" "Shhh, don't tell nobody." We laugh and joke for a while as I try to get a reading on this man. He's doing the same with me, but I don't know what he's looking for. As for myself, I may have half an ally in the office. A man who has a tendency to buck the system would do well to cultivate such a friendly relationship.

Today three people are getting out which is the most dangerous time inside any prison. Jealousy and envy conspire to make sure one does not get out. One man with hope surrounded by thousands without. Here we have no such worries. Nothing but congrats and back slaps. A vato named Jesus is asking me questions about my religion. His daughter married a Muslim and converted to Islam. He wants to know the difference between Catholicism and Islam. I point out the similarities so he can see they're not that different which allows him to be more at ease with her transition, " Same Adam and Eve, same Abraham, same Moses, same Jesus, Mary and Joseph. Same virgin birth. We just don't deify Jesus, Mary or Saints. For us, all worship and praise is due to Allah." "I heard a man can have more than one wife." "Yeah, but it's not what you think. It came about in communities with a shortage of men. War, famine, disease and drought sometimes leaves a people with an uneven population, so multiple wives is out of necessity more than anything else. There are however provisions. A man can only take more than one wife if he can afford it. Also, he must treat them equally." We talk for a while longer. I hope I've been of some help. It must be tough on him, but he looks like he's taking it in stride.

Two guards enter the tank with facial expressions we recognize - sullen, mournful eyes cast downward with official paperwork in hand notifying another prisoner his mother has passed. Every inmate is hoping it isn't their turn. The guard hands the notice to the inmate in the bunk across from me. Without speaking he jumps down off the bunk and begins packing his belongings just like the last three who received this letter.

Coming back from a taleem with my Muslim brothers, I'm in good place mentally. I get to the tank door and the COs fails to open it. I'm interrupting their conversation, but don't rush them. I'm in no rush to be locked up again. They're discussing the ills of the correctional system and the criminal education one receives when forced to congregate and cohabitate with criminals, "Yeah and you can't separate them cuz that makes them crazy. What do thay call that? You know, when you don't see or hear nothin' different and don't talk to nobody for a long time?" I'm listening to these two pundits profess with the combined cognitive abilities of a corpse, "You're talking about sensory deprivation." Both of them turn and look at me as if I just won Final Jeopardy, "Well lookie here, a college man. What college did you go to?" "What difference does it make man? Open the door." I didn't have the heart to tell them what they were discussing was not a scholarly nor collegiate subject matter. I remember not paying attention to an 8th grade lecture when I learned of sensory deprivation, but I did remember the words sounded funny to me and that's what stuck.

Listening to COs with high school diplomas struggling with grade school subject matter reminds me of my childhood. Upon hearing I was moving to California, my 4th grade special education teacher was concerned that California's public school curriculum was more advanced than Texas. My teacher feared I couldn't keep up. I had no such misgivings. I never did a damn thing in class then and I was sliding by. I figured I'd have to work a little harder on my studies or on conjuring new ways of getting around working on my studies. It takes great work and thinking to keep from thinking and working. Now, I find myself surrounded by the fruits of that dumbed down curriculum because people from rural areas and backgrounds have no need of a first rate education. As a dyslexic child, by the time I was 9 years old I hated anything that smelled like school. I knew the bullshit logic was convoluted, but I didn't have the words to say so at the time. Any first year child psychologist graduate student can discuss in length the detrimental effects of low expectations. Now after all I've seen and experienced of this great state, I can only think Texas prefers its populous to be ignorant. Why else would this state's elected officials go out of their way to ensure their constituent's children stay behind? If they never left Texas they wouldn't even know they were behind. Who's profiting off their stupidity?

Another one of us lost his mother. This is starting to become an epidemic. He's an older brotha. Still, his age doesn't make it any easier. As he's packing to go to the funeral his grief is palpable. People are finding it difficult to look in his direction. The sight of him attempting to deal cuts too close to the bone. No one wants to think of this day we all got coming.

On the way back to the tank I see Mr. B., "Say man, you'll never know what you did for me with that Tupac CD." "Yeah I do. That's why I did it." "Man, I was back on the coast all weekend. Just wanted you to know I appreciate what you did." "No problem. Someone couldn't keep their mouth shut and now y'all have to share the radio with the other tanks." "What? Who?" "I don't know, but that tank has it next weekend. Well, no matter what, too much of that makes me want to break out." "Shh, don't let anyone hear you say that." "You act like you spent some time." "I plead the 5th." "A'ight man, you ain't gotta tell me twice." I knew there had to be a reason this dude was so cool. I found an ally.

40 of us in a room are making parole preparations which amounts to standing in lines and filling out redundant paper work. I'm glad to do it. Seeing my name on paper with the word parole next to it has an uplifting effect you would not believe. We`re light hearted and full of smiles. I can't imagine any other time such blatant happiness would be tolerated. Everyone in this room will be getting out at the same time. All of us have less than 5 months in the wakeup. Hector and I seem to be joined at the hip, at least on paper. If they call my name, they call his next. Dave's in here, too. It's good to see all the people we'll be making our exits with.

I'm in the chow hall and the flood gates are open. The kitchen received a shipment today and someone left the wrong lock unlocked. Suffice to say, if the kitchen got it, we got it. They won't even know anything is missing until tomorrow. It also happens to be chicken day. I have my big clothes on and a pocket full of stamps. The guards are preoccupied with shaking down the tank where the weed is being smoked. Me, Parra, Navarez, Hector and the new vato Morano look like chipmunks in October. Everyone is B-lining it back to their respective tanks.

It's the weekend and the tank has decided to spread tonight. We just went to store on Thursday, so everyone is breaking out their best dishes including me. I'm making chicken tamales and Spanish rice. The rice is easy enough - V8 juice, salsa, salt, pepper and spices to taste. Navarez is making the beans while me and Parra are deboning the chicken. Morano is grinding corn chips into a powder for the masa and laying open Raman soup bags. I add butter and hot water in a bowl with the powered corn chips, mix into a paste the consistency of peanut butter. I spread the masa on an opened Raman bag, fill with chicken, chopped onion, garlic and nacho cheese. Then I roll them up like a cigar, pack the rolls tightly in a plastic bag, heat bag in hot water and enjoy. Damn if they don't look, smell and taste like tamales! Good thing we made enough. The tank is tripping. There's no way they should taste this good and there's no way a black man should be making tamales for

Mexicans in a Texas prison. Ricky wastes no time in reminding me so, "A'ight nigga, you pushin' it. If they wasn't so good I wouldn't say a damn thang, but these muthafuckas is good! And you ain't got no bid'ness knowin' how to make tamales like this. Just ain't right!" "If it just ain't right then stop eatin' nigga." Naw, I'll get over it." My Celly hasn't said anything because his mouth is full. Mike, Matt and Dave look like they want some more, but don't want to ask. Parra and Navarez just look at each other, "Pinche Cubano?" "Si, pinche Cubano."

It's late Saturday and we're watching TV. Just before count time one of the COs made popcorn. When they left to count the next tank they didn't close the door all the way. No one here is looking to break out, but that popcorn is a bit too much to take. As the door to the next tank closes, Morano slides out into the hall, pulls the popcorn bag through the bars of the guard's pod and back in the tank. Some of these guys haven't had popcorn in decades. After 45 seconds, the popcorn is gone and the bag is flushed. It's Monday morning and we're back in group programming. Inmates from other tanks are teaching the program today. There are four of them; I hope they don't have stories to tell. They put forth the effort and then it was over. The civilian counselors are ask our opinion and to critique our peer's performance. I elect to abstain from the vote, but it seems the ayes have it. They let us know we'll have inmate counselors throughout the program. I guess it's better than the old crabby ladies.

Matt, Mike and I are discussing new computer technology, a subject we seem to be alone in having any interest. Before it all went to shit, Mike was working on a way to totally automate new homes under construction, "Yes, any digital appliance in or around your home, I can integrate them and have them controlled by a laptop. That means alarms, garage doors, thermostats, stoves, sprinkler systems and washer/dryers. Anything with a chip." This dude might be good to know when I get out. Getting a regular job is an improbability for me. It sounds like Mike is going right back into business. My job said they would be there for me. I'm not holding my breath. My other option would be to start cultivating criminal opportunities. That means coming to grips with the probability of coming back here. No thanks, I think I'll stick to computers.

Matt is packing up and moving. He's on his way to be an inmate counselor, "What the fuck you wanna do that shit for?" "Because I get my own cell with my own door, get to move around from tank to tank, get to sleep in and I don't have to program." "Say what? "Yeah and all I gotta do is talk to people about their drug problems." "Damn Matt, how can I be down?" "As people get released they'll ask for new volunteers. They asked me if I knew anyone and the first person I told them about was you." "Is that right? What made you think of me? I mean good lookin' out, but why me?" "I just thought you'd be good at it." "Appreciate it man." "No problem." Dave is looking like Matt just stole his lunch money. He's wondering why his homeboy didn't have his back, "I did tell them about you Dave. I just mentioned Cali first." This is my get out of jail free card. Well, almost. My get- out-of- programming free card for sure.

My thoughts are consumed with more freedom. A private cell means a private toilet which means I can close the door and enjoy some peace and quiet. This also means no more 6 am wake up call to make my bunk. No more listening to crotchety old white ladies offer their opinion and having to obey them like the law. All of this means I can get over on the Warden and his program. I've been recommended. Now it's up to me to make it happen.

My Muslim brothers and I are talking about the new inmate counselor program and how we can get in on it. Back in the tank and the Golden Girls are telling us the warden has visitors coming to inspect the progress of his program. They say we need to step up our r. They want us looking real sharp for the warden's guests. They even want us to sing out loud while marching in cadence for the visiting dignitaries. The warden expects inmates to make him look good. I don't know about the rest of these inmates, but this is one monkey that doesn't dance to that tune.

It's Friday and Mr. B was nice enough to leave a Tupac CD in the player for our enjoyment. He must've heard me recite Tupac's "I ain't mad at yuh." I find a small 4 x 8 Plexiglas empty store room, close the door, close my eyes, turn it up and I'm back on my beloved coast. This man sang the soundtrack to my life. The memories descend from the heavens like the monsoon. Painful, but it hurts so good. Before long this little room is filled with brothas. We're silent with reflective introspection. From start to finish not one song is skipped or even talked over. The last song on the CD is "Dear Momma." As the song fades out, the silence is broken with a single sniffle. Every head in unison turns in that direction. It's the last brotha who lost his mother earlier this month. The clearing of throats, sniffling and the rubbing of eyes caused us to disperse quickly and act as if nothing happened, so as to not linger in this tearful state. All of us tried to regain composure before the rest of the tank sees. Tupac reduced a room full of hardened convicts to tears - tears we were unable to fight back, tears for their mamas. No one cracks a joke or makes light of the situation. We're ashamed of our inability to control our emotions, but we understand.

A few of the younger brothas turn on feel good hip hop, but the older brothas are through with the radio. Parra and Navarez want me to hang out on the block. Not tonight. Tupac has my mind on the California coast. I'm home sick and I want to be alone. Like everything in prison the radio has been divided up racially. The Mexicans get it Saturday and the white boys get it Sunday. I hope I can find some Latin Jazz tomorrow. No wonder Parra keeps beating me up and down this chess board. He reads books on chess strategies. Now I don't feel so bad. Shit, he's supposed to kick my ass. I got lucky beating him that one time. I guess I could pick up a book or two on the subject. My innate aversion to books precludes such an eventuality from being likely or even probable. But I'm learning. Albeit the hard way.

Terry told me someone snitched on me after I blew up in our counseling class when we were left to our own devices, "Yeah, he went and told the counselors you called them bitches and said fuck them." "You bullshitin'?" "No I ain't. I was out in the hall, moppin' up. He walked right in and just started talkin'." "Thanks man. Good lookin' out." This couldn't come at a worse time. I'm trying to get on their good side so I can out flank this program. The whole time I thought the enemy was on the other side of the bars. Now there's evidence to support the hypothesis there's a fungus among us. Parra told me what I already knew, "Man, Cuba, everybody is talking about that pinche maricone who snitched on you. How did he survive on the cell block?" Parra knows this situation calls for blood shed. He also knows I'm not stupid enough to lose my parole over this puto, so he really wants to know what I'm going to do. I've been abstaining from any active involvement and I've decided to use the program to officially call him a punk bitch house nigger to his face.

It's been two weeks since Matt recommended me for the counseling program. When I see him, I bug the shit out of him, "What's up man, what's the damn deal?" A few days later I was called to a meeting with the counselors. They asked if I have something positive to contribute to the program. This is my time to shine. Mr. B. gives me a look as if to say don't trip, you got this. Mrs. Garrett is looking at me like I owe her rent money. Another one is giving me her best Bela Lugosi look. Rose and Blanche seem to have taken it all in stride. They understand an inmate bad mouthing his jailers is just par for the course. Blanche used to be a looker. She still has her petite and dainty little frame, a fact she is more than aware of. Why else would she come to work in a prison wearing cut off shorts? I'm not complaining. I leave the meeting in a good place.

Finally someone for me to smack around the chess board. Morano has a fools rush in style of play. Plus he doesn't mind getting beat. I'm only too happy to oblige. He's one of those guys who likes to talk shit while he's losing. Unfortunately he has about as much skill and aptitude for it as he has for chess. He's funny and means well. I'm saved by the chow bell. Mate in 2.

I received a letter from my home girl in the L.A. She's getting married and bubbly with joy. Rightfully so. She's waited a long time for this. She's a good person and it's nice to see her get what she wants. Another important moment I'll miss, so I'll give her a unique wedding present. I asked her to send me photos of her and her man. I commissioned Parra to draft a portrait. She's the kind of woman who will appreciate an authentic Texas penitentiary rendition of her nuptials and something none of her bougie friends and relations could possibly get her.

For the first time since his new appointment, Matt finally begins teaching and counseling. He's a car salesman in the free world and has decided to teach us the ins and outs of buying and selling cars. He notes how car sales is a good trade for an ex-con. Car lots don't care about criminal records as long as you move metal. We have questions mostly about commission and how it works, "Yes, you eat what you kill." "Oh hell naw! You mean we don't get paid if we don't sell anything?" "Yeah, but you'll know if you have what it takes pretty quick. If you can move metal then you can make a lot of money." Lord knows I don't want to work on commission. I prefer a steady check for steady work, but I have to do what I can to get by.

After class Matt and I discuss car sales. He thinks I'll do well in the industry, "Selling cars is more about you than the car. If a person is at a car lot, they want a car. The only question is whether or not they want to buy from you. All about whether or not the customer likes you. I think you could get people to like you." "That's the second time you've called me affable. What the fuck gave you that impression?" That's not the vibe I was attempting to project." "Yeah, but you can turn it on when you want." I understand how he sells cars. His con is subtle and well camouflaged. The only difference between a con man and a salesman is when you leave a con man you feel like you've been had. After you leave a good salesman you feel lucky. Either way, you've been conned. Mike and a few white boys bait me into joining their conversation.

"Cali thinks the world has gone to shit. He says I have no street, whatever that means."

"That's not what I said. I'm being misquoted. I didn't say the world is going to shit. I said the world has always been shit. I didn't say you haven't any street. I said you ain't got no street."

"You still haven't told me what that means."

"It means you lack a fundamental understanding of the con. It means you have a tendency to take things at face value."

"How do you figure?"

"If you see a person in uniform, whether it be a policeman, a man of the cloth or even a judge, you give that man a certain measure of respect."

"Sure I do."

"You've been conned."

"What do you mean?"

"Giving a man in uniform respect is a mistake."

"I say the uniform is to be respected."

"The man is to earn his measure of respect. When I see a cop, I see a cowardly bully with control issues like the hall monitors in grade school. Why do you think the judge wears that long black robe? It's to give you the impression of official propriety."

"What do you have against the reverend?"

"Any man who chooses religion as his profession is automatically suspect. That's why people like you always get caught unaware and off guard when respectable people get caught out of pocket. When the truth is celibate men of the clergy have been fucking little kids, nuns and each other for centuries. Truth is a judge is simultaneously a lawyer and a politician who has spent his entire professional career neck deep in the very worst humankind has to offer. Now his benefit package is to the point where payoffs and bribery from prison officials to keep them well stocked are almost taxable income. Somehow he's in a position to pass judgment. As far as the police, shit, they've been corrupt for so long the phrase "dirty cop" is redundant. Yet these are the people who automatically and unquestionably have your respect? Like I said, no street. Don't get it twisted, I ain't condemning every person who has chosen to serve his fellow man. All I'm saying is ain't none of us wearing halos."

I saw Blanche in the hallway. She told me to pack it up. I'm moving. It must be all over my face when I walk into the tank because Parra and Navarez know right away, "You get it Cuba?" Si!" No more group programming at 6 am. I can't get this smile off my face. Celly and Ricky are rife with envy, "Damn Cali, how you swing this?" "Yeah, hook a nigga up." "I ain't got no hook up man. Ain't sure how I got in myself." Parra and Navarez didn't waste any time putting their bid in. I've packed my stuff up more than 15 times during my tenure and this is the quickest I've done it. Morano says I'm moving because I don't want him to beat me, "Morano, if the creator himself helped you cheat, you still couldn't beat me in a dream." Dave and Mike are looking like it should've been them. I'm going to miss my crew. I don't know anyone but Matt in the counselor's tank which means I have to get to know yet more convicts. I keep thinking how this is going be the last time I have to do this, not to mention I now have a cell to myself. As I'm standing at the door, Parra tells me he'll finish my home girl's picture and put it in the mail tomorrow. There's so much detail in his drawing. The hammer indentations around bent nails in wood grain are impressive. I know she'll like it. Somehow Navarez has talked the CO into letting him help me carry my stuff across the unit. He's got some conniving to do. This will give him the mobility he requires. The door is open and I'm out.

16

This tank is an improvement from the last one. It's quiet. There are 2 TVs and VCRs. Instead of 32 bunks, there are 10 portable cells, 5 to a row. There are 10 people in here. Did I mention it's quiet? I have my own cell and toilet, and door. This is almost as good as Mineral Wells. Except for having to profess this rehab program to drug offending convicts, I got it made. Matt comes around the corner all smiles. I thank him one more time for dropping my name. He's headed out to do a little reconnaissance. It's strange how Matt's conniving is a surprise to me. It's hard to imagine him doing anything illegal. That must come in real handy with the cops. Navarez and I take our time and talk shit while I unpack,

"Man Cuba, this ain't bad. Can't wait 'till they move me in here."

"Any word on when that might be?"

"No, they just said they'd get back to me."

"Yeah, that's what they told me too. If that's any indication you got about 2 weeks."

"What about Parra?"

"Same time."

"Cool, I'll have this place hooked up by then. You and Parra can just get in where you fit in."

"If you wanna do something for us, let us have some of that salsa you just made."

The CO presence is almost nonexistent. As Navarez leaves on his one man excursion, I take this time to take in the new found solo silence. I haven't been alone in a while. I open and close my cell door because I can. The simple things.

I wake up from a nap in the dark and a bit disorientated. It takes me a second to get my bearings. I have no sense of the continuum. I take a minute to relish in the aloneness. As a young child I had trepidation about the dark. Who knows what lurks and all that. Lying here now, in the recesses of self-imposed and all-encompassing shadows, I have found a measure of peace. The TV says it's almost 11 pm. I slept through chow and then some. It's still quiet in here. No asinine arguments about nothing, no loud and mindless chatter. No wonder I slept for hours.

On the other side of the tank there's a Muslim brother of mine who happens to be in the same cell as Matt. He's old school and wears it well. Picture John Coltrane at 70. He's well-adjusted, mellow and content in his skin. He's getting out in a week. It's late and I can't sleep, so I'm scrubbing this cell from top to bottom. I can't get comfortable when I'm surrounded by unknown filth. The first time I close the door and shit by myself will be a momentous occasion. It's 6 am and I'm finally falling asleep. I feel sorry for the inmates who have to get up to make their beds at this fine hour.

Navarez hooked us up with more groceries from the kitchen. We have so much food I need the help of some local cons to carry everything back to the tank. This will cost me, but there's plenty to go around so it's all good. These dudes happen to be black. One of them is nicknamed Old School. He's confused with Navarez calling me Cuba and me speaking Spanish. Old School says one word, "Akee?" "Naw Old School, I ain't Cuban." He cracks a little smile. A brotha who hears all of this decides to give me a shit about it, "Shit nigga, I cain't tell!" "Really. How many Cubanos you know?" Old School leans back and says, "He got you there. Now let's get these groceries back to the tank." Old School is getting out Monday, so we're celebrating. He's got a box full of food and not wanting to take it with him, he puts it in the pot. We enlist prep cooks including a murderer. He's putting his unique trade skills to good use by chopping and dicing vegetables. We eat, laugh, talk shit and tell lies deep into the wee hours. A good time is had by all. Old School and I hang out in the background. He's always watching and studying. I will learn a lot from him. The rest are just run of the mill criminals. Old School is giving me an in depth psychological profile of every man in the room. His thoughts are accurate and insightful. I wish he wasn't getting out the day after tomorrow.

It's late Monday morning and I find myself standing in front of 65 ill-mannered inmates. I'm observing today or so I thought. Lugosi is testing me by leaving me alone with these men. She thinks I can't handle these hoodlums and that I'm way out of my league. She doesn't know I spent my entire childhood in special education classrooms filled with the same exact people I see here before me today. Brer Rabbit is back in the briar patch,

"A'ight look! I don't give a fuck what you do. Just keep it down and if that bitch shows up act like y'all is payin' attention."

"Man, fuck you and fuck that bitch!"

"See that's the kind of nearsighted thinkin' that got yo' dumb ass locked up in the first place. If she comes back by here and y'all actin' a fool, she's gonna stay in here with us. Then we're gonna have to program for real."

"Yeah vato, callate! What you think about this pinche program vato?"

"Para me, basura!"

"Oh, tu hablas?"

"Mas o menos."

"Donde vivas homes?"

"Califas."

"Ok, well if you don't give a fuck about the program then why you teachin it?"

"So I don't have to program. So I can have my own cell. So I can sleep in. So I can shit in private. So I can do what the fuck I want."

"Damn nigga, how you swing dat?"

"You see, that's what a little thinkin' can get you. Don't

know if you give a fuck but that's what this program is supposed to teach you."

"You said this program is garbage."

"No, I said this program is garbage for me. Some of y'all can use it."

"Like who?"

"That's for you to decide, but some of you could really use help with your thinking."

"How you figure?"

"First clue is you're in here. Second is for most of you, this ain't your first time or your last for that matter. Now unless you like it in here the logical conclusion is you need help with your thinking."

"You in here, too!"

"Yeah, well ain't none of us perfect. Let me ask you how many times you been down?"

"Dis miy third time."

"You comin' back?"

"Hell naw!"

"Did you say that the last time you got out?"

"Uh, yeah."

"What's changed since the first time? Another thing, when I asked you, you said "dis my third time." You said it with pride. That's penitentiary thinking. The problem with penitentiary thinking is it's only good in the penitentiary. It might be helpful if you learned how to think like a free man."

As soon as I have their undivided attention and hanging on to every word I say, here she comes, the widow of Dracula. She's beside herself as inmates stay after class to thank and show genuine appreciation for my words. She intended to showcase my incompetence and it back fired. On the way back to our suite, the other 2 inmate counselors are curious,

"How'd you do that?"

"What'd you say to them?"

"How'd you get them to listen?"

They let me know that this tank has a rather nefarious reputation for being incorrigible,

"Oh, so you knew it was a setup?"

"Yeah, but what could we do?"

"She done this before?"

"Not that I know of. Why is she gunnin' for you anyway? What'd you do to piss her off?"

"I said fuck her and called her a bitch."

"What, and she still let you in?"

"I doubt she was the swing vote. Did you see her face? Look like it was gonna slide right off her skull. She had it coming after going out of her way to fuck with me like that. Shit, if you looked like her, you'd be a pissed old bitch, too."

"Sho'e you right."

I'm still receiving accolades for my performance this morning. Inmates are telling me they like what I said and asked when I'm coming back. I'm uncomfortable with this level of attention. Being prison, this isn't the place for smiling faces. I dig them feeling compelled to tell me. Lord knows all my insecurities needed to hear it, but I don't like random and spontaneous encroachment into my personal space.

I put in a request to go to the library. Too much free time is making the clock slow down. I'm thinking about reading an autobiography and maybe science fiction. Back in the county, when I first started reading books, I didn't think I'd like sci-fi or fantasy novels. I came to discover that if a book is well-written, no matter the subject matter, I will most likely enjoy it. My favorites by far are the true stories.

As I'm leaving, I run into Mr. B. in the hall. I smile and give him a dap.

"Ain't seen you for a minute. Where you been?"

"I had some family things."

"Every thang, everthang?"

"Yeah, it's all good."

"Good. Say man, on the real, I appreciate what you did for me. Those old ladies must'uh given you mad shit behind what I said."

"No, just one."

"Did you hear what she tried to do to me?"

"Yeah and I also heard about you."

"What'd you hear?"

"Heard you were like Malcolm Farrakhan."

"That's funny. Boyz N The Hood?"

"Yeah."

"What the hell is you doin' watchin' Boyz n The Hood?"

"Shh, don't tell nobody."

"I have one more ask of you."

"Sure."

"I have access to 2 VCRs."

"Say no more. I've got more movies than I know what to do with." Any requests?"

"Come on man, you brought me a Tupac CD, sang a John Lee Hooker and a Little Walter song. Then you made a Boyz N The Hood reference. I trust your taste."

I'm walking by the rec yard when a white boy calls me over to the fence. He tells me how much he liked what I said the other day. I have no idea who he is, but I'm glad I could help. As I head back inside, I run into Steve from my first stay in Bowie County.

"Say man, how the fuck you end up in here?"

"Been a long time Cali."

"Yeah, real long. You been down since we were in the county?"

"Yep. You?"

"Bout' a year and a half. When you get here?"

"I've been here almost 3 months."

"I just got here on Monday."

"Damn Steve, you didn't even make the list of the last persons I expected to see down here."

"Well hell Cali, I ain't expect to see you ever again. Figured you'd got the hell out of Texas and went back home."

"I tried, but Bowie County kept fuckin with me."

"Yeah, they been known to do that from time to time."

"What's up with old Cuz?"

"He passed."

"Sorry to hear that. How'd he go?"

"In bed with a 25 year old girl."

"Is that right? What was he - 75, 80 years old?"

"Yep, bout that."

"Way to go cuz...literally."

"Yeah, hell I figure if I gotta go, that's bout' the best way. Anyway, I'll see you around Cali."

"I'll see if I can teach a few classes in your tank. Then we can talk about old times."

"Yeah, do that."

The downside of living in a pre-release tank is people are always leaving. Watching my cellmates pack up and leave every few days is starting to chafe. The administration has us doing more paper work required prior to our release. I see Hector and Dave in the crowd. Now that I think about it, everyone here arrived to Hamilton on the same bus. It looks like we're going out on the same bus, too. Hector and Dave missed me,

"Hey Cuba, been hearin' about you vato."

"Is that right?"

"Yeah Cali, everybody's talking about you teaching those classes. You got a little fan base."

"Glad they dig it. Makes it a hell of a lot easier and almost fun."

"Yeah, you look like you'd like that shit vato."

"Fuck all that. When y'all comin' over to the dark side?"

"I don't know. Matt said I gotta wait."

"Chingao vato, I ain't doin' that. I ain't standing up there in front of everybody like that."

"Oh, so you'll break into a jewelry store and rob them blind, but you won't stand up and talk in front of a few people? You can be in a high speed motorcycle chase with the cops, but a little public speaking got you shook. What type shit is that?"

"Fuck you Cuba!"

Mr. B. came through with a few movies - New Jack City, Scarface, Angels with Dirty Faces, Goodfellas, The Good, the Bad and the Ugly, Little Caesar, Shaft, High Sierra and Boyz n the Hood. I knew he'd choose the right ones. The movies will help me pass the time since I worked it out where I don't have to teach classes anymore. The rest of the time, I'm getting my nap on. Parra and Navarez are moving on up as counselors.

"What took y'all so long?"

"Ay Cuba! Thought we'd never get over here. Muthafucha's in trouble now! We ain't gonna do shit white folks say."

"I told you I'd have it hooked up by the time y'all got over here. I worked it to where we can play hooky. We ain't gotta go and teach shit if we don't want to. I got a couple muthafuckas runnin' a little interference. Just got a gang of gangster flicks from Mr. B., too. Parra, you got your board right?"

"You know I do."

I'm scheduled to teach today, but instead Steve and I are shooting the shit reminiscing about our time in the county,

"Remember that ice storm? Freezin' our nuts to the pole. Remember that little muthafucka stole that weed? Almost got yo' ass thrown down the staircase?"

"Hell yeah I remember! I remember we smoked all that weed, too. I thought for sure they was gonna open his moon roof fur'em."

"Yeah, he slid right out of that noose and got the fuck out of Dodge! Say what you want about that boy, but he knew when to walk away."

The recounting of our recollections is brought to a loud conclusion. Someone is on the floor bleeding about the head and shoulders while someone else is standing over him talking shit, "Got yo ass now bitch! Thought you'd get away wit it again?" "Oh my head." "Shut the fuck up. Shoulduh cracked yo' skull wide open!" "Damn Kin foke, what'd he do?" "Caught his ass in my box." Here come the COs, "A'ight, what the fuck is goin' on in here?" "I slipped." "Oh yeah, well get yo slippin' ass up and go to the infirmary! If anybody else slips in here, we're gonna have a problem! One of y'all clean up this blood. You, get your shit and go back to your own tank." That's my curtain call. My celly is going home Friday. He's all smiles which is something I haven't seen. Ricky and the brothas think they're going home Friday, too. They're talking big shit and telling lies. It's good to see genuine joy on some of their faces.

I've been summoned to a meeting for a performance evaluation. I'm in a little room with Mr. B. and the Golden Girls. Blanche is killing me with those shorts. She makes me feel like a dirty younger man. The other one still throws me the evil eye like she caught me looking at Blanche's ass or something. Mrs. Garrett looks like she always does - drunk but not drunk enough. Mr. B. looks like he's annoyed with the process. After a barrage of bullshit questions and the equally bullshit answers they require, I thought I was finished. Lugosi wants me to recite the program's mantra. I worked hard at not being able to so I don't recite it. She sits up and interjects more venom in her speech. She thinks she's got me, "Maybe he doesn't deserve to be a counselor. Maybe he needs to go back and learn it. If we put you back in there maybe you'll learn it then." This is personal so I make it about the job, "If you doubt my ability, as you know, you're more than welcome to sit in and listen to my classes." Blanche smiles and says "No, that won't be necessary." Mr. B. speaks up, "I think what he's saying is he doesn't have to memorize those words to understand and teach it." They ask a few more questions, I'm thanked and sent on my way. As I leave, I can't help but wonder if Lugosi is tired of fucking with me.

I've commissioned Parra to do a one of a kind rendering for Mother's Day. He did a brilliant job on my friend's wedding portrait, so I've decided to issue him a professional challenge to see if he's got any freestyle skills in the third dimension.

I say, "A'ight Parra, see if you can dig this. A slim glass vase with 3 flowers and a Mother's Day card in an window open to a pastoral seen filled with butterflies and bubbles. My mom has an affinity for butterflies. I want it done in ink, but this is the kicker. I want the bubbles and all that lies within done in color. Think you can handle that?"

Parra says, "Yeah Cuba, I got it."

I say, "Oh yeah, one more thing, if you think you can, draw one of the bubbles in mid pop."

Parra exclaims, "Chingale Cuba!"

I jokingly say, "What, I thought you was good?"

Parra is a perfectionist. He won't accept my challenge if he can't do it right, so calling his artistic reputation into question will awaken his ego. I can't wait to see what he creates.

Matt is getting out tomorrow. I should be happy for him. I am, but it's more and more difficult to express my enthusiasm. Matt's a good dude. I wish I could be bigger about this, but I'm full of impatient envy. I shake his hand and wish him well. On his way out he tells me I'd do well selling cars and I should give it a shot when I get out. The day his only homeboy gets out, Dave gets moved up as a counselor. Matt spent almost every day with him. He could've gone anywhere in the unit, but chose to hang with his homie. Dave is the more abstract of the two and now his co-pilot is gone. A weird white boy in Texas travels a hard, lonely road.

Parra is a little upset with me, or rather with the bubbles I requested he recreate. His exacting standards have yet to be satisfied. The bending and reflecting of light is giving him fits.

He says if he could see it he could draw it. To help him I lather soap with water and begin blowing bubbles so he can see exactly how the light bends. I wonder what he sees that allows him to reproduce it so accurately. He's talked about his lifelong fascination with light and shadow and how he would spend hours studying the reflective properties on an object. Pretty soon he learned how. As I watch his pen deposit ink on the poster board, it's still hard for me to comprehend how he's does it.

Parra's grandfather

Mother's Day Gift

Parra's artwork

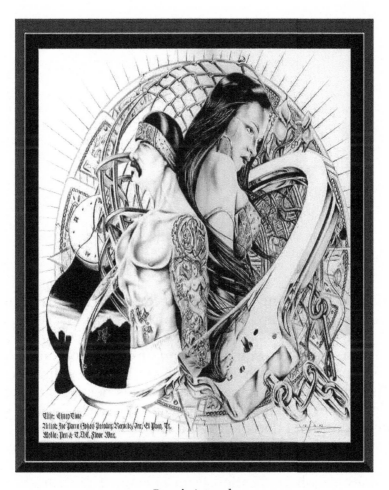

Parra's Artwork

17

My time is drawing near and I'm finding it more and more difficult to fall asleep. Focusing long enough to accomplish much of anything is a challenge. I spend my time with Navarez and Parra, most of which is spent in quiet contemplation. We're returning to vastly different lives. Parra is going back to El Paso to get his art thing on. Navarez is being sent back to Mexico where he'll live with his family. I'm going back to Dallas to do what I don't know. I'll have to contend with a little more than 2 years on parole. I'm not tripping about that. What keeps me staring up at the ceiling is having to check that little box on every job application from now on. The realization, if by some celestial miracle, I do happen upon some form of gainful employment, I'll have to act like the second coming just to keep it. The labels which now apply to me – ex-con, felon and parolee somehow don't seem fitting. I'm attempting in vain to come to grips with having to lace up. I've been a dirty, rotten, and low down scoundrel a time or two in my day, but that soil was easy to wash off. Now, with these insoluble stains, I don't know.

Navarez is packing up. He's on deck. La Migra is waiting to take him back to Mexico. I asked him if he wants to go back home. He says he's looking forward to visiting with his family and friends, but he wants to stay here. The law says he can't come back for 10 years. Before he goes, we exchange contact info. If I ever get down Mexico way again I will look up Navarez. Parra being in El Paso, on my way out of Texas, I plan to stop and hang out on the boarder. He says we'll have a hell of a time on both sides. Today is Parra's turn. Saying goodbye is routine, so we don't make a big deal of it. There goes the last of my compadres. I have two weeks to go. The anticipation is giving me agita. There's no such thing as sleep. My thoughts travel on the four winds.

We're going on lockdown at the end of the week. I'm scheduled to leave the day after it's over. I can't believe I have to spend the last week here on 24/7 lockdown without running water or electricity. It means one more public rectal inspection for good measure. It means soggy Johnny sacks 3 times a day. It means time will stand still. This almost seems personal as if the warden is taking one last shot at me. I moved to the prerelease tank which consists of five 2 man cells along the wall. I'm given the cell in the back corner. My celly is Hector, again.

"Damn Hector! Can't get rid of you if I tried. Came in together. Looks like we're goin' out the same way."

"Ay Cuba, que onda, I heard we're goin' on lockdown."

"Yeah, I heard Saturday. Fucked up Homes. I've been in 5 different units. This will be my 3rd lockdown."

"My 4th. At least this time it won't be cold or raining."

"Yeah, outside butt ass naked in the cold ain't cool at all. I suppose we should be happy this is our last one."

"Ain't gonna be happy until I get the fuck out of here vato."

"Heard that!"

There's an inmate in here named K.J. We taught a couple of classes together and we got along right away. He's the kind of brotha who'd be in for a white collar crime. He's a street dude who made the transition to corporate. Out in the world he's in Special Finance; a middle man between banks and persons with challenged credit. He works out of a Chevy dealership in north Dallas and tells me to look him up when I get out. I'm hoping to get back into computers. My job told me I could come back when I got out, but they've been bought-out since. My homeboy wrote and told me the new company has prohibitions against felons, something I must get used to. I guess I'll give positive thinking and optimism try. I never had any trouble getting a job. I do well in interviews and I always knew I could get another job. A felony drug conviction could possibly prove slight impedance. This is why this optimism shit doesn't work for me. The words sound self-delusional even before they leave my mouth.

We're back from chow and there she is, pretty little Billie. She's busy talking and joking with inmates. I've never seen her look an inmate in the eye before. This is the first time I've seen her smile. My eyes don't leave hers as I roll up on her. She looks at me and says, "You need a haircut." In that instant, every last trace of affectionate affinity evaporates like a rain drop in Death Valley. I'm getting out in a week and she's telling me my hair isn't within regulations? Fuck her and fuck them goddamn regulations! She can kiss my nappy black ass. And just like that the sight of her invokes hostilities. I'm angry at her for the deception. My disdain for her is as rational as my desire. Now all I see is another CO. I should've known better. It's Friday and I'm at my last prison Jummah. I'm giving away most non-essential prison property and paraphernalia. Zakat (charity) is required of all Muslims and I want to do what I can for those I leave here. In prison, the smallest measure of creature comfort can make all the difference.

I'm two days in to the last lockdown I'll have to deal with. I'm going through pictures and letters that have been sent me. Hector's bugging me about pictures. He must be bored to want to look at pictures of people and places he has no knowledge of. I must be just as bored to show and tell it like in grade school.

"Look at you Cuba all young and skinny and shit."

"Yeah man, I was in the clubs 4 or 5 nights a week on the dance floor damn near til sunrise. In that picture I was the same age you are now."

"You goin' back to Cali when you get out?"

"Soon as I get off paper. Don't want to go back home dirty and draggin' this parole shit with me."

"How long you got on paper?"

"A little more than 2 years. When I leave Texas, I leave this shit behind."

That's what I say, yet there's a persistently pervasive thought and feeling I won't be able to shake this X off my back. I have no intention of becoming a productive member of our society. At my angriest, I've seriously considered a life of crime. It wouldn't be difficult at all.

I'm in the rec yard in the morning air, butt naked and waiting on my last public colonoscopy. Look who they put in charge of assholes - pretty little Billie. I can't look at her anymore. Oddly enough, if she hadn't pissed me off the other day, this might have proved a bit awkward. To be exposed in front of the object of ones lust could invoke a little self-consciousness. The way I feel now, I'm happy to shove my asshole in her face. I have three days left.

One of the COs got the power and water turned back on. No more stench of hundreds of men. I'll be sitting in front of the TV and pass more hours. Early tomorrow morning I'll be getting on a prison bus for the last time. Tonight I'm doing all I can not to do any thinking. Hector and I are packing up to leave. We're all awash with nervous excitement and finding it difficult to perform the most basic of hand eye coordination. Both of us are dropping shit and bumping into each other. I'm leaving most of my stuff behind, but Hector wants to take some of his stuff with him. I can't wait to dump all this shit.

It's sunrise and we're lined up outside the prison bus. I'm handcuffed to Hector with a smile on my face. Dave has been talking since we got out here. He's asking questions that no one has the answers to. He doesn't realize some men on this bus aren't getting out today, "Say nigga, tell that white boy to shut the fuck up!" The directive was received and now he's apologizing. He's a nice guy to a fault, so I give him an elbow to the ribs. Hector hits him with a "Callate vato!" Dave gets the point.

Hector and I have developed a rhythmically simpatico, almost conjoined relationship with these cuffs. Being cuffed is dehumanizing enough. Being cuffed to someone else compounds the humiliation. Cuffed to the wrong person is hazardous. This is the 14th time in 18 months I've been on a prison bus. This is the first time I've been concerned with it's speed. This motherfucker can't go fast enough. There are 20 men on this bus and every head is turned, every pair of eyes is cast outward toward the sea of rippling grasslands. Memories of the first time I got on this bus come over me. Strange, the same apprehensive feelings of trepidation and insecurity are now inverted and have doubled back on me.

18

I'm back in Huntsville, back at The Walls for the 5th time. The last time I was in one of these cells I was on my way to Mineral Wells. I remember thinking then that was going to be the last time I would ever be in a cell. I can't help but think of the recidivism rate. I'd say about 40% of the inmates I encountered were parole violators. To be fair, most of them had it coming. There are those, and more than you might think, who simply fell victim to the system. From bullshit bureaucracy to fucked up parole officers, an ex-con's life is in many different hands. Soon my life will be in such hands. I'm not worried. I usually don't have run-ins with the police or the courts. Not because I'm a model citizen, but because I go out of my way not to get caught. I was out on bail for 4 years and smoked weed every one of those days, not to mention the 20 years I ran amuck in California. If I come back, it won't be my doing. I suspect this fact would be then as now, of little consolation. As I lay here in this cell for what I hope will be the last time, I'm attempting to set my mind to walking on rice paper. The heat in the cells is unholy. The humidity is almost drinkable. I'm advising Hector and Dave on how to deal with it. I tell them to strip and put their boxers in the sink, wet them and put them back on, "Then wet your sheets and lay them on the bunk. Now lay on those sheets and don't move." Dave says, "Ahhh, now that makes it mo'e better."

A CO is walking the tier, handing out release paper work. I remember seeing COs handing out this paperwork to what seemed like everyone but me. I remember thinking one day it'll be my turn. Today is that day. I thought I'd be more joyous. Looking at these papers now in my hand brings to mind the paperwork the judge was shuffling that sent me here in the first place. How the fates of all of mankind are beholden and subject to the whims of the shuffling of paperwork. Dave is in the next cell. He's having an experience with those fates right now. The CO didn't give him release paperwork. He's in a bit of a panic. We're hoping there's been some mistake. I have a sinking feeling the mistake was made long ago when they told him he was getting out. I know he's in that cell going through it. I hate it for him. I can hear his quiet contemplation. Now he's has to sit in his cell and wait until the CO comes back with an update. Though I'm inclined, I don't have the slightest idea of what to say to him. I could say this type of thing happens all the time, but I don't think he wants to hear that shit. He's got to be the sickest man in Texas.

We're being let out for chow. I'm finding it difficult to look at Dave. He's having the same difficulty. Hector is standing behind me and whispers two words, "Chingao Cuba!" "Yeah man, I know. Shit's fucked up." We walk up the tier, down the stairs and past all the cells in an almost mournful silence. We're thinking the same thing - what if it was me or I'm glad it ain't me. Dave is not a person you would like to see shit like this happen to. Hector and I make sure we sit and eat with him. We don't want to subject him to a table of happy convicts who are still getting out in the morning, so we eat without saying a word. I think of him alone in that cell all night with just his thoughts. Allah be merciful.

It's July and the sun is going down. A different CO is passing out more release papers. I can't see him, but I can feel Dave at the cell bars dealing with the evaporation of his last vestiges of hope. He asks the CO for an act of kindness and a little information. He's still wishing for a miracle and working that positive thinking shit. This CO doesn't waste any time. He comes right back and tells Dave he's scheduled to return on Monday. The silence is painful. I can hear him surrendering and climbing in his bunk, succumbing to the repugnant truth. What does one say? What and where is the bright side to be looked upon? Does he give a fuck about the bright side? An indeterminate and untold amount of time passes in complete silence, when Dave suddenly breaks it with a low, prayer-filled moaning sigh, "Oh God." The dude in the next cell offers a sobering comment, "Don't know what you callin' on him fo'e. He ain't gonna help yuh."

It's way past lights out when I hear a hollow reverb within the silence.

"Cali, Cali, you awake?"

"Yeah Dave, what's up?"

"Since you're going home can I have your shower shoes?"

"Uh, yeah sure man. You can have anything I got."

"Thanks man, just the shoes."

I wish I could do more for him. The thought the same thing might still happen to me has not left the back of my mind which is why I'm toting my shit around. I remember not having any shower shoes when I first came to prison. I remember not having anything. Imprisonment is dehumanizing enough. Being in prison and having less than every other prisoner is beyond my ability to explain.

Now that Hector knows I'm awake he's full of questions about the release process. He wants to know what time they're coming to let us out.

"About an hour after breakfast."

"Then what happens?"

"Shit man, I don't know."

"Thought you'd been here before?"

"I have but I can't tell you what happens after they leave the cells. They always left me in the here."

I'm trying not to talk about it too much. I feel like I'm being rude to Dave. After a couple more questions Hector gets the drift. Our conversation tapers off back to that vacant quiet.

It's 3:30 am and I'm eating my last prison breakfast. Dave decided not to come. He has his reasons. When the cell doors opened he was still on his bunk. He didn't say anything, neither did I. I figured he wanted to be left alone. The only good day in prison is the day you're getting out. It's what makes surviving prison possible. It's the only thing to hold on to when the walls and bars start fucking with you. The sight of Dave and his blues is not conducive to the mood.

We're led from the cells out into the dungeonous day room. I say goodbye to Dave and keep on moving. Hector and I are damn near skipping down the tier. A CO tries to get us to calm down, "Alright goddamnit! You ain't out yet." His word have no sway. No more, not any longer. He knows it and I think it pisses him off. One more reason to smile. I'm told we're in for an all-day wait.

"It's almost 5 am and they won't start letting y'all out 'till 'bout 12 or 1."

"Muthafucka, I been waitin' fo'e 18 years. Now you talkin' bout a few hours. Shit, I'll wait all goddamn day. Long as I'm waitin' at the back do'e."

"Shit nigga, sho'e you right! I don't give a fuck!"

CO gives as good as he gets, "Don't know why y'all so happy. Most y'all commin' right back!"

Every man here knows he's telling the truth, but today is our day, so fuck him and whatever he's got to say. By this time tomorrow, every swingin' dick here will be balls deep in pussy. Then everything will be right with the world.

Hector and I are feeding the pigeons while being lectured to. We're told to go directly to the bus station and to not hang around town. We're told there will be prostitutes, drug dealers and liquor store workers who are undercover. A CO says, "If you violate the terms and conditions of your parole they will bring you right back. I know it sound pretty stupid to all of you, but every day we catch at least one or two. Please don't be one of those two." Sounds like entrapment.

I'm given more paperwork. This time the papers have our parole information with restrictions, prohibitions and level of supervision; how often we are to report and how often we can expect a parole officer to pop up at our house. Some have to go to halfway houses. Some have ankle monitors, alcohol monitors and once a week parole visits. I'm on minimum supervision which means reporting once a month and home visits once every 6 months for me. It's for this reason I worked so hard and went out of my way to stay out of all the fighting and fucking up so prevalent in prison life. I won't bring prison home with me. Hector has an ankle monitor and has to report twice a month. Plus he's got 4 years on paper. That's a long time to have parole officers all up in your shit. Hector tells me he already knows how to get out of the ankle monitor. When he leaves home, he'll put the monitor around his dogs neck and put him on a leash in the back yard, "If that dog gets lose, you fucked Homes." "He ain't gonna get loose." "Better get two leashes." The right thing for me to do is talk some sense into him. This vato is 19 and getting out of prison. The last thing he wants to hear is another convict telling him what he shouldn't do when he gets out. He's a grown man. All I can do is drop a seed and infer he think about it.

It's 10:30 am and we're back in the chow hall for the last time. We were told they'll start letting us out in about an hour. I can't eat. I can't get enough to drink. I can't sit still. I can't keep a thought in my head. In a matter of hours this will all be a memory, past tense, to be forgotten. The closer it gets the less real it feels. I'm thinking about Dave still sitting up there in that cell with all his beliefs liquefied into salty tears he dare not shed.

It's 3:30pm and I'm still here. They just called another group to begin out processing. They called Hector's name, but not mine. We say our goodbyes and he's on his way out. I'm more than a little concerned. Since Mineral Wells if they called Hector's name, they called mine. Not to mention there aren't but 2 of us left. They told him there's been some mistake. He's been down here with us since 5 am and they're just now getting around to telling him that they stop letting people out at 4:30 pm. It's Friday and they don't release on the weekends. According to all this paperwork, today is the last possible day for my release. Now I'm the only remaining inmate in this dungeon; just me, the pigeons and a little bit of panic.

A CO comes running in looking as if he's misplaced me.

He says, "There you are!"

I reply, "Yeah, same place I've been since y'all left me here at 5:00 in the goddamn morning! Where the fuck should I be?"

He says, "Ah, shut the fuck up and come on here."

I reply, "Bout goddamn time!"

I've been down in this holding hole for damn near 12 hours.

I watched all 200 of the other parolees get out. Half an hour before they close up shop they send a CO looking for me like I've been lost in plain sight. It's almost unbelievable. I'm finally getting out of this white prison jumpsuit and buying clothes donated to the prison with the stamps I hung onto.

Huge aged oak double doors open to a beautifully bright summer afternoon. The sky is bluer, the grass is greener and the air is sweeter. I cast my eyes skyward, breathing slow and deep. I regain my composure and look out into the street. Mom is standing there waiting for me. I hug her, take the keys and hit the streets. Everything is new again. Sitting behind the wheel again for the first time, sitting at a red light watching people go about their day. You know that moment in a dream when you realize it's too good not to be a dream, and then you wake up? I expect to wake up any moment now.

On the other side of the overpass is a sign that bares the crest of all things American and civilized – Starbucks, "Yes, can I have a venti, vanilla bean, caramel and coconut cream Frappuccino with mocha drizzle? Oh, and a quad espresso please." I throw the quad shot in the back of my throat and hit the highway. I have 300 miles to go at 5:30 pm on Friday. Before today I wouldn't have thought it possible to enjoy being stuck in traffic.

Before I can get out of Huntsville my thoughts turn to Siler. I never found out what happened to him. I Hope it's not as bad as I think. On the way back to Dallas, I swing through Babygirl's hood to see what's up. "She's gone, better learn how to face it." I figured as much. Life is seldom that easy. I'm not doing anything tonight. I'm going home to shit, shower, shave, shine and shampoo in private and eat everything until the reverse gear kicks in.

The next morning I'm on the phone, reconnecting with what's left of my network. Everyone can't wait to see me, but right now I'm only interested in one good feeling – pussy. My homie from Dallas is on the phone.

"I know you want some pussy."

"You goddamn right!" He tells me his girl has a friend who saw me at a party once and inquired on more than one occasion.

"Shit nigga, how come this is the first I'm hearin' bout this?"

"She was fuckin' wit my cousin back then. He moved back to Ohio about 2 months ago."

"She know I just got out?"

"I don't think so. I ain't told her."

"Cool, what's her number?"

It's been a little more than 8 months since my release. I was forced to attend a once a week, 3 month rehab class, the exact same class I just spent the previous 6 months teaching. It was remedial and redundant the first time. I never wanted a joint so bad! One good thing came of it though. My homie KJ was in my class and kept after me to come see him at the job. I didn't want to sell cars and work on commission, so I spent 6 months trying to get back into the computer field. Interview after interview, it's the exact same result. I would wait until I was sure I had the job just to see the reaction, "Oh, uh, well, uh." Having no job and no money after getting out is like not getting out. I'm stuck in the house, so out of desperation I went to see KJ. I was offered job that day which happened to be the day after Christmas.

I'm good at selling cars. The first two months I damn near made salesman of the month. There are a lot of ex-cons selling cars. It's one of the only jobs where skill is the only determining factor. There are 18 salesmen on this lot. 10 of them are ex-cons. All of us had the same experience. We've tried in vain to return to whatever we were doing before. I'm making a killing in this game.

It's mid-October. I completed parole without incident and I'm busy packing for my trip back home to California. I never had intentions of staying in Texas longer than a year. Instead, I spent 2 years in prison and 6 years on paper for a crime I didn't commit; I lost my life as it was. They burnt down my lawyer's office and locked him up for being a nigger lover. Corruption and racism are the norm not the exception. This is America.

I have a first class window seat at full recline and a complementary drink in hand. Across the aisle sits a pretty Polynesian woman giving me a demure, coy come hither smile. It's a long flight and right now I need a moment to myself. I look at my last Texas sunrise. It's beautiful, but there will be no more. I've had my fill of southern comfort. I'm heading home to a new life as a felon. 4 hours later SFO sprawls out from beneath the clouds. I'm finally back on my beloved coast, back amongst the free.

ABOUT THE AUTHOR

DW Hennington was born in 1972 in San Antonio, Texas and raised on United States Air Force bases around the world before settling in California with his family at the age of 10. He lives with his wife Belisa (Babydoll) in Northern California. *Yellow Meat Watermelon* is DW Hennington's first publication.

Made in the USA
Monee, IL
26 June 2021